HOUGHTON BOOKS IN LITERATURE

KENNETH S. LYNN · ADVISORY EDITOR

DESIGNS FOR READING

- ○ Plays
- ○ Poems
- ○ Short Stories
- ○ Nonfiction Prose

THE RANGE OF LITERATURE

- ○ Drama
- ○ Poetry
- ○ Fiction
- ● Nonfiction Prose

HOUGHTON
BOOKS IN
LITERATURE

THE RANGE OF LITERATURE:

Nonfiction

Prose

FRED B. MYERS

HOUGHTON MIFFLIN COMPANY • BOSTON

NEW YORK   ATLANTA   GENEVA, ILLINOIS   DALLAS   PALO ALTO

ABOUT THE AUTHOR AND EDITOR

Fred B. Myers is an English teacher who has served as lecturer in methods and as supervising teacher for the University of California at Berkeley. As Chairman of the English Department at Katella High School in Anaheim, California, Mr. Myers is the author of a non-graded, elective curriculum in English.

Kenneth S. Lynn, advisory editor for the Houghton Books in Literature, is an authority in American literature. The author of *Mark Twain and Southwestern Humor* and *The Dream of Success: A Study of the Modern American Imagination,* he is also preëminent for his editing of classic American writers. Dr. Lynn is now Professor of History at Johns Hopkins University.

CONTENTS

I Introductory

II Personalities

III Exposition

IV Persuasion

I

Introductory

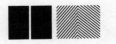

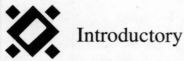

Introductory

Nonfiction prose includes all the ways in which we tell each other something in writing—letters, editorials, articles, and essays, for example. These writings may be, but need not be, literature. Often, as in the case of letters and memos, such writing is not even published.

In this introductory section you will sample some of the varieties of nonfiction. You will find a personal letter from a grandmother, an editorial on travel in contemporary America, the confession of a young man whose emotions are torn by the fact of racial discrimination, an excerpt from the travel journal of an archaeologist, a semanticist's explanation of symbols, and a satirical essay on modern man's egotism.

In each case the writer has a different purpose in writing and is writing to a somewhat different audience. The grandmother, writing to a grandson, is concerned only with communicating her feelings of love in the simplest, most natural language; the young man caught in a conflict of emotions seems almost to be writing to himself; the newspaper editorialist wants the reading public to realize what they have lost in the progress of travel technology; the archaeologist is providing his reader with a backdrop for the book he has written; the semanticist wants to explain an academic idea to the public; and the satirist, if possible, would like to rid man of his arrogant pride.

In each case the writer tries to adjust his methods and approach to his particular purpose and audience. The intimate, casual tone* of the grandmother's letter would not do for the semanticist's or the archaeologist's purpose, for example. Neither would the more formal tone and organization used by these scholars work for the young man who is trying to sort out his own feelings. And the wicked and witty style of the satirist would serve nobody's purpose but his own.

To become a skillful reader of nonfiction is to become sensitive to both the writer's purpose and to the role he is playing. Understanding these things will help to explain the tone of the writing, whether it is casual or formal, or something in between, whether it is grave or playful, intense or detached. And the tone, in turn, will control the author's choice of words and expressions—even his usage and sentence structure.

*All terms so marked appear in the Glossary.

3

A personal letter may serve many purposes, but the most important is to express the *person* — his thoughts, attitudes, and, especially, his feelings. The quality of the feeling is something one usually senses from the way the letter is written rather than from the literal* meaning of the separate words on the page. The following excerpt is from a letter written by a grandmother to her grandson, serving in the Peace Corps. As you read, try to imagine the person who is writing.

A Letter from a Grandmother

(An excerpt)

May, 1967

. . . we are doing very well just old. I miss seeing you I hope you are well and happy. Grand Pa still remember the good times we all had fisheing to gather. I guess all things comes to a end some times but times flyes and you get old and you can't do things you did when you was younger. I still go to church most ever Sunday I have made good friends Yes I enjoy life. I am not sorry I am old I have had a good life. God bin good to me I am proud of my Grand Children they are very dear to me. Dan I want you to all way know I love you very mutch. Wher ever you are if I can be of any help to you let me know I pray for you often I will try to write to you when I am not so mushey.

lots
Granny

INTERPRETATION

1. Describe the "person" that comes through in this letter. What kind of life has she led? How does she *feel* about it? about herself? about her family?

4

2. Is the writer aware of the way her letter may sound to her grandson? How do you know?

STYLE AND METHOD
1. Taken sentence by sentence, the letter seems disjointed. Does this tend to help or hinder the expression of the writer's feeling? What errors in grammar, usage, punctuation, and spelling do you notice? Does the letter succeed in communicating *in spite of,* or *because of,* these?
2. On the basis of your answers to these questions, try to answer the following: Which seems to be more important to writing a good personal letter: honest thought and sincere emotion or correctness? Do you think the same thing holds true for other kinds of writing? Discuss.

FOR WRITING
Try rewriting Grandmother's letter, correcting the spelling, punctuation, and syntax. Make the sentence structure more "mature." What is the effect compared to the original? What further light is shed on question 2 above?

It is a truism that technology provides us with speed and power and convenience — at the expense of first-hand contact with life. (A person may eat bread all his life without ever seeing or feeling a kernel of wheat; cross the continent in four hours without touching the earth.) In the following editorial, the columnist takes the occasion of the Apollo 8 mission to reflect on the effects of "progress" on travel — and on Americans as people. What he says reflects his personal feelings and values, and leads him to make a judgment about our national behavior. That is the usual formula of an editorial — from facts to argument to judgment or conclusion. Its success will be judged in terms of the objectivity with which the facts are chosen, the logic of the argument, and the soundness of the writer's moral judgments.

On Not Seeing America

JENKIN LLOYD JONES

A couple of weeks after our three men went around the moon it was announced that the last Pullman conductors in America were being retired. Why not? The newest Pullman car is 13 years old and is on its way to join the canal boat and the stagecoach.

So I weep. And not because I'm a grumpy gaffer with a perverse penchant for the past, but because it is ironic that as Americans are about to know the moon better they will know America less well.

The Pullman car is not, as the college crowd imagines, merely a collection of narrow sleeping boxes in which one is banged and jolted through the night for the purpose of crawling across the landscape at a ridiculously slow 60 or 70 miles an hour.

It is that, of course. But it is a way of going to sleep in Michigan or Iowa and waking up in New York State or Wyoming. You doze off amid cornfields and dawn finds you looking out at the broad Hudson or the hunting grounds of the Ogallala Sioux. It is a way of understanding the immensity and glory of this great country.

It is also the only practical way of watching America roll by in moonlight. You can't do it in an automobile, blinded as you are by the oncoming headlights and paying attention to the tailgate up ahead. But propped up on two pillows in a cozy roomette you see the stars wheel over the Great Smokies and the moon dance on the great Salt Lake.

At night the wheatlands of western Kansas are a rolling sea. The firs of Idaho, the palms of Florida and the saguaro cacti of Arizona march by in the half-light. You sense the rich variety of America and you go off into dreams with some long forgotten tune keeping time to the rail joints.

The Pullman made you think about time. I remember my first trip East as a pop-eyed 13-year-old. Dusk fell in western Ohio and through the night I was aware of rugged mountains, ghostly coal tipples[1] and once the glare and heat of a blast furnace. And then it was morning and there were the fat Dutch barns and the stone two-gabled houses of Lancaster County, Pa.

Hessians had stolen chickens from those barns and Washington's troops had begged food at those houses—or maybe they stole, too. But the western kid knew that during the night he had traveled back 150 years.

There was the first trip South, gathering dust and cinders behind the burnished brass railings of the Panama Limited's open-ended club car. And in the morning there was Spanish moss and old slave cabins and swamps that had known the buccaneers of Jean Lafitte. You knew you had gone somewhere.

The modern kid, tucked up six miles high in a Boeing with his pop and comic books, is cheated of his country. The Twin Cities airport looks a lot like the one in Seattle and in between there are clouds or maybe a brown-green carpet in which Pipestone Pass and Maria's Pass and the three forks of the Yellowstone are lost.

The super highway isn't going to cure things, either, even though it's wonderful for getting there and long overdue. Because, you see, it's really a tunnel through the land. There are the twin ribbons of white flanked by the broad right-of-way, and the towns are gone and even the barns are far away.

[1] **tipples:** apparatus or locations for tipping loaded cars.

Last fall, zooming across Indiana, my wife and I followed for many boring miles a highballing tractor-trailer bearing on its back the word, "Spector". And it occurred to me that I was seeing a spectre, indeed—the vision of Americans rushing hell-bent between birth and death with nothing in between.

So we wheeled off the interstate and got on the old National Road with its inns and villages and stop lights. But at least we were back in Indiana once more, and it was wonderful.

It is easy—too easy—to snivel over the past. A generation now long dead mourned the day when three banks of packets lined the levee at Memphis, and the cry "Steamboat 'round the bend" brought the people with beaver hats and hoopskirts a-flying.

But at 9 a.m. in the great Pullman Age the St. Louis Union Station was, indeed, a sight to remember—a dozen lighted drumhead markers, a dozen gleaming observation platforms, and all America a day, two days, three days away.

In a way, it was a more awesome country then. The turbine and the paver hadn't shrunk it. You had time to sniff it and marvel at its moods and wait upon its sidetracks. And it took a long, long time to cross.

Perhaps it was that kind of America that made it hard for us to burn our draft cards or drop out of her traditions.

INTERPRETATION

1. Why does the author say, "So I weep"? What does he think has been lost? What is "ironic" about our going to the moon?
2. Explain the full meaning of the "spectre" the writer sees while following the tractor-trailer. Does he concede any good in modern modes of transportation? Explain.
3. Explain the meaning of the last sentence of the editorial. Why does it stand alone?

STYLE AND METHOD

1. The "facts" of this editorial take the form of the author's observations— reminiscences, mainly. How does the author's language blend these facts with feelings? Is the tone sad, angry, sarcastic? something other than these?
2. What values are important to the author? (Could equally valid values be discovered in space flight? high speed transportation?) Do you accept the author's values?

3. How logical is the conclusion of this editorial?

FOR WRITING
1. If you have taken a memorable trip recently, describe some of the things you saw. Use language that will reveal the meaning or significance of people, places, events.
2. Discuss some other aspect of technological living, making clear your attitude toward it.

"Can I turn myself off and on like a machine to suit the situation?"
This was only one of many probing questions Thedford Slaughter
asked himself before starting home for Alabama after a summer
in the Yale University Summer High School. He speaks with an
introspective voice, searching his own experience and raising
questions — questions the answers to which may affect not only
his own life but those of all Americans.

Up from Hate

THEDFORD SLAUGHTER

Sometimes I still feel uneasy, completely out of place when I'm
the only Negro in a crowd of *them*. I find it difficult to believe
that there is no "catch" to my seeming absorption into the Yale
Summer High School community. At home, sometimes they pass
by with pretended innocence and unconcern, and then spit on the
sidewalk behind us to demonstrate their contempt; or they
scream "black nigger" from the relative safety of passing cars.
I hated them for their open arrogance and viciousness, but I
hated them even more for their estimate of *us* — their certainty
that we were ignorant and bestial. I could not see a Lindsay, or a
Bill, or a Bob among them; they were white and therefore evil.

Here, I have begun to differentiate. I see John and Bob instead
of two whites. But when I go back, in the old surroundings of my
hate, will they no longer be evil? If I wasn't mistaken about those
at home, can I set aside the old image and wait hopefully until I
return up North, or move to some other place where there is no
civil strife, to find the new image again? Can I turn myself off
and on like a machine to suit the situation? Now that I know how
different places are, how will I take the shock of being called
"nigger" again; or will it actually be a shock? Has the summer
program really awakened me to an extent that I am purged of all
the hatred toward the whites that I have harbored?

Not having attended an integrated school and knowing full well the strength of Jim Crowism, I don't know how I felt when the first white kid challenged me on an issue and proved me wrong. Did I feel that I could never be right because I was inferior? Did my submerged hatred almost compel me to bridge the gap in one leap and give Whitey a good kick in the ass? Or did I concede, "OK, next time I'll be right"? Even now I'm not sure what my initial reaction was.

It is difficult to write these things for fear of being misinterpreted. I don't want to create the impression that I'm appealing for sympathy with the old line, "God help the poor, depressed Negro of the ghetto!" I make no such appeal, nor am I an advocate of Black Power. These are just questions I ask myself relentlessly. I don't know the answers. If there is anything I hate, it is the idea that the Negro must be pitied. If you really want to help a Negro, don't bathe him in self-pity or he'll probably drown in it.

Chances are that my present conflicts will subside as soon as I return home because my guard will be up. I may be able to take their verbal attacks without flinching.

Would it really be possible to adopt a whole new set of ideals in seven weeks? Can I destroy in a moment sixteen years of hatred? Is it as great here as I think? I have nothing against the guys at Yale Summer High School, but I constantly wonder if prejudice doesn't linger behind some surreptitious face. I find it almost inconceivable that two places could be so different — one a hellport of sore spots, the other a Utopia. Then, too, I wonder if here is really Utopia. Do I value the things I have here only because I have been deprived of them for so long at home down South?

As the end of the term approaches, I ask myself, "Can I really still hate so much? Is all of the hate still there just waiting to be awakened by some kind of white backlash? Do I hate as an act of self-defense because I know that I'm hated? Or do I hate because I'm evil, too?" Will I ever be entirely free of this hatred, or has it grown in me for so long that it *is* me, now and inseparable? I'll find out soon. Yes, real soon. But as of now, I don't know. I just don't know.

INTERPRETATION

1. What differences does the writer find between his home town and his

summer experience? What inner conflicts result from these differences?

2. What does the second sentence of the second paragraph tell about the kind of differentiation the writer has learned to make? Why are distinctions of this kind important?

3. At what points does the writer reveal an intimate knowledge of himself? What is your attitude toward the writer? Is your attitude affected by (a) his attitude toward himself? (b) his attitude toward Negroes? (c) his values or ideals? What are they?

STYLE AND METHOD

How many questions are there in the essay? How many declarative sentences with the words "I wonder" imbedded in them? Are the latter really questions or statements? How does the questioning approach affect the general tone of the essay? What is the tone*?

FOR WRITING

1. Write an extended definition or explanation of race prejudice as you understand it from your own experience or reading.

2. Write an essay in which you expand on Thedford Slaughter's notion of "turning off and on to suit the situation."

In recent years scientists, scholars, politicians, and everyone concerned with the effects of language on human thought and behavior, have paid increasing attention to semantics, the science of meaning. Semanticists understand that words, as symbols, *stand for* certain objects or ideas and that they evoke in the reader specific kinds of responses. The choice of a word, then, may be crucial.

In the following essay, the writer explains the basic idea of semantics, the symbol. But as you read, be aware of the plan of the essay as well. In each short section the exposition* proceeds from concrete examples to definitions, which are then illustrated. The author's purpose here is to make a concept as clear to the reader as possible.

Symbols

S. I. HAYAKAWA

I find it difficult to believe that words have no meaning in them- selves, hard as I try. Habits of a lifetime are not lightly thrown aside. — STUART CHASE

Signal and Symbol Reaction

Animals struggle with each other for food or for leadership, but they do not, like human beings, struggle with each other for things that *stand for* food or leadership: such things as our paper symbols of wealth (money, bonds, titles), badges of rank to wear on our clothes, or low-number license-plates, supposed by some people to stand for social precedence. For animals the relationship in which one thing *stands for* something else does not appear to exist except in very rudimentary form. For example, a chimpanzee can be taught to drive a car, but there is one thing wrong with its driving: its reactions are such that if a red light shows when it is halfway across a street, it will stop in the middle of the crossing, while if a green light shows while another car is stalled in its path, it will go ahead regardless of consequences. In other words, so far as a chimpanzee is concerned, the red light can hardly be said to *stand for* stop; it *is* stop.

Let us then introduce two terms to represent this distinction between the "red light *is* stop" relationship, which the chimpanzee understands, and the "red light *stands for* stop" relationship, which the human being understands. To the chimpanzee, the red light is, we shall say, a *signal,* and we shall term its reaction a *signal reaction; that is, a complete and invariable reaction which occurs whether or not the conditions warrant such a reaction.* To the human being, on the other hand, the red light is, in our terminology, a *symbol,* and we shall term his reaction a *symbol reaction; that is, a delayed reaction, conditional upon the circumstances.* In other words, the nervous system capable only of signal reactions *identifies the signal with the thing for which the signal stands;* the human nervous system, however, working under normal conditions, understands *no necessary connection* between the symbol and the thing for which the symbol stands. Human beings do not automatically jump up in the expectation of being fed whenever they hear an icebox door slam.

The Symbolic Process

Human beings, because they can understand certain things to *stand for* other things, have been able to develop what we shall term the *symbolic process.* Whenever two or more human beings can communicate with each other, they can, by agreement, make anything stand for anything. Feathers worn on the head can be made to stand for tribal chieftainship; cowrie shells[1] or rings of brass or pieces of paper can stand for wealth; crossed sticks can stand for a set of religious beliefs; buttons, elks' teeth, ribbons, special styles of ornamental haircutting or tattooing, can stand for social affiliations. The symbolic process permeates human life at the most savage as well as at the most civilized levels. Warriors, medicine men, policemen, doormen, telegraph boys, cardinals, and kings wear costumes that symbolize their occupations. Savages collect scalps, college students collect dance programs and membership keys in honorary societies, to symbolize victories in their respective fields. There are very few things that men do or want to do, possess or want to possess, that have not, in addition to their mechanical or biological value, a symbolic value.

[1] **cowrie shells:** shells used as money in Africa and some Asiatic countries.

an

All fashionable clothes, as Thorstein Veblen has pointed out in his *Theory of the Leisure Class,* are highly symbolic: materials, cut, and ornament are dictated only to a slight degree by considerations of warmth, comfort, or practicability. The more we dress up in fine clothes, the more do we restrict our freedom of action. But by means of delicate embroideries, easily soiled fabrics, starched shirts, high heels, long and pointed fingernails, and other such sacrifices of comfort, the wealthy classes manage to symbolize the fact that they don't have to work for a living. The not so wealthy, on the other hand, by imitating these symbols of wealth, symbolize their conviction that, even if they do work for a living, they are just as good as anybody else. Again, we select our furniture to serve as visible symbols of our taste, wealth, and social position; we trade in perfectly good cars for later models, not always to get better transportation, but to give evidence to the community that we can afford such luxuries; we often choose our residential localities on the basis of a feeling that it "looks well" to have a "good address"; we like to put expensive food on our tables, not always because it tastes better than cheap food, but because it tells our guests that we like them, or, just as often, because it tells them that we are well fixed financially.

Such complicated and apparently unnecessary behavior leads philosophers, both amateur and professional, to ask over and over again, "Why can't human beings live simply and naturally?" Perhaps, unconsciously, they would like to escape the complexity of human life for the relative simplicity of such lives as dogs and cats lead. But the symbolic process, which makes possible the absurdities of human conduct, also makes possible language and therefore all the human achievements dependent upon language. The fact that more things can go wrong with motorcars than with wheelbarrows is no reason for going back to wheelbarrows. Similarly, the fact that the symbolic process makes complicated follies possible is no reason for wanting to return to a cat-and-dog existence.

Language as Symbolism

Of all forms of symbolism, language is the most highly developed, most subtle, and most complicated. It has been pointed out that human beings, by agreement, can make anything stand for anything. Now, human beings have agreed, in the course of centuries of mutual dependency, to let the various noises that they can produce with their lungs, throats, tongues, teeth, and lips systematically stand for specified happenings in their nervous systems. We call that system of agreements *language*. For example, we who speak English have been so trained that when our nervous systems register the presence of a certain kind of animal, we may make the following noise: "There's a cat." Anyone hearing us would expect to find that by looking in the same direction, he would experience a similar event in his nervous system — one that would have led him to make an almost identical noise. Again, we have been so trained that when we are conscious of wanting food, we make the noise, "I'm hungry."

There is, as has been said, *no necessary connection between the symbol and that which is symbolized*. Just as men can wear yachting costumes without ever having been near a yacht, so they can make the noise, "I'm hungry," without being hungry. Furthermore, just as social rank can be symbolized by feathers in the hair, by tattooing on the breast, by gold ornaments on the watch chain, by a thousand different devices according to the culture we live in, so the fact of being hungry can be symbolized by a thousand different noises according to the culture we live in: "J'ai faim," or "Es hungert mich," or "Ho appetito," or "Hara ga hetta," and so on.

Linguistic Naïveté

However obvious these facts may appear at first glance, they are actually not so obvious as they seem except when we take special pains to think about the subject. Symbols and things symbolized are independent of each other; nevertheless, all of us have a way of feeling as if, and sometimes acting as if, there were necessary connections. For example, there is the vague sense that we all have that foreign languages are inherently absurd. Foreigners have "funny names" for things: why can't they call things by their "right names"? This feeling exhibits itself most strongly in those American and English tourists who seem to believe that they can make the natives of any country understand English if they shout it at them loud enough. They feel, that is, that the symbol *must necessarily* call to mind the thing symbolized.

Anthropologists[2] report similar attitudes among primitive peoples. In talking with natives, they frequently come across unfamiliar words in the native language. When they interrupt the conversation to ask, *"Guglu? What is a guglu?"* the natives laugh, as if to say, "Imagine not knowing what a *guglu* is! What amazingly silly people!" When an answer is insisted upon, they explain, when they can get over laughing, "Why, a *guglu is a* GUGLU, of course!" Very small children think in this respect the way primitive people do; often when policemen say to a whimpering lost child, "All right, little girl, we'll find your mother for you. Who is your mother? What's your mother's name?" the child can only bawl, "My muvver is *mummy*. I want *mummy!"* This leaves the police, as they say in murder mysteries, baffled. Again, there is the little boy who is reported to have said, "Pigs are called pigs because they are such *dirty* animals."

Similar naïveté regarding the symbolic process is illustrated by an incident in the adventures of a theatrical troupe playing melodramas to audiences in the western ranching country. One night, at a particularly tense moment in the play, when the villain seemed to have the hero and the heroine in his power, an overexcited cowpuncher in the audience suddenly rose from his seat and shot the villain. The cowpuncher of this story, however, is no more ridiculous than those thousands of people today, many of them adults, who write fan letters to a ventriloquist's dummy, or those goodhearted but impressionable people who send presents to the broadcasting station when two characters in a radio serial get married, or those astonishing patriots who rushed to recruiting offices to help defend the nation when the United States was "invaded" by an "army from Mars."

These, however, are only the more striking examples of primitive and infantile attitudes towards symbols. There would be little point in mentioning them if we were uniformly and permanently aware of the independence of symbols from things symbolized. But we are not. Most of us retain many habits of evaluation ("thinking habits") more appropriate to life in the jungle than to life in modern civilization. Moreover, all of us are capable of reverting to them, especially when we are overexcited or when subjects about which we have special prejudices are mentioned.

[2] **anthropologists:** scholars who study the physical, social, material, and cultural development of man, his origin, evolution, distribution, ethnology, and communal forms.

Worst of all, various people who have easy access to such instruments of public communication as the press, the radio, the lecture platform, and the pulpit actively encourage primitive and infantile attitudes towards symbols. Political and journalistic charlatans,[3] advertisers of worthless or overpriced goods, and promoters of religious bigotry stand to profit either in terms of money or power or both, if the majority of people can be kept thinking like savages or children.

INTERPRETATION

1. In the first part of his essay, the author makes a distinction between "signal reaction" and "symbol reaction." Can you supply examples from your experience that illustrate the difference as clearly as the author's do?
2. Thorstein Veblen's theories are mentioned as an example of our application of the symbolic process. Discuss examples from your own experience in which the symbolic value for buying something or doing something was more important than the practical value — for example, your choice of clothing, the importance of an automobile in your circle of friends, your reasons for joining or not joining certain clubs or organizations.
3. What concept is the author emphasizing in his comments about language as symbolism? Can you think of any evidence which tends to refute this concept?
4. What is the meaning of "linguistic naïveté"? Act out the ways a naïve person would behave in each of these situations: asking about membership in an exclusive club; eating in a restaurant; asking about the clothes others wear; communicating with someone new to the school who doesn't speak English.

STYLE AND METHOD

1. The language and examples a writer chooses can reveal his own prejudices, level of thinking, and conception of audience. Dr. Hayakawa is writing here in a relatively formal style which helps to maintain an objective point of view on a serious subject. Can you point to places where the author's *persona** nevertheless shows how he "feels"? Consider the examples used in the essay. Would any of them be likely to offend anyone? If so, would the reaction be a signal reaction or a symbol reaction?
2. Develop explanations of "signal reaction," "symbol reaction," and "linguistic naïveté" for three different audiences: in a letter or telephone

---

[3] **charlatans:** impostors.

conversation to a good friend; a teacher other than your English teacher; a classmate you don't know well who has asked you for help because he missed the class discussion on this essay. Discuss the differences that distinguish these three statements.

FOR WRITING

1. Write your own definitions for each of the following: "signal reaction," "symbol reaction," "symbolic process," and "linguistic naïveté." Try them out on other people. How do they compare with Hayakawa's definitions?

2. Drawing on your own reading and experience, explain how "political and journalistic charlatans . . ." etc. can use the symbolic process in language to gain money or power or both. Be sure to give examples.

In *The Bull of Minos,* Leonard Cottrell retraces the quest of
archaeologists — assisted by the theories of historians, linguists,
and literary critics — to discover the origins of the ancient Greek
and Cretan civilizations, and the relation between the two. (It
was at Crete where, according to legend, the Greek hero
Theseus slew the Minotaur and freed his companions from being
sacrificed to the monster.)

In this journal-like Prologue to his book, the author describes
his singular impressions and his deep sense of personal
excitement as he approaches "golden Mycenae," the starting
point of his investigation and the fabled stronghold of Homer's
Agamemnon, leader of the Greek armies against Troy.

Prologue from
The Bull of Minos

LEONARD COTTRELL

I left Athens at midday in the *Automatrice,* a reasonably fast
Diesel train, which trundled along for four hours beside the sun-
glittering Gulf of Salamis, through pale green valleys hemmed in
by low, treeless hills of gray limestone, past dust-gray villages set
among the dark spearlike cypresses. The light was white and intense, the magical light of Hellas, which shadows impartially the
fluting of a Doric column or the hard lines of a peasant's face. We
passed Megara, near which the hero Theseus kicked the giant
Sciron into the sea (where he turned into a tortoise), and then,
after miles of gnarled olive trees, slowed and stopped at New
Corinth.

I had over an hour to wait at the squalid railway station,
which seemed designed to destroy all romantic preconceptions of
Greece. On the dirty, paper-littered platform sat sad-eyed women
in drab, shapeless clothes, and a few listless men, cloth-capped

and collarless. Among them was a sullen youth with a strained, handsome face, who looked older than his years. He had lost a leg in the Civil War and hobbled painfully on crutches. A few meagre-looking fowl pecked between the tracks, and a small ragged boy moved along the platform with a trayful of "souflakia" — fragments of meat on wooden skewers — but he had few customers.

So this was Greece. It served me right for my selfish preoccupation with the past. What else had I any right to expect in postwar Greece? Invaded in turn by Italians and Germans, then, when other countries had gained peace, subjected to a bitter Civil War, Greece was now impoverished and exhausted. Was this a time for half-baked romantics to come poking about among her ruins? So I reproached myself, wishing either that I could have visited the country in happier times, or that I had the temperament of a contemporary reporter who could apply himself fearlessly and frankly to her present-day problems.

Another train took me southward again, crawling slowly round the skirts of the two-thousand-foot mountain on which stands the Acrocorinthus.[1] Dramatically it rose from the darkening plain, a dome of limestone capped by the ruins of the Temple of Athena, and the citadel from which the ancient Corinthians commanded the Isthmus. By the time its black silhouette had passed out of view, the sun had set, and only an occasional cluster of lights revealed a village among the folded hills. My fellow passengers were mostly peasants, the women usually in black, with head scarves, and laden baskets resting on their broad laps. They chatted, but the suntanned men usually sat silent. Occasionally a pipe would be removed from beneath a curled moustache; a brief remark would accompany a flash of strong white teeth; then the pipe would be replaced, the arms folded, and dark eyes beneath round black turbans would resume their detached but unhostile contemplation of the stranger.

As I watched them, my spirits rose a little. In fact, so fascinating were those grave, contemplative faces that I almost forgot to get out at my destination. Glancing up when the train had been halted for nearly a minute, I happened to see a station name board in the yellow light of an oil lamp. It was *Mycenae*. Even as I snatched my bag from the rack and scrambled out of

[1] **Acrocorinthus:** hill of impregnable rock rising behind the town of Corinth; a medieval fortress now a monument.

the carriage, the absurdity of the situation struck me. To see the name of Agamemnon's[2] proud citadel, Homer's "Mycenae,[3] rich in gold," the scene of Aeschylus's epic tragedy, stuck on a station platform, was too bizarre. And yet there it was. And there was I, the sole occupant of the platform, watching the red rear light of the little train as it slowly receded into the night.

A full moon was rising, and the groves of olive trees rustled gently in the night wind, which brought with it the faint scent of thyme. I looked around for the car which my friends in Athens had told me *might* be waiting to take me to the village inn at Charvati, two miles away. It was not there. So, hitching my bag on my shoulder, I set off along the straight, olive-bordered lane towards the hills which showed clearly in the moonlight. As I walked I felt happier. Without knowing why, I began to believe that Mycenae would not disappoint me.

A few lights gleamed through the trees ahead. Some way off a dog barked and another answered. The hills were quite close now, and I could see the scattered houses of the village clustered on the lower slopes. The houses lay on the left of the road. On the right the plain of Argos stretched open to the sea, which, although I could not see it, I knew was only a few miles away. The inn, I had been told, was by the roadside, set back behind a break in the trees. Could this be it, this small, dark, flat-fronted building without a light showing? Yes, there was the sign, hung from a tree by the roadside. I shone my torch and read, "La Belle Hélène de Menelaüs."

If it had adorned a large, neon-lit hotel with a car park and a gold-braided porter, the inn's sign would have seemed smart aleck and vulgar; but not as it was, hung in front of this unpretending house in an unpretending village. I knocked, waited, knocked again; but the house seemed deserted. There was no sound within, and not a light showed. The dog barked again, a long way off. The oleanders stirred in the slight breeze, and again came that faint, fresh smell of thyme. I felt curiously elated and

[2] **Agamemnon:** legendary king of Mycenae, or Argos, who led the Greek army that laid siege to Troy. His wife Clytemnestra and her lover Aegisthus killed him upon his return home, and his son Orestes killed them in revenge. The tragedy of Agamemnon is told by the Greek playwright Aeschylus in his trilogy the *Oresteia.*

[3] **Mycenae:** city in ancient Greece, located six miles north of Argos; leading political and cultural center of mainland Greece from 1450 to 1100 B.C.

expectant, not at all cast down by this apparent indifference to my arrival. My Athenian hosts had warned me that, although they had sent a telegram to the proprietor of the inn, there was no certainty that it would arrive.

Then came a light step crossing the hall; the door opened, and there emerged, first a slim white arm holding aloft an oil lamp, then the owner of the arm. She was about twenty-three, fair-skinned, with a wide, firm mouth; strong, rounded chin; and deep, dark eyes under a smooth brow. She stood for a moment on the top step, looking down at me. Her dress was that of a peasant, a simple cream-colored frock with a scarlet jacket carelessly thrown over it, but her face was like one of the sculptured maidens of the porch of the Erechtheum[4] on the Athenian Acropolis.[5] It was too absurdly romantic — the plain of Argos — Helen of Troy had been called "Argive Helen" — the name on the inn sign, the Homeric setting.

In the inn there were two men, and an older woman who seemed to be the mother of the girl who had admitted me. Evidently the telegram had not come and my arrival had taken them unawares, but now, recovering from their surprise, they bustled about the house, up and down the stairs, in and out of dining room and kitchen, eager to make me comfortable. The older of the two men, tall, lean and dark, with stubble on his long chin, appeared to be in charge. As he shouted orders, lamps were brought into the stone-flagged dining room, the girl spread a cloth and laid the table, while her mother hurried upstairs to prepare my bed. The other man, who seemed to be the brother of the first, then entered carrying a three-legged shallow brazier filled with glowing coals. This he placed beneath the table so that I might warm my feet. As the brazier carrier was hurrying out again, his brother caught him by the arm and, pointing to him, said to me, "Orestes!" And then, indicating himself, he added, "Agamemnon!"[6]

We all bowed and smiled. I did not dare inquire the name of the girl. It would have been too disappointing if she had not

[4] **Erechtheum:** temple on the Acropolis of Athens, closely associated with origins of Athenian religion; masterpiece of Ionic architecture.

[5] **Athenian Acropolis:** hill towering 200 feet above Athens on which several beautiful buildings, including the Parthenon and the Erechtheum, are situated.

[6] **Agamemnon ... Orestes** (see note page 22): king of Mycenae and the son who avenged his murder.

been named Helen[7] or Andromache.[8] Now she entered again, bearing my meal—a superb omelette, a fine cheese and a bottle of pale golden wine—the familiar resin-flavored *retzina* which is drunk all over Greece.

Dinner over, I wandered around the room, examining the photographs on the walls: pictures of the citadel of Mycenae, with its Lion Gate, its Cyclopean[9] walls and the huge beehive-shaped "tholos" tombs which I had studied so often in weighty volumes at home. To think that these glories lay only a mile away in the dark hills, awaiting exploration tomorrow, filled me with excitement. On a table lay a copy of Professor Wace's book on Mycenae, with his written greetings to my cheerful hosts. Wace, they had told me in Athens, had stayed here during the previous year while superintending his latest "dig" at Mycenae.

While turning Wace's pages I found Agamemnon, my host, standing at my elbow with the inn's Visitors' Book. He held it under the light, pointing with a brown finger at an entry on a page dated 1942. It was a foreign signature, difficult to read at first. Then, with a start, I recognized it—Hermann Goering.[10] My host flicked the pages and pointed to another signature— Heinrich Himmler.[11] Somewhat shaken, I took the book from his hand, sat down and carefully read through the names entered during the early years of the war. I also found Goebbels,[12] together with many scores of officers and men of *Panzerdivizionen,*[13] from generals to privates.

What had attracted the Nazi chiefs and so many German soldiers to this spot? They had come to pay tribute to the memory of Heinrich Schliemann.[14] Eighty years ago that great German

[7] **Helen:** daughter of Zeus and Leda and wife of Menelaus of Sparta; her abduction by Paris started the Trojan War.

[8] **Andromache:** in Greek legend, the faithful wife of Hector taken captive to Greece after the fall of Troy.

[9] **Cyclopean walls:** ancient style of architecture characterized by use of massive blocks of stone.

[10] **Hermann Goering:** second to Adolph Hitler as leader of Nazi Germany, reich marshal, and commander of the German air force.

[11] **Heinrich Himmler:** head of German police including the Gestapo, minister of the interior, and minister of home defense in Nazi Germany.

[12] **Goebbels:** Joseph Paul Goebbels, official propagandist of Nazi Germany.

[13] **Panzerdivizionen:** mechanized unit of German army organized for rapid attack.

[14] **Heinrich Schliemann:** German archaeologist who discovered and excavated the ruins of Troy and other ancient cities; he uncovered five royal graves at Mycenae in 1876.

archaeologist had come here after his triumphs at Troy, and dug from beneath the citadel treasures which proved that Homer's "golden Mycenae" had been aptly named. Schliemann had died more than sixty years ago, yet his influence was still felt. Was it not a habit of Schliemann to call his workmen by Homeric names, and often to stand godfather to their children? No doubt the Agamemnon who stood watching me now had been so sponsored.

For a time I lay awake, reading Wace's book by candlelight and listening to the faint sound of the night wind, and the occasional croak of a frog. When I snuffed the candle, I was too excited to sleep. Again and again my thoughts kept returning to the parson's son from Mecklenburg who believed in the literal truth of Homer; the self-made merchant turned archaeologist whose instinct proved more accurate than the learning of scholars; that exasperating, bewildering, yet likable mixture of shrewdness and naïvety — Doctor Heinrich Schliemann. From Schliemann my thoughts turned to Homer, the poet whom he idolized and by whom he was led to make those discoveries which set up such a fluttering in the academic dovecotes.

INTERPRETATION

1. With the help of Bulfinch's *Age of Fable,* Edith Hamilton's *Mythology,* or other references, find out about Agamemnon, Clytemnestra, Orestes, Menelaus, Helen, and other personalities mentioned by the author. Give a report on the discoveries of Heinrich Schliemann. (In addition to Schliemann's own writings, three good sources are E. Ludwig's *Schliemann of Troy,* C. W. Ceram's *Gods, Graves and Scholars,* as well as Cottrell's *The Bull of Minos,* especially chapters II-IV and VI.)
2. The "facts" in the Prologue seem to be more the author's personal impressions of his immediate experience than a discussion of the book's subject. What do you learn about Greece from the author's observations? Discuss passages that provide information about ancient Greece; about contemporary Greece. What is the purpose of these passages — to show differences or similarities?
3. How is the author's *persona* * revealed by this Prologue?

STYLE AND METHOD

1. Prologues usually discuss the facts, ideas, issues, or theories that are going to be developed in a book. What does Cottrell gain by his personal narrative approach? What does the Prologue lead you to expect from the rest of the book?

2. How much does the description add to the personal quality of Cottrell's writing? Discuss the effectiveness of the descriptive details dealing with each of the following: a) the people waiting for the train, b) the passengers on the train, c) the family at the inn, d) the food served, e) the countryside.

3. At one point the author writes, "It was too absurdly romantic . . . ." What does this comment mean? What does it reveal about the writer's frame of mind? How does it relate to the general tone* of the Prologue and to the later comment, "When I snuffed the candle, I was too excited to sleep"?

FOR WRITING

1. Revise the Prologue in such a way as to exclude the expression of the author's personal feelings entirely. What kinds of material must be eliminated?

2. The time span of the Prologue is from midday to late evening, but it is more than an account of the events of those hours. Allusions* to the past and to the future constantly enlarge the perspective.

Recall some event—or look forward to a forthcoming one—that was very important to you. Record in journal form your thoughts and observations as you prepared for the event itself.

A fable can be defined as a very brief story with a moral, in which
animals talk and act like humans. "The Human Being and the
Dinosaur" fits the definition on two counts: first, there is a
stated moral at the end; and second, at least one of the characters
is an animal that talks. James Thurber, however, has given the
traditional notion of the fable his own unique treatment and
has created something that is different. The dialogue between
the man and dinosaur becomes a short, whimsical essay which
satirizes modern man and his society much more directly than
the fable. To follow the argument* of the essay, you will have to
pay attention to the style — to the meaning and effects of
individual words.

The Human Being
and the Dinosaur

JAMES THURBER

Ages ago in a wasteland of time and a wilderness of space,
Man, in upper case, and dinosaur, in lower, first came face to
face. They stood like stones for a long while, wary and watchful,
taking each other in. Something told the dinosaur that he beheld
before him the coming glory and terror of the world, and in the
still air of the young planet he seemed to catch the faint smell of
his own inevitable doom.

"Greetings, stupid," said Man. "Behold in me the artfully
articulated architect of the future, the chosen species, the certain
survivor, the indestructible one, the monarch of all you survey,
and of all that everyone else surveys, for that matter. On the
other hand, you are, curiously enough, for all your size, a member
of the inconsequent ephemera.[1] You are one of God's moderately
amusing early experiments, a frail footnote to natural history, a

---

[1] **ephemera:** short-lived, transient things.

contraption in a museum for future Man to marvel at, an excellent example of Jehovah's jejune juvenilia."[2]

The dinosaur sighed with a sound like thunder.

"Perpetuating your species," Man continued, "would be foolish and futile."

"The missing link is not lost," said the dinosaur sorrowfully. "It's hiding."

Man paid the doomed dinosaur no mind. "If there were no Man it would be necessary to create one," said Man, "for God moves in mysterious, but inefficient, ways, and He needs help. Man will go on forever, but you will be one with the mammoth and the mastodon, for monstrosity is the behemother[3] of extinction."

"There are worse things than being extinct," said the dinosaur sourly, "and one of them is being you."

Man strutted a little pace and flexed his muscles. "You cannot even commit murder," he said, "for murder requires a mind. You are capable only of dinosaurslaughter. You and your ilk are incapable of devising increasingly effective methods of destroying your own species and, at the same time, increasingly miraculous methods of keeping it extant. You will never live to know the two-party system, the multi-party system, and the one-party system. You will be gone long before I have made this the best of all possible worlds, no matter how possible all other worlds may be. In your highest state of evolution you could not develop the brain cells to prove innocent men guilty, even after their acquittal. You are all wrong in the crotch, and in the cranium, and in the cortex. But I have wasted enough time on you. I must use these fingers which God gave me, and now probably wishes He had kept for Himself, to begin writing those noble volumes about Me which will one day run to several hundred billion items, many of them about war, death, conquest, decline, fall, blood, sweat, tears, threats, warnings, boasts, hopelessness, hell, heels, and whores. There will be little enough about you and your ilk and your kith and your kin, for after all, who were you and your ilk and your kith and your kin? Good day and goodbye," said

---

[2] **Jehovah's jejune juvenilia:** God's insipid first attempts; His earliest creations lacking in sophistication and interest.

[3] **behemother** (bi hē′ muth ər): word coined from *behemoth,* a huge beast mentioned in the Bible, and *mother,* to suggest that monstrous size is the cause of its own extinction.

Man in conclusion. "I shall see to it that your species receives a decent burial, with some simple ceremony."

Man, as it turned out, was right. The dinosaur and his ilk and his kith and his kin died not long after, still in lower case, but with a curious smile of satisfaction, or something of the sort, on their ephemeral faces.

MORAL: *The noblest study of mankind is Man, says Man.*[4]

INTERPRETATION
1. Discuss the meaning of the dinosaur's comments to the Man. What effect do they have on him?
2. What is Man's attitude toward the dinosaur? toward himself? With which do you sympathize, the Man or the dinosaur? Why? Judging from the moral, with which does the author sympathize?

STYLE AND METHOD
1. *Hyperbole* is a term used to describe extreme exaggeration — for rhetorical* effect. Find several instances of hyperbole in the selection. What is the point, or effect, of each?
2. In the introductory note, it was suggested that Thurber was being satirical.* What specific quality(ies) of Man is the target of his ridicule? (Notice that except for the moral, Thurber never directly criticizes Man; how, then, is the satire accomplished? What part does Man's *language* play in producing the desired effect?)
3. How does the tone* of the author reveal itself in the first and last paragraphs?

FOR WRITING
1. Write a fable of your own which demonstrates some universal human fault or weakness.
2. Write an expository* essay in which you make clear the meaning of some of the expressions Man uses in his references to himself and the relationship between his species and other animals, the world, and God.

---

[4] An allusion to Alexander Pope's line, "The proper study of mankind is man," from *An Essay on Man.*

II

Personalities

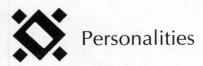

Personalities

Some forms of writing—the diary, the personal letter, and the personal essay, for example—invite the writer to reveal himself in a personal way. Reading such writing, we can almost imagine that we are overhearing a soliloquy* or a confidential chat. When we take up the diary of a Dag Hammarskjöld or read E. M. Forster's confession of personal belief, we feel that we have touched the inner self that is at the core of every personality.

Yet, even though each selection in this section of the book allows you to read a personality, skillful readers will guard against the assumption that the voice they hear in any essay is always and necessarily identical with the author at his desk. Just as we all do in everyday speaking situations, writers will adjust their "voice" (*persona** is the technical term) according to their attitude toward their subject and their view of their audience. Just as you adopt one tone in speaking to friends about last night's movie and another when speaking to a guidance counselor about college, so an author may adopt—among others—a formal, dignified tone, a casual, bantering tone, or a detached, ironic tone—depending on his artistic purpose, his audience, and his subject. Thus Mark Twain, in writing for a general magazine audience about the turning point of his life, is clearly winking at the reader, while E. B. White, in reflecting on a boyhood episode, fondly regards his adolescent gaucheness at the same time as he recognizes the ridiculousness of his behavior. So rather than say that writing *is* the man, it might be better to say that it expresses one aspect of the writer's person-ality, or one of the writer's *potential* personalities—the one best suited to the writing situation. It is, in other words, the projection of a *persona*.

Personality is expressed in many ways in writing, but especially through the choice and use of words. Does the writer's expression tend to be concrete or abstract, literal* (factual) or figurative* (metaphorical)? Then, how does the author order his material—logically, chronologically, according to fancy or association, or according to some original or novel plan? And, finally, what values and sensibilities does the writing express? Continuing to ask questions like these as you read will not only heighten your ap-preciation of writing as an expression of personality, but make you aware of what you can bring to your own writing.

33

The following selection is from the diary of Dag Hammarskjöld, Secretary General to the United Nations from 1953 to 1961. He himself described his thoughts as "negotiations with myself — and with God." But after Hammarskjöld had become a public figure and recognized the possibility that the diary might some day be published, some of the entries seem to have been addressed to a different audience.

Markings was published after the author's death in an airplane accident, which occurred in the execution of his peace-keeping duties as Secretary General to the U. N.

From *Markings*

DAG HAMMARSKJÖLD

At every moment you choose yourself. But do you choose *your* self? Body and soul contain a thousand possibilities out of which you can build many *I*'s. But in only one of them is there a congruence of the elector and the elected. Only one — which you will never find until you have excluded all those superficial and fleeting possibilities of being and doing with which you toy, out of curiosity or wonder or greed, and which hinder you from casting anchor in the experience of the mystery of life, and the consciousness of the talent entrusted to you which is your *I*.

*

While performing the part which is truly ours, how exhausting it is to be obliged to play a role which is not ours: the person you must really be in order to fulfill your task, you must not appear to others to be, in order to be allowed by them to fulfill it. How exhausting — but unavoidable, since mankind has laid down once and for all the organized rules for social behavior.

*

Respect for the word is the first commandment in the discipline by which a man can be educated to maturity — intellectual, emotional, and moral.

Respect for the word — to employ it with scrupulous care and an incorruptible heartfelt love of truth — is essential if there is to be any growth in a society or in the human race.

To misuse the word is to show contempt for man. It undermines the bridges and poisons the wells. It causes Man to regress down the long path of his evolution.

"But I say unto you, that every idle word that men speak. . . ."[1]

*

Humility is just as much the opposite of self-abasement as it is of self-exaltation. To be humble is *not to make comparisons.* Secure in its reality, the self is neither better nor worse, bigger nor smaller, than anything else in the universe. It *is* — is nothing, yet at the same time one with everything. It is in this sense that humility is absolute self-effacement.

To be nothing in the self-effacement of humility, yet, for the sake of the task, to embody *its* whole weight and importance in your bearing, as the one who has been called to undertake it. To give to people, works, poetry, art, what the self can contribute, and to take, simply and freely, what belongs to it by reason of its identity. Praise and blame, the winds of success and adversity, blow over such a life without leaving a trace or upsetting its balance.

Towards this, so help me, God —

*

To have humility is to experience reality, not *in relation to ourselves,* but in its sacred independence. It is to see, judge, and act from the point of rest in ourselves. Then, how much disappears, and all that remains falls into place.

In the point of rest at the center of our being, we encounter a world where all things are at rest in the same way. Then a tree becomes a mystery, a cloud a revelation, each man a cosmos of

[1] Matthew 12:36: "But I say unto you, That every idle word that men shall speak, they shall give account thereof in the day of judgment."

whose riches we can only catch glimpses. The life of simplicity is simple, but it opens to us a book in which we never get beyond the first syllable.

INTERPRETATION

1. There is no topical or thematic organization to *Markings,* since it is a chronological record of the author's daily reflections. What thematic titles would you suggest for each of these five selections? Which selection speaks most directly to your experience? Explain.
2. We know who is speaking in each of these selections, but whom is he addressing? Does the writer seem to have the same or a different audience in mind in each selection? Who do the pronouns refer to in each selection? How do you know?

STYLE AND METHOD

1. Discuss the use of the concept of "self" in the fourth and fifth selections. How does the change from "self" to "ourselves" affect the meaning and tone*? Despite these shifts in tone and *persona*, does a single personality show through these selections? If so, describe it.
2. In the fourth selection there is an increased use of the infinitive construction ("to be humble," "to be nothing," "to give to people.") Does this style express a heightened sense of discovery? of aspiration? To what climax does this series of parallel thoughts rise?

FOR WRITING

1. In one or two thoughtful paragraphs try to state your conception of yourself.
2. Explain your conception of any of the following terms: honesty, faith, humility, pride, or integrity. Make clear any difference between your view and the popularly held notion of the term.

A good novel is not only a reflection of life, but a comment on it, a criticism. If you can project yourself into the novel's world and characters, the experience of your reading will often illuminate your own life, clarifying the problems and heightening your responses to the world. In the following essay, a sixteen-year-old girl analyzes the effect of J. D. Salinger's novel *The Catcher in the Rye* on her view of herself and the world.

On *The Catcher in the Rye*

SANDRA CHRISTENSON

(A student essay)

The Catcher in the Rye is a story concerned with self-identity; the search of a boy for himself, for his place, and for his reason. It is at a time when childhood and its innocence are at one end, and the patterned stamp of adulthood lurks at the other. Holden Caulfield represents the person caught in the vacuum, an offspring of its emptiness. He is someone who is trying to find out who he is and what he is looking for so that he will have some pattern to fit in and something permanent and real to identify with and to cling to when he is left alone to make his own way.

Holden's migration from one world and its values to another brings about an ugly bitterness. The bitterness is derived in part from the uncertainty of the future. It is the fear that you are looking forward to something that won't exist that makes you acrid and spiteful. Maybe the future will consist of rehashed memories; you are only closer to dying each day as you wallow in your rut remembering how you and the gang played kick-the-can when you were twelve. When you are sixteen, you wait until your life becomes miraculously transformed into something worthwhile,

"On *The Catcher in the Rye*," by permission of Sandra Christenson.

and you can become cynical about the future and life in general in order to protect yourself from the let-down.

Bitterness comes, too, when you look around in order to find something or someone real to see your reflection in, and everything and everyone that you touch is phoney. You witness people respecting the wrong thing for the wrong reason; teachers laughing at the "right" jokes that aren't even funny; neighbors grinning at one another under a guise of interest and friendship instead of the indifference and dislike they really feel; snobs acting humble while everyone utters, "What a great guy," in the background, great guys with artificial reputations; kindhearted souls with their synthetic sympathy; and well-trained boys and girls who mumble mimeographed conversational niceties to adults when they feel like telling them, "go to hell." "If you want to stay alive, you have to say those things, though," Holden reflects. The greatest disappointment comes when you find yourself a part of the phoniness and see yourself in that mirror. There is bitterness at the realization that adulthood and maturity offer no guarantee against falseness — that nothing does.

Bitterness evolves when you grope for a helping hand in the chaos, and there is none. ". . . nobody cared . . . you could be a dope fiend and nobody'd care . . . ," Holden tells himself. You wait for people to stop testing you, to stop making judgments on you, and to quit giving advice, hoping for someone who will look further than your reflection — someone who will touch you inside where you are you. Yes, you wait and you wait and you wait.

There is resentment, too, when your childhood is dirtied by life, and your innocence is gone. The dirtiness is indelibly inscribed in your mind, and you are changed inside and on the surface, too, like a wall with a profanity scratched on it with a knife. You can turn profanity and ugliness around and use them for your own weapons, but it is small defense against the hurt and confusion that you feel.

Phoebe, Holden's ten-year-old sister, represents something pure and authentic; someone who is young enough to be Benedict Arnold in a school play and still be excited about it. She is the one thing in Holden's life (besides his dead brother Allie) who is still genuine and unchanged, at least for the time being. The bond between them is something for Holden to clutch onto in his wanderings; something silly and infantile and very "nice" like his red hunting hat that he bought on a whim and later gave to Phoebe. "My red hunting hat really gave me a lot of protection, in a way . . . ," Holden reflects.

To be a catcher in the rye would be to watch all the little children as they play and prevent their falling over the cliff and becoming older and wiser. That is what Holden wanted to be. It may sound ironic for someone sixteen to talk about the protection of childish innocence, but sixteen is still too old to ride a merry-go-round — to ride it and enjoy it as you used to.

You can't go around wiping off all the dirty words from all the walls, because no matter what is done, the words will be discovered. Change within a person is inevitable, but there will always be more children, more Christmas grins, and more grade-school patriotic plays. "That's one nice thing about carrousels, they always play the same songs," Holden tells himself. The more things change, the more they stay the same. Just as Holden is searching for himself and for a definition that will link his present to his past and his past with his future, so will Phoebe. "The thing with kids is, if they want to grab for the golden ring, you have to let them do it and not say anything to them," Holden decides.

I accept *The Catcher in the Rye* as part of myself. It leaves you in the middle of a search that is as formless, as indefinite, and as unexplainable as the book is to me. Holden's perambulating thoughts and abusive language help paint the picture of bitter confusion which surrounds this boy as he gropes about for stable bearings, wondering if there are any.

The book — often compared to *Huckleberry Finn* because of the use of colorful language — seems to me also to be sensitive without being sentimental and dramatic without being melodramatic. The book is so startling in its frankness that you can't help laughing at the character's candor despite your well-trained sense of middle-class decency (or carefully cultivated phoniness, if you like). I think it was Mary McCarthy who compared Salinger and Hemingway in their ability to implant their own attitudes deep within the characters in their books — to be revealed in telling acts or expressions. It is clear, then, that if you can speak the language of Salinger's characters, you also have a bond with the author.

The subject matter and treatment of *The Catcher in the Rye* suggest that the book is very personal to the author. You can't write about loneliness if you haven't felt it or if your experience isn't genuine. Salinger has challenged my power of understanding by writing frankly and intricately simply about events and ideas that are very complex in their causes and effects.

Salinger writes about feelings and attitudes without explaining them. There is no need to, for you either understand the character or you don't. Empathy makes the fine line between *The Catcher in the Rye* being profound or just vulgar; between its being authentic or an exaggeration. I thought the book was magnificently written. Salinger made the theme and the book's protest shine subtly through the lens of Holden's frankness and confusion. *The Catcher in the Rye* is a very personal book, and if you can find a part of yourself in it, then Holden Caulfield lives!!!

INTERPRETATION

1. Which aspects of Holden Caulfield's experience does the writer most strongly identify with? If you have read the novel, discuss the accuracy of the writer's interpretation. Has she picked the essential points to stress in her essay?

2. Explain the writer's "I accept *The Catcher in the Rye* as part of myself." Does the writing confirm the truth of this statement?

3. In the last paragraph, the writer states: "Empathy makes the fine line between *The Catcher* being profound or just vulgar; between its being authentic or an exaggeration." Explain this statement. Then try to explain what makes you empathize with a character in fiction.

STYLE AND METHOD

1. This essay is both a personal comment and an explanation of a personal quality in the novel. How does the writer combine "facts" from the novel with personal comment?

2. The writer uses some words and phrases which may seem extreme or even illogical—but which express an intensely personal vision of both the novel and the real world. Find as many examples as you can and discuss the meanings and attitudes they imply.

3. The essay makes extensive use of first and second person pronouns. Discuss the effectiveness of this technique. Does it make the essay seem more personal? Who might the "you" be in this paper?

FOR WRITING

The writer feels that the novelist told the truth about many elements in teen-age living. Choose something you have read which impressed you with its authenticity. Discuss its effect on you. Write as though for the audience of a good teen-age magazine.

This statement of personal belief was composed at a time when World War II was threatening to destroy European civilization — including the freedom of self-expression. The author begins his essay, surprisingly, with the comment, "I do not believe in belief." Why does he say that? Are militant creeds and causes as much a threat today as they were at the time Forster wrote? Try to discover whether the author offers any defense against them, any coherent set of beliefs with which to confront the chaotic forces that are always threatening to disrupt civilization.

What I Believe

E. M. FORSTER

I do not believe in belief. But this is an age of faith, where one is surrounded by so many militant creeds that, in self-defense, one has to formulate a creed of one's own. Tolerance, good temper, and sympathy are no longer enough in a world which is rent by religious and racial persecution, in a world where ignorance rules, and science, who ought to have ruled, plays the subservient pimp. Tolerance, good temper, and sympathy — well, they are what matter really, and if the human race is not to collapse they must come to the front before long. But for the moment they don't seem enough, their action is no stronger than a flower, battered beneath a military jack boot. They want stiffening, even if the process coarsens them. Faith, to my mind, is a stiffening process, a sort of mental starch, which ought to be applied as sparingly as possible. I dislike the stuff. I do not believe in it, for its own sake, at all. Herein I probably differ from most of the contributors to this volume, who believe in belief, and are only sorry they can't swallow even more than they do. My lawgivers are Erasmus and Montaigne,[1] not Moses and St. Paul.[2] My tem-

[1] **Erasmus and Montaigne:** humanists skeptical of Roman Catholic dogma who advocated charitable action as the primary expression of Christian truth.
[2] **Moses and St. Paul:** strict interpreters of God's law, in the Old and New Testaments, respectively.

ple stands not upon Mount Moriah[3] but in the Elysian Field[4] where even the immoral are admitted. My motto is "Lord, I disbelieve — help thou my unbelief."

I have, however, to live in an age of Faith — the sort of thing I used to hear praised and recommended when I was a boy. It is damned unpleasant, really. It is bloody in every sense of the word. And I have to keep my end up in it. Where do I start?

With personal relationships. Here is something comparatively solid in a world full of violence and cruelty. Not absolutely solid, for psychology has split and shattered the idea of a "person," and has shown that there is something incalculable in each of us, which may at any moment rise to the surface and destroy our normal balance. We don't know what we're like. We can't know what other people are like. How then can we put any trust in personal relationships, or cling to them in the gathering political storm? In theory we can't. But in practice we can and do. Though A isn't unchangeably A or B unchangeably B, there can still be love and loyalty between the two. For the purpose of living one has to assume that the personality is solid, and the "self" is an entity, and to ignore all contrary evidence. And since to ignore evidence is one of the characteristics of faith, I certainly can proclaim that I believe in personal relationships.

Starting from them, I get a little order into the contemporary chaos. One must be fond of people and trust them if one isn't to make a mess of life, and it is therefore essential that they shouldn't let one down. They often do. The moral of which is that I must myself be as reliable as possible, and this I try to be. But reliability isn't a matter of contract — that is the main difference between the world of personal relationships and the world of business relationships. It is a matter for the heart, which signs no documents. In other words, reliability is impossible unless there is a natural warmth. Most men possess this warmth, though they often have bad luck and get chilled. Most of them, even when they are politicians, *want* to keep faith. And one can, at all events, show one's own little light here, one's own poor little trembling flame, with the knowledge that it's not the only light that is shining in the darkness, and not the only one which the

[3] **Mount Moriah:** place name of ancient Palestine, usually identified with the site of the Temple at Jerusalem.
[4] **Elysian Field:** in Greek mythology, land of sunlight, flowers, and meadows where good souls went after death.

darkness doesn't comprehend. Personal relations are despised today. They are regarded as bourgeois luxuries, as products of a time of fair weather which has now passed, and we are urged to get rid of them, and to dedicate ourselves to some movement or cause instead. I hate the idea of dying for a cause, and if I had to choose between betraying my country and betraying my friend, I hope I should have the guts to betray my country. Such a choice may scandalize the modern reader, and he may stretch out his patriotic hand to the telephone at once, and ring up the police. It wouldn't have shocked Dante,[5] though. Dante places Brutus and Cassius in the lowest circle of Hell because they had chosen to betray their friend Julius Caesar rather than their country Rome. Probably one won't be asked to make such an agonizing choice. Still there lies at the back of every creed something terrible and hard for which the worshiper may one day be required to suffer, and there is even a terror and a hardness in this creed of personal relationships, urbane and mild though it sounds. Love and loyalty to an individual can run counter to the claims of the state. When they do—down with the state, say I, which means that the state will down me.

This brings me along to democracy, "even Love, the Beloved Republic, which feeds upon Freedom and lives." Democracy isn't a beloved republic really, and never will be. But it is less hateful than other contemporary forms of government, and to that extent it deserves our support. It does start from the assumption that the individual is important, and that all types are needed to make a civilization. It doesn't divide its citizens into the bossers and the bossed, as an efficiency regime tends to do. The people I admire most are those who are sensitive and want to create something or discover something, and don't see life in terms of power, and such people get more of a chance under democracy than elsewhere. They found religions, great or small, or they produce literature and art, or they do disinterested scientific research, or they may be what is called "ordinary people," who are creative in their private lives, bring up their children decently, for instance, or help their neighbors. All these people need to express themselves, they can't do so unless society allows them liberty to do so, and the society which allows them most liberty is a democracy.

[5] **Dante:** Italian poet and author of *The Inferno,* which describes a journey through hell.

Democracy has another merit. It allows criticism, and if there isn't public criticism there are bound to be hushed up scandals. That is why I believe in the press, despite all its lies and vulgarity, and why I believe in Parliament. The British Parliament is often sneered at because it's a talking shop. Well, I believe in it because it is a talking shop. I believe in the private member who makes himself a nuisance. He gets snubbed and is told that he is cranky or ill-informed, but he exposes abuses which would otherwise never have been mentioned, and very often an abuse gets put right just by being mentioned. Occasionally, too, in my country, a well-meaning public official loses his head in the cause of efficiency, and thinks himself God Almighty. Such officials are particularly frequent in the Home Office. Well, there will be questions about them in Parliament sooner or later, and then they'll have to mend their steps. Whether Parliament is either a representative body or an efficient one is very doubtful, but I value it because it criticizes and talks, and because its chatter gets widely reported.

So two cheers for democracy: one because it admits variety and two because it permits criticism. Two cheers are quite enough: there is no occasion to give three. Only Love, the Beloved Republic deserves that.

What about force, though? While we are trying to be sensitive and advanced and affectionate and tolerant, an unpleasant question pops up: Doesn't all society rest upon force? If a government can't count upon the police and the army, how can it hope to rule? And if an individual gets knocked on the head or sent to a labor camp, of what significance are his opinions?

This dilemma doesn't worry me as much as it does some. I realize that all society rests upon force. But all the great creative actions, all the decent human relations, occur during the intervals when force has not managed to come to the front. These intervals are what matter. I want them to be as frequent and as lengthy as possible and I call them "civilization." Some people idealize force and pull it into the foreground and worship it, instead of keeping it in the background as long as possible. I think they make a mistake, and I think that their opposites, the mystics, err even more when they declare that force doesn't exist. I believe that it does exist, and that one of our jobs is to prevent it from getting out of its box. It gets out sooner or later, and then it destroys us and all the lovely things which we have made. But it isn't out all the time, for the fortunate reason that the strong are so stupid. Consider their conduct for a moment in the Nibelung's *Ring*.[6] The giants there have the guns, or in other words the gold; but they do nothing with it, they do not realize that they are all-powerful, with the result that the catastrophe is delayed and the castle of Walhalla,[7] insecure but glorious, fronts the storms for generations. Fafnir,[8] coiled around his hoard, grumbles and grunts; we can hear him under Europe today; the leaves of the wood already tremble, and the Bird calls its warnings uselessly. Fafnir will destroy us, but by a blessed dispensation he is stupid and slow, and creation goes on just outside the poisonous blast of his breath. The Nietzschean[9] would hurry the monster up, the mystic would say he didn't exist, but Wotan,[10] wiser than either, hastens to create warriors before doom declares itself. The Valkyries[11] are symbols not only of courage but of intelligence; they represent the human spirit snatching its opportunity while the going is good, and one of them must be accepted as true if we are to go on the recurrence of love, and since it is the privilege of art to exaggerate she goes even further, and proclaims the love which is eternally triumphant and feeds upon freedom, and lives.

So that is what I feel about force and violence. It is, alas! the ultimate reality, on this earth, but — hooray! — it doesn't always get to the front. Some people call its absences "decadence"; I call them "civilization" and find in such interludes the chief justification for the human experiment. I look the other way until fate strikes me. Whether this is due to courage or to cowardice in my own case I cannot be sure. But I know that if men hadn't looked the other way in the past nothing of any value would survive. The people I respect most behave as if they were immor-

[6] **Nibelung's Ring:** magic ring of a dwarf people taken from them by Siegfried in Teutonic mythology.

[7] **Walhalla:** Valhalla. In Norse mythology, the great hall into which souls of heroes fallen in battle were borne by Valkyries and feasted by the god Odin.

[8] **Fafnir:** giant turned dragon who guards the stolen treasure in Wagner's opera *Siegfried* based upon Scandinavian and Germanic mythology.

[9] **Nietzschean:** one who, following the German philosopher Nietzsche, has abandoned traditional Christian ethics in favor of the Superman, the strong man who is motivated by the will to power.

[10] **Wotan:** chief of ancient gods in Scandinavian mythology; also called Odin.

[11] **Valkyries:** armed goddess maidens who rode to battlefields and chose slain heroes for Valhalla.

tal and as if society were eternal. Both assumptions are false: both of them must be accepted as true if we are to go on eating and working and loving, and are to keep open a few breathing holes for the human spirit. No millennium seems likely to descend upon humanity; no better and stronger League of Nations will be instituted; no form of Christianity and no alternative to Christianity will bring peace to the world or integrity to the individual; no "change of heart" will occur. And yet we needn't despair, indeed we cannot despair; the evidence of history shows us that men have always insisted on behaving creatively under the shadow of the sword; that they have done their artistic and scientific and domestic stuff for the sake of doing it, and that we had better follow their example under the shadow of the airplanes. Others, with more vision or courage than myself, see the salvation of humanity ahead, and will dismiss my conception of civilization as paltry, a sort of tip-and-run game. Certainly it is presumptuous to say that we *can't* improve, and that man, who has only been in power for a few thousand years, will never learn to make use of his power. All I mean is that, if people continue to kill one another at the rate they do, the world cannot get better than it is, and that since there are more people than formerly, and their means for destroying one another more diabolic, the world may well get worse. What's good in people — and consequently in the world — is their insistence on creation, their belief in friendship, in loyalty, for its own sake; and though violence remains and is indeed the major partner in this muddled establishment, I believe that creativeness remains too, and will always assume direction when violence sleeps. So, though I am not an optimist, I cannot agree with Sophocles[12] that it were better never to have been born. And although I see no evidence that each batch of births is superior to the last, I leave the field open for this happier view. This is such a difficult time to live in, especially for a European, one can't help getting gloomy and also a bit rattled.

There is of course hero worship, fervently recommended as a panacea in some quarters. But here we shall get no help. Hero worship is a dangerous vice, and one of the minor merits of a democracy is that it does not encourage it, or produce that unmanageable type of citizen known as the Great Man. It produces instead different kinds of small men, and that's a much finer

[12] **Sophocles:** Greek writer of tragedies. Allusion is to *Oedipus Coloneus*, "Not to be born is best."

achievement. But people who can't get interested in the variety of life and can't make up their own minds get discontented over this, and they long for a hero to bow down before and to follow blindly. It's significant that a hero is an integral part of the authoritarian stock in trade today. An efficiency regime can't be run without a few heroes stuck about to carry off the dullness — much as plums have to be put into a bad pudding to make it palatable. One hero at the top and a smaller one each side of him is a favorite arrangement, and the timid and the bored are comforted by such a trinity, and, bowing down, feel exalted by it.

No, I distrust Great Men. They produce a desert of uniformity around them and often a pool of blood, too, and I always feel a little man's pleasure when they come a cropper. Every now and then one reads in the newspapers some such statement as, "The *coup d'état* appears to have failed, and Admiral Boga's whereabouts is at present unknown." Admiral Boga had probably every qualification for being a great man — an iron will, personal magnetism, dash, flair — but fate was against him, so he retires to unknown whereabouts instead of parading history with his peers. He fails with a completeness that no artist and no lover can experience, because with them the process of creation is itself an achievement, whereas with him the only possible achievement is success. I believe in aristocracy though — if that's the right word, and if a democrat may use it. Not an aristocracy of power, based upon rank and influence, but an aristocracy of the sensitive, the considerate, and the plucky. Its members are to be found in all nations and classes, and all through the ages, and there is a secret understanding between them when they meet. They represent the true human tradition, the one permanent victory of our queer race over cruelty and chaos. Thousands of them perish in obscurity; a few are great names. They are sensitive for others as well as for themselves, they are considerate without being fussy, their pluck is not swankiness but the power to endure, and they can take a joke. I give no example — it is risky to do that — but the reader may as well consider whether this is the type of person he would like to meet and to be, and whether (going further with me) he would prefer that the type should *not* be an ascetic one. I'm against asceticism myself. I'm with the old Scotchman who wanted less chastity and more delicacy. I don't feel that my aristocrats are a real aristocracy if they thwart their bodies, since bodies are the instruments through which we register and enjoy the world. Still, I don't insist here. This isn't a major point. It's clearly possible to be sensitive, considerate, and plucky and yet be an ascetic too, and if anyone possesses the first three qualities, I'll let him in! On they go—an invincible army, yet not a victorious one. The aristocrats, the elect, the chosen, the best people—all the words that describe them are false, and all attempts to organize them fail. Again and again authority, seeing their value, has tried to net them and to utilize them as the Egyptian priesthood or the Christian Church or the Chinese civil service or the Group Movement, or some other worthy stunt. But they slip through the net and are gone; when the door is shut they are no longer in the room; their temple, as one of them remarked, is the holiness of the heart's imagination, and their kingdom, though they never possess it, is the wide open world.

With this type of person knocking about, and constantly crossing one's path if one has eyes to see or hands to feel, the experiment of earthly life cannot be dismissed as a failure. But it may well be hailed as a tragedy, the tragedy being that no device has been found by which these private decencies can be transferred to public affairs. As soon as people have power they go crooked and sometimes dotty, too, because the possession of power lifts them into a region where normal honesty never pays. For instance, the man who is selling newspapers outside the Houses of Parliament can safely leave his papers to go for a drink, and his cap beside them: anyone who takes a paper is sure to drop a copper into the cap. But the men who are inside the Houses of Parliament—they can't trust one another like that; still less can the government they compose trust other governments. No caps upon the pavement here, but suspicion, treachery, and armaments. The more highly public life is organized the lower does its morality sink; the nations of today behave to each other worse than they ever did in the past, they cheat, rob, bully, and bluff, make war without notice, and kill as many women and children as possible; whereas primitive tribes were at all events restrained by taboos. It's a humiliating outlook—though the greater the darkness, the brighter shine the little lights, reassuring one another, signaling, "Well, at all events I'm still here. I don't like it very much, but how are you?" Unquenchable lights of my aristocracy! Signals of the invincible army! "Come along— anyway let's have a good time while we can." I think they signal that too.

The savior of the future — if ever he comes — will not preach a new gospel. He will merely utilize my aristocracy; he will make effective the good will and the good temper which are already existing. In other words he will introduce a new technique. In economics, we are told that if there was a new technique of distribution, there need be no poverty, and people would not starve in one place while crops were dug under in another. A similar change is needed in the sphere of morals and politics. The desire for it is by no means new; it was expressed, for example, in theological terms by Jacopone da Todi over six hundred years ago. *"Ordina questo amore, O tu che m'ami,"* he said. "O thou who lovest me — set this love in order." His prayer was not granted and I do not myself believe that it ever will be, but here, and not through a change of heart, is our probable route. Not by becoming better, but by ordering and distributing his native goodness, will man shut up force into his box, and so gain time to explore the universe and to set his mark upon it worthily. At present he only explores it at odd moments, when force is looking the other way, and his divine creativeness appears as a trivial by-product, to be scrapped as soon as the drums beat and the bombers hum.

Such a change, claim the orthodox, can only be made by Christianity, and will be made by it in God's good time: man always has failed and always will fail to organize his own goodness, and it is presumptuous of him to try. This claim — solemn as it is — leaves me cold. I cannot believe that Christianity will ever cope with the present worldwide mess, and I think that such influence as it retains in modern society is due to its financial backing rather than to its spiritual appeal. It was a spiritual force once, but the indwelling spirit will have to be restated if it is to calm the waters again, and probably restated in a non-Christian form. Naturally a great many people, and people who are not only good but able and intelligent, will disagree with me here; they will vehemently deny that Christianity has failed, or they will argue that its failure proceeds from the wickedness of men, and really proves its ultimate success. They have Faith, with a large F. My faith has a very small one, and I only bring it into the open because these are strenuous and serious days, and one likes to say what one thinks while speech is still free: it may not be free much longer.

These are the reflections of an individualist and a liberal who has found his liberalism crumbling beneath him and at first felt ashamed. Then, looking around, he decided there was no special reason for shame, since other people, whatever they felt, were equally insecure. And as for individualism—there seems no way out of this, even if one wants to find one. The dictator-hero can grind down his citizens till they are all alike, but he can't melt them into a single man. That is beyond his power. He can order them to merge, he can incite them to mass antics, but they are obliged to be born separately and to die separately and, owing to these unavoidable termini, will always be running off the totalitarian rails. The memory of birth and the expectation of death always lurk within the human being, making him separate from his fellows and consequently capable of intercourse with them. Naked I came into the world, naked I shall go out of it! And a very good thing too, for it reminds me that I am naked under my shirt. Until psychologists and biologists have done much more tinkering than seems likely, the individual remains firm and each of us must consent to be one, and to make the best of the difficult job.

INTERPRETATION
1. Why does Forster mistrust Faith? How does Faith get connected with force? What *does* Forster believe in? Describe the qualities of his "aristocracy" of the best people. How do they differ from earlier aristocracies? Would you add to or change any of the characteristics Forster gives them?
2. What strengths does Forster find in democracy that make it better than other forms of government? Why does he accord only *two* cheers for democracy?
3. Discuss Forster's idea that all society rests upon force; his definition of civilization. Some people have held that war ennobles man. What answer would Forster give to this argument?

STYLE AND METHOD
1. Much writing about abstractions such as *democracy, aristocracy,* and *friendship* is dull and lifeless. Forster avoids this pitfall—how? How does Forster give color and concreteness to these ideas?
2. Diction* is one of the most important ways in which tone is established. In this essay Forster writes about the most serious matters in colloquial* language usually reserved for more casual conversation. For example, "... They have done their artistic and scientific and domestic stuff ..." (page 46) and "... as soon as people have power they go crooked and

sometimes dotty, too" (page 48). Can you find others? How do such phrases affect the tone* of the writing?

3. Does Forster's attitude seem more positive or negative? How is his general outlook influenced by his allegiance to Erasmus and Montaigne above Moses and St. Paul? Describe the personality that comes through this writing. How does it differ from the personality of Dag Hammar-skjöld, as revealed in *Markings* (pages 34-36)?

FOR WRITING

1. Discuss one of the ideas advanced in Forster's essay. For example:
   a) I do not believe in belief.
   b) It is better to betray your country than your friend.
   c) The people I respect most behave as if they were immortal.
2. Forster states that it is tragic that no way has been found to organize the "private decencies" of people for political good. Describe some ways in which you think this might be accomplished.

George Orwell's essay is a personal experience that is much more than an anecdote from the past. In it the author tells you what it is like to have to be a part of a social system and to hold an official position which requires you to "do what is expected." Pay special attention to what Orwell says about the relationship between himself and the natives and about his attitude toward his job. These set the stage for his important question: how free can a person in a position of authority be? As you read, consider whether the social compulsions he describes have an even wider application.

Shooting an Elephant

GEORGE ORWELL

In Moulmein, in Lower Burma, I was hated by large numbers of people — the only time in my life that I have been important enough for this to happen to me. I was sub-divisional police officer of the town, and in an aimless, petty kind of way anti-European feeling was very bitter. No one had the guts to raise a riot, but if a European woman went through the bazaars alone somebody would probably spit betel juice[1] over her dress. As a police officer I was an obvious target and was baited whenever it seemed safe to do so. When a nimble Burman tripped me up on the football field and the referee (another Burman) looked the other way, the crowd yelled with hideous laughter. This happened more than once. In the end the sneering yellow faces of young men that met me everywhere, the insults hooted after me when I was at a safe distance, got badly on my nerves. The young Buddhist priests were the worst of all. There were several thousands of them in the town and none of them seemed to have anything to do except stand on street corners and jeer at Europeans.

[1] **betel juice:** juice from the chewing of betel nuts, the seeds of a palm tree grown in Asia.

All this was perplexing and upsetting. For at that time I had already made up my mind that imperialism was an evil thing and the sooner I chucked up my job and got out of it the better. Theoretically — and secretly, of course — I was all for the Burmese and all against their oppressors, the British. As for the job I was doing, I hated it more bitterly than I can perhaps make clear. In a job like that you see the dirty work of Empire at close quarters. The wretched prisoners huddling in the stinking cages of the lock-ups, the gray, cowed faces of the long-term convicts, the scarred buttocks of the men who had been flogged with bamboos — all these oppressed me with an intolerable sense of guilt. But I could get nothing into perspective. I was young and ill-educated and I had had to think out my problems in the utter silence that is imposed on every Englishman in the East. I did not even know that the British Empire is dying, still less did I know that it is a great deal better than the younger empires that are going to supplant it. All I knew was that I was stuck between my hatred of the empire I served and my rage against the evil-spirited little beasts who tried to make my job impossible. With one part of my mind I thought of the British Raj as an unbreakable tyranny, as something clamped down, in *saecula saeculorum*[2] upon the will of prostrate peoples; with another part I thought that the greatest joy in the world would be to drive a bayonet into a Buddhist priest's guts. Feelings like these are the normal by-products of imperialism; ask any Anglo-Indian official, if you can catch him off duty.

One day something happened which in a roundabout way was enlightening. It was a tiny incident in itself, but it gave me a better glimpse than I had had before of the real nature of imperialism — the real motives for which despotic governments act. Early one morning the sub-inspector at a police station the other end of the town rang me up on the 'phone and said that an elephant was ravaging the bazaar. Would I please come and do something about it? I did not know what I could do, but I wanted to see what was happening and I got on to a pony and started out. I took my rifle, an old .44 Winchester and much too small to kill an elephant, but I thought the noise might be useful *in terrorem*.[3] Various Burmans stopped me on the way and told me about the

---

[2] **saecula saeculorum:** for all time.
[3] **in terrorem:** in the event of fright.

elephant's doings. It was not, of course, a wild elephant, but a tame one which had gone "must."[4] It had been chained up, as tame elephants always are when their attack of "must" is due, but on the previous night it had broken its chain and escaped. Its mahout,[5] the only person who could manage it when it was in that state, had set out in pursuit, but had taken the wrong direction and was now twelve hours' journey away, and in the morning the elephant had suddenly reappeared in the town. The Burmese population had no weapons and were quite helpless against it. It had already destroyed somebody's bamboo hut, killed a cow and raided some fruit-stalls and devoured the stock; also it had met the municipal rubbish van and, when the driver jumped out and took to his heels, had turned the van over and inflicted violences upon it.

The Burmese sub-inspector and some Indian constables were waiting for me in the quarter where the elephant had been seen. It was a very poor quarter, a labyrinth of squalid bamboo huts, thatched with palm-leaf, winding all over a steep hillside. I remember that it was a cloudy, stuffy morning at the beginning of the rains. We began questioning the people as to where the elephant had gone and, as usual, failed to get any definite information. That is invariably the case in the East; a story always sounds clear enough at a distance, but the nearer you get to the scene of events the vaguer it becomes. Some of the people said that the elephant had gone in one direction, some said that he had gone in another, some professed not even to have heard of any elephant. I had almost made up my mind that the whole story was a pack of lies, when we heard yells a little distance away. There was a loud, scandalized cry of "Go away, child! Go away this instant!" and an old woman with a switch in her hand came round the corner of a hut, violently shooing away a crowd of naked children. Some more women followed, clicking their tongues and exclaiming; evidently there was something that the children ought not to have seen. I rounded the hut and saw a man's dead body sprawling in the mud. He was an Indian, a black Dravidian coolie, almost naked, and he could not have been dead many minutes. The people said that the elephant had come suddenly upon him round the corner of the hut, caught him

---

[4] **must:** dangerous frenzy to which male elephants are occasionally subject.
[5] **mahout:** elephant driver.

with its trunk, put its foot on his back and ground him into the earth. This was the rainy season and the ground was soft, and his face had scored a trench a foot deep and a couple of yards long. He was lying on his belly with arms crucified and head sharply twisted to one side. His face was coated with mud, the eyes wide open, the teeth bared and grinning with an expression of unendurable agony. (Never tell me, by the way, that the dead look peaceful. Most of the corpses I have seen looked devilish.) The friction of the great beast's foot had stripped the skin from his back as neatly as one skins a rabbit. As soon as I saw the dead man I sent an orderly to a friend's house nearby to borrow an elephant rifle. I had already sent back the pony, not wanting it to go mad with fright and throw me if it smelt the elephant.

The orderly came back in a few minutes with a rifle and five cartridges, and meanwhile some Burmans had arrived and told us that the elephant was in the paddy fields below, only a few hundred yards away. As I started forward practically the whole population of the quarter flocked out of the houses and followed me. They had seen the rifle and were all shouting excitedly that I was going to shoot the elephant. They had not shown much interest in the elephant when he was merely ravaging their homes, but it was different now that he was going to be shot. It was a bit of fun to them, as it would be to an English crowd; besides they wanted the meat. It made me vaguely uneasy. I had no intention of shooting the elephant — I had merely sent for the rifle to defend myself if necessary — and it is always unnerving to have a crowd following you. I marched down the hill, looking and feeling a fool, with the rifle over my shoulder and an ever-growing army of people jostling at my heels. At the bottom, when you got away from the huts, there was a metalled road and beyond that a miry waste of paddy fields a thousand yards across, not yet ploughed but soggy from the first rains and dotted with coarse grass. The elephant was standing eight yards from the road, his left side towards us. He took not the slightest notice of the crowd's approach. He was tearing up bunches of grass, beating them against his knees to clean them and stuffing them into his mouth.

I had halted on the road. As soon as I saw the elephant I knew with perfect certainty that I ought not to shoot him. It is a serious matter to shoot a working elephant — it is comparable to destroying a huge and costly piece of machinery — and obviously one ought not to do it if it can possibly be avoided. And at that distance, peacefully eating, the elephant looked no more dangerous than a cow. I thought then and I think now that his attack of "must" was already passing off; in which case he would merely wander harmlessly about until the mahout came back and caught him. Moreover, I did not in the least want to shoot him. I decided that I would watch him for a little while to make sure that he did not turn savage again, and then go home.

But at that moment I glanced round at the crowd that had followed me. It was an immense crowd, two thousand at the least and growing every minute. It blocked the road for a long distance on either side. I looked at the sea of yellow faces above the garish clothes—faces all happy and excited over this bit of fun, all certain that the elephant was going to be shot. They were watching me as they would watch a conjurer about to perform a trick. They did not like me, but with the magical rifle in my hands I was momentarily worth watching. And suddenly I realized that I should have to shoot the elephant after all. The people expected it of me and I had got to do it; I could feel their two thousand wills pressing me forward, irresistibly. And it was at this moment, as I stood there with the rifle in my hands, that I first grasped the hollowness, the futility of the white man's dominion in the East. Here was I, the white man with his gun, standing in front of the unarmed native crowd—seemingly the leading actor of the piece; but in reality I was only an absurd puppet pushed to and fro by the will of those yellow faces behind. I perceived in this moment that when the white man turns tyrant it is his own freedom that he destroys. He becomes a sort of hollow, posing dummy, the conventionalized figure of a sahib.[6] For it is the condition of his rule that he shall spend his life in trying to impress the "natives," and so in every crisis he has got to do what the "natives" expect of him. He wears a mask, and his face grows to fit it. I had got to shoot the elephant. I had committed myself to doing it when I sent for the rifle. A sahib has got to act like a sahib; he has got to appear resolute, to know his own mind and do definite things. To come all that way, rifle in hand, with two thousand people marching at my heels, and then to trail feebly away, having done nothing—no, that was impossible. The crowd would laugh at me. And my whole life, every white man's life in the East, was one long struggle not to be laughed at.

[6] **sahib:** native title for European gentleman.

But I did not want to shoot the elephant. I watched him beating his bunch of grass against his knees, with that preoccupied grand-motherly air that elephants have. It seemed to me that it would be murder to shoot him. At that age I was not squeamish about killing animals, but I had never shot an elephant and never wanted to. (Somehow it always seems worse to kill a *large* animal.) Be-sides, there was the beast's owner to be considered. Alive, the elephant was worth at least a hundred pounds; dead, he would only be worth the value of his tusks, five pounds, possibly. But I had got to act quickly. I turned to some experienced-looking Burmans who had been there when we arrived, and asked them how the elephant had been behaving. They all said the same thing: he took no notice of you if you left him alone, but he might charge if you went too close to him.

It was perfectly clear to me what I ought to do. I ought to walk up to within, say, twenty-five yards of the elephant and test his behavior. If he charged, I could shoot; if he took no notice of me, it would be safe to leave him until the mahout came back. But also I knew that I was going to do no such thing. I was a poor shot with a rifle and the ground was soft mud into which one would sink at every step. If the elephant charged and I missed him, I should have about as much chance as a toad under a steam-roller. But even then I was not thinking particularly of my own skin, only of the watchful yellow faces behind. For at that moment, with the crowd watching me, I was not afraid in the ordinary sense, as I would have been if I had been alone. A white man mustn't be frightened in front of "natives"; and so, in general, he isn't frightened. The sole thought in my mind was that if any-thing went wrong those two thousand Burmans would see me pursued, caught, trampled on and reduced to a grinning corpse like that Indian up the hill. And if that happened it was quite probable that some of them would laugh. That would never do. There was only one alternative. I shoved the cartridges into the magazine and lay down on the road to get a better aim.

The crowd grew very still, and a deep, low, happy sigh, as of people who see the theatre curtain go up at last, breathed from innumerable throats. They were going to have their bit of fun after all. The rifle was a beautiful German thing with cross-hair sights. I did not then know that in shooting an elephant one would shoot to cut an imaginary bar running from ear-hole to ear-hole. I ought, therefore, as the elephant was sideways on, to have aimed straight at his ear-hole; actually I aimed several inches in front of this, thinking the brain would be further forward.

When I pulled the trigger I did not hear the bang or feel the kick — one never does when a shot goes home — but I heard the devilish roar of glee that went up from the crowd. In that instant, in too short a time, one would have thought, even for the bullet to get there, a mysterious, terrible change had come over the elephant. He neither stirred nor fell, but every line of his body had altered. He looked suddenly stricken, shrunken, immensely old, as though the frightful impact of the bullet had paralyzed him without knocking him down. At last, after what seemed a long time — it might have been five seconds, I dare say — he sagged flabbily to his knees. His mouth slobbered. An enormous senility seemed to have settled upon him. One could have imagined him thousands of years old. I fired again into the same spot. At the second shot he did not collapse but climbed with desperate slowness to his feet and stood weakly upright, with legs sagging and head drooping. I fired a third time. That was the shot that did for him. You could see the agony of it jolt his whole body and knock the last remnant of strength from his legs. But in falling he seemed for a moment to rise, for as his hind legs collapsed beneath him he seemed to tower upward like a huge rock toppling, his trunk reaching skywards like a tree. He trumpeted, for the first and only time. And then down he came, his belly towards me, with a crash that seemed to shake the ground even where I lay.

I got up. The Burmans were already racing past me across the mud. It was obvious that the elephant would never rise again, but he was not dead. He was breathing very rhythmically with long rattling gasps, his great mound of a side painfully rising and falling. His mouth was wide open — I could see far down into caverns of pale pink throat. I waited a long time for him to die, but his breathing did not weaken. Finally I fired my two remaining shots into the spot where I thought his heart must be. The thick blood welled out of him like red velvet, but still he did not die. His body did not even jerk when the shots hit him, the tortured breathing continued without a pause. He was dying, very slowly and in great agony, but in some world remote from me where not even a bullet could damage him further. I felt that I had got to put an end to that dreadful noise. It seemed dreadful to see the great beast lying there, powerless to move and yet powerless to die, and not even to be able to finish him. I sent back for my small rifle and poured shot after shot into his heart and down his throat. They seemed to make no impression. The tortured gasps continued as steadily as the ticking of a clock.

In the end I could not stand it any longer and went away. I heard later that it took him half an hour to die. Burmans were bringing dahs[7] and baskets even before I left, and I was told they had stripped his body almost to the bones by the afternoon.

Afterwards, of course, there were endless discussions about the shooting of the elephant. The owner was furious, but he was only an Indian and could do nothing. Besides, legally I had done the right thing, for a mad elephant has to be killed, like a mad dog, if its owner fails to control it. Among the Europeans opinion was divided. The older men said I was right, the younger men said it was a damn shame to shoot an elephant for killing a coolie, because an elephant was worth more than any damn Coringhee coolie. And afterwards I was very glad that the coolie had been killed; it put me legally in the right and it gave me a sufficient pretext for shooting the elephant. I often wondered whether any of the others grasped that I had done it solely to avoid looking a fool.

INTERPRETATION

1. What is the author's position in the community and the attitude of the community toward him? What is *his* attitude toward his position and the community? What is the tone* of his remark (page 53): "But I could get nothing into perspective. I was young and ill-educated . . ."?
2. Why does Orwell decide that he must shoot the elephant even though it is probably harmless? What meaning does he derive from the decision? (Was there another alternative open to him? Explain what you might have done if you had been Orwell.)

STYLE AND METHOD

To appreciate the craftsmanship in Orwell's prose, try to assess the effects of each of the following: the use of anecdotal material rather than discussion of generalities; the use of concrete detail in describing action; the use of figures of speech to heighten the effect of statements; the use of colloquialisms* for their personal flavor; and the effects of short and long sentences.

[7] **dahs:** bowls.

FOR WRITING

1. Rewrite a paragraph from the narrative, changing it from first person to third person narrative. Then, write a short paper discussing the difference in the effectiveness of the two versions.

2. Relate some experience of your own in which you felt compelled to do what was expected of you. Try to make your writing as vivid as Orwell's.

How well do you remember things that happened to you some
time ago, particularly embarrassing things? Can you recall the
details or only the general outlines? In this reminiscence,
E. B. White recalls some painful moments in an event that took
place thirty-five years earlier. His selection of detail, his
interpretation, and his style show that both the main actor and the
narrator of this piece are interesting persons.

Afternoon of
an American Boy

E. B. WHITE

When I was in my teens, I lived in Mount Vernon, in the same
block with J. Parnell Thomas, who grew up to become chairman
of the House Committee on Un-American Activities. I lived on
the corner of Summit and East Sidney, at No. 101 Summit
Avenue, and Parnell lived four or five doors north of us on the
same side of the avenue, in the house the Diefendorfs used to
live in.

Parnell was not a playmate of mine, as he was a few years older,
but I used to greet him as he walked by our house on his way to
and from the depot. He was a good-looking young man, rather
quiet and shy. Seeing him, I would call "Hello, Parnell!" and he
would smile and say "Hello, Elwyn!" and walk on. Once I remember dashing out of our yard on roller skates and executing a
rink turn in front of Parnell, to show off, and he said, "Well!
Quite an artist, aren't you?" I remember the words. I was delighted at praise from an older man and sped away along the
flagstone sidewalk, dodging the cracks I knew so well.

"Afternoon of an American Boy," from *The Second Tree From the Corner* by E.B. White. Copyright,
1947 by E.B. White. Originally appeared in *The New Yorker*. Reprinted by permission of Harper &
Row, Publishers.

The thing that made Parnell a special man in my eyes in those days was not his handsome appearance and friendly manner but his sister. Her name was Eileen. She was my age and she was a quiet, nice-looking girl. She never came over to my yard to play, and I never went over there, and, considering that we lived so near each other, we were remarkably uncommunicative; nevertheless, she was the girl I singled out, at one point, to be of special interest to me. Being of special interest to me involved practically nothing on a girl's part—it simply meant that she was under constant surveillance. On my own part, it meant that I suffered an astonishing disintegration when I walked by her house, from embarrassment, fright, and the knowledge that I was in enchanted territory.

In the matter of girls, I was different from most boys of my age. I admired girls a lot, but they terrified me. I did not feel that I possessed the peculiar gifts or accomplishments that girls liked in their male companions—the ability to dance, to play football, to cut up a bit in public, to smoke, and to make small talk. I couldn't do any of these things successfully, and seldom tried. Instead, I stuck with the accomplishments I was sure of: I rode my bicycle sitting backward on the handle bars, I made up poems, I played selections from "Aïda" on the piano. In winter, I tended goal in the hockey games on the frozen pond in the Dell. None of these tricks counted much with girls. In the four years I was in the Mount Vernon High School, I never went to a school dance and I never took a girl to a drugstore for a soda or to the Westchester Playhouse or to Proctor's. I wanted to do these things but did not have the nerve. What I finally did manage to do, however, and what is the subject of this memoir, was far brassier, far gaudier. As an exhibit of teen-age courage and ineptitude, it never fails to amaze me in retrospect. I am not even sure it wasn't un-American.

My bashfulness and backwardness annoyed my older sister very much, and at about the period of which I am writing she began making strong efforts to stir me up. She was convinced that I was in a rut, socially, and she found me a drag in her own social life, which was brisk. She kept trying to throw me with girls, but I always bounced. And whenever she saw a chance she would start the phonograph and grab me, and we would go charging around the parlor in the toils of the one-step, she gripping me as in a death struggle, and I hurling her finally away from me through greater strength. I was a skinny kid but my muscles were hard, and it would have taken an unusually powerful woman to have held me long in the attitude of the dance.

One day, through a set of circumstances I have forgotten, my sister managed to work me into an afternoon engagement she had with some others in New York. To me, at that time, New York was a wonderland largely unexplored. I had been to the Hippodrome[1] a couple of times with my father, and to the Hudson-Fulton Celebration, and to a few matinées; but New York, except as a setting for extravaganzas, was unknown. My sister had heard tales of tea-dancing at the Plaza Hotel. She and a girl friend of hers and another fellow and myself went there to give it a try. The expedition struck me as a slick piece of arrangement on her part. I was the junior member of the group and had been roped in, I imagine, to give symmetry to the occasion. Or perhaps Mother had forbidden my sister to go at all unless another member of the family was along. Whether I was there for symmetry or for decency I can't really remember, but I was there.

The spectacle was a revelation to me. However repulsive the idea of dancing was, I was filled with amazement at the setup. Here were tables where a fellow could sit so close to the dance floor that he was practically on it. And you could order cinnamon toast and from the safety of your chair observe girls and men in close embrace, swinging along, the music playing while you ate the toast, and the dancers so near to you that they almost brushed the things off your table as they jogged by. I was impressed. Dancing or no dancing, this was certainly high life, and I knew I was witnessing a scene miles and miles ahead of anything that took place in Mount Vernon. I had never seen anything like it, and a ferment must have begun working in me that afternoon.

Incredible as it seems to me now, I formed the idea of asking Parnell's sister Eileen to accompany me to a tea dance at the Plaza. The plan shaped up in my mind as an expedition of unparalleled worldliness, calculated to stun even the most blasé girl. The fact that I didn't know how to dance must have been a powerful deterrent, but not powerful enough to stop me. As I look back on the affair, it's hard to credit my own memory, and I sometimes wonder if, in fact, the whole business isn't some dream that has gradually gained the status of actuality. A boy

[1] **Hippodrome:** indoor playhouse in New York, the largest in the world until it closed in 1928; it could seat about 5,200 persons.

with any sense, wishing to become better acquainted with a girl who was "of special interest," would have cut out for himself a more modest assignment to start with—a soda date or a movie date—something within reasonable limits. Not me. I apparently became obsessed with the notion of taking Eileen to the Plaza and not to any darned old drugstore. I had learned the location of the Plaza, and just knowing how to get to it gave me a feeling of confidence. I had learned about cinnamon toast, so I felt able to cope with the waiter when he came along. And I banked heavily on the general splendor of the surroundings and the extreme sophistication of the function to carry the day, I guess.

I was three days getting up nerve to make the phone call. Meantime, I worked out everything in the greatest detail. I heeled myself with a safe amount of money. I looked up trains. I overhauled my clothes and assembled an outfit I believed would meet the test. Then, one night at six o'clock, when Mother and Father went downstairs to dinner, I lingered upstairs and entered the big closet off my bedroom where the wall phone was. There I stood for several minutes, trembling, my hand on the receiver, which hung upside down on the hook. (In our family, the receiver always hung upside down, with the big end up.)

I had rehearsed my first line and my second line. I planned to say, "Hello, can I please speak to Eileen?" Then, when she came to the phone, I planned to say, "Hello, Eileen, this is Elwyn White." From there on, I figured I could ad-lib it.

At last, I picked up the receiver and gave the number. As I had suspected, Eileen's mother answered.

"Can I please speak to Eileen?" I asked, in a low, troubled voice.

"Just a minute," said her mother. Then, on second thought, she asked, "Who is it, please?"

"It's Elwyn," I said.

She left the phone, and after quite a while Eileen's voice said, "Hello, Elwyn." This threw my second line out of whack, but I stuck to it doggedly.

"Hello, Eileen, this is Elwyn White," I said.

In no time at all I laid the proposition before her. She seemed dazed and asked me to wait a minute. I assume she went into a huddle with her mother. Finally, she said yes, she would like to go tea-dancing with me at the Plaza, and I said fine, I would call for her at quarter past three on Thursday afternoon, or whatever afternoon it was — I've forgotten.

I do not know now, and of course did not know then, just how great was the mental and physical torture Eileen went through that day, but the incident stacks up as a sort of unintentional un-American activity, for which I was solely responsible. It all went off as scheduled: the stately walk to the depot; the solemn train ride, during which we sat staring shyly into the seat in front of us; the difficult walk from Grand Central across Forty-second to Fifth, with pedestrians clipping us and cutting in between us; the bus ride to Fifty-ninth Street; then the Plaza itself, and the cinnamon toast, and the music, and the excitement. The thundering quality of the occasion must have delivered a mental shock to me, deadening my recollection, for I have only the dimmest memory of leading Eileen onto the dance floor to execute two or three unspeakable rounds, in which I vainly tried to adapt my violent sister-and-brother wrestling act into something graceful and appropriate. It must have been awful. And at six o'clock, emerging, I gave no thought to any further entertainment, such as dinner in town. I simply herded Eileen back all the long, dreary way to Mount Vernon and deposited her, a few minutes after seven, on an empty stomach, at her home. Even if I had attempted to dine her, I don't believe it would have been possible; the emotional strain of the afternoon had caused me to perspire uninterruptedly, and any restaurant would have been justified in rejecting me solely on the ground that I was too moist.

Over the intervening years (all thirty-five of them), I've often felt guilty about my afternoon at the Plaza, and a few years ago, during Parnell's investigation of writers, my feeling sometimes took the form of a guilt sequence in which I imagined myself on the stand, in the committee room, being questioned. It went something like this:

PARNELL: Have you ever written for the screen, Mr. White?

ME: No, sir.

PARNELL: Have you ever been, or are you now, a member of the Screen Writers' Guild?

ME: No, sir.

PARNELL: Have you ever been, or are you now, a member of the Communist Party?

ME: No, sir.

Then, in this imaginary guilt sequence of mine, Parnell digs deep and comes up with the big question, calculated to throw me.

PARNELL: Do you recall an afternoon, along about the middle of the second decade of this century, when you took my sister to the Plaza Hotel for tea under the grossly misleading and false pretext that you knew how to dance?

And as my reply comes weakly, "Yes, sir," I hear the murmur run through the committee room and see reporters bending over their notebooks, scribbling hard. In my dream, I am again seated with Eileen at the edge of the dance floor, frightened, stunned, and happy — in my ears the intoxicating drumbeat of the dance, in my throat the dry, bittersweet taste of cinnamon.

I don't know about the guilt, really. I guess a good many girls might say that an excursion such as the one I conducted Eileen on belongs in the un-American category. But there must be millions of aging males, now slipping into their anecdotage, who recall their Willie Baxter[2] period with affection, and who remember some similar journey into ineptitude, in that precious, brief moment in life before love's pages, through constant reference, had become dog-eared, and before its narrative, through sheer competence, had lost the first, wild sense of derring-do.[3]

INTERPRETATION

1. Discuss White's view of himself as a teen-ager. Do you think he views himself objectively? How many similarities can you find between his teen years and your own? How many differences?
2. Why does he consider that his act might somehow have been "un-American"? What does he mean by the term "un-American" and what is the origin of the connection?

STYLE AND METHOD

1. How does the writer's diction* help show his view of himself in each of the following cases: his conversation as a boy; his description of the situation from the present; and his interrogation as a witness? Describe the personality that is revealed by these three facets of White's experience.
2. How does White achieve the effect of moving back and forth in time? Discuss the organizational plan of the essay.

---

[2] **Willie Baxter:** adolescent hero of Booth Tarkington's novel *Seventeen*.
[3] **derring-do:** daring action; used as an archaic term.

FOR WRITING

1. Imagine yourself in E. B. White's place. Describe your handling of the situation.
2. Re-tell one experience of your own in which you felt terribly ill-at-ease. Try structuring it in White's manner.

A letter like this one of Lincoln's can yield an insight into the personality of the writer that might never be acquired from any other source. For reading a personal letter is like overhearing a confidential chat; the writer speaks his mind without hedging because he knows his audience and how his audience will react. The *persona** we hear, then, is as close to the actual person as we are likely to get.

In this letter you will discover exactly what Lincoln thought about his stepbrother Johnston and Johnston's problem, but the *persona* also speaks worlds about the character of the letter writer. The letter, then, imaginatively read, becomes a kind of script for a scene from an intimate family drama.

A Letter from Abraham Lincoln

December 24, 1848

Dear Johnston:

Your request for eighty dollars, I do not think it best to comply with now. At the various times when I have helped you a little, you have said to me, "We can get along very well now," but in a very short time I find you in the same difficulty again. Now this can only happen by some difficulty in your conduct. What the defect is, I think I know. You are not lazy, but still you are an idler. I doubt whether since I saw you, you have done a good day's work, in any one day. You do not very much dislike to work, and still you do not work much, merely because it does not seem to you that you would get much for it.

This habit of uselessly wasting time, is the whole difficulty; it is vastly important to you, and still more to your children, that you should break this habit. It is more important to them, because they have longer to live, and can keep out of an idle habit before they are in it, easier than they can get out after they are in.

68

You are now in need of some ready money; and what I propose is, that you shall go to work, "tooth and nail," for somebody who will give you money for it.

Let father and your boys take charge of things at home — prepare for a crop, and make the crop, and you go to work for the best money wages, or in discharge of any debt you owe, for what you can get. And to secure you a fair reward for your labor, I promise you that for every dollar that you will, between this and the first of May, get for your own labor either in money or in your own indebtedness, I will then give you one other dollar.

By this, if you hire yourself at ten dollars a month, from me you will get ten more, making twenty dollars a month for your work. In this, I do not mean that you shall go off to St. Louis, or the lead mines, or the gold mines, in California, but I mean for you to go at it for the best wages you can get close to home — in Coles County.

Now if you do this, you will soon be out of debt, and what is better, you will have a habit that will keep you from getting into debt again. But if I should now clear you out, next year you will be just as deep in as ever. You say you would almost give your place in Heaven for $70 or $80. Then you value your place in Heaven very cheaply, for I am sure you can with the offer I make you get the seventy or eighty dollars for four or five months' work. You say if I furnish you the money you will deed me the land, and if you don't pay the money back, you will deliver possession —

Nonsense! If you can't live now *with* the land, how will you then live without it? You have always been kind to me, and I do not mean to be unkind to you. On the contrary. If you will but follow my advice, you will find it worth more than eight times the eighty dollars to you.

Affectionately

Your Brother

A. Lincoln

INTERPRETATION

1. What are Johnston's weaknesses as Lincoln sees them? Does the criticism seem too harsh? Why or why not?
2. Discuss the solution to Johnston's problem recommended by Lincoln. Do you agree or disagree with Lincoln's prediction that the course of

action he recommends will produce the stated results? Would they if you were Johnston?

3. Lincoln indicates that he does not mean to be "unkind" to Johnston. Is he? Discuss the meaning of *unkind* in the context of this letter.

STYLE AND METHOD

1. How closely does the *persona* in this letter resemble your earlier impressions of Lincoln's character? Do any new or unexpected qualities appear in this letter? If so, are these new qualities connected with the way Lincoln expresses himself? Explain.
2. Explain how the following elements affect the *persona* of the letter: the vocabulary and sentence structure; the organization of the letter; the nature of the suggested solution to Johnston's problem.

FOR WRITING

1. Write a personal letter to a specific person in your class in which you give your honest advice and helpful criticism on some actual situation. The purpose should be to help the person improve his behavior, attitude, or performance in some specific way. Try to follow the same pattern of development used by Lincoln.
2. Write a character sketch of either Lincoln or Johnston based solely on the information and personality clues provided in the letter.

The topic of this essay was one that was treated very seriously by many others who were invited to write for the *Bazar,* but Mark Twain approaches it with the mock-serious attitude that was his trademark. He begins in a straightforward enough manner, but soon finds the subject too pretentious to resist spoofing. At the same time he seriously develops a new and different conception of a turning point. But it is not so much what Twain says that sets the tone as the way he says it — his style. Pay attention to the unexpected twists and incongruous statements which develop from an otherwise perfectly straightforward discussion of a serious subject.

The Turning Point
of My Life

MARK TWAIN

I

If I understand the idea, the *Bazar* invites several of us to write upon the above text. It means the change in my life's course which introduced what must be regarded by me as the most *important* condition of my career. But it also implies — without intention, perhaps — that that turning point *itself* was the creator of the new condition. This gives it too much distinction, too much prominence, too much credit. It is only the *last* link in a very long chain of turning points commissioned to produce the cardinal result; it is not any more important than the humblest of its ten thousand predecessors. Each of the ten thousand did its appointed share, on its appointed date, in forwarding the scheme, and they were all necessary; to have left out any one of them would have defeated the scheme and brought about *some other* result. I know we have a fashion of saying "such and such an event was the

"The Turning Point of My Life," from *What Is Man* by Mark Twain. Reprinted by permission of Harper & Row, Publishers.

turning point in my life," but we shouldn't say it. We should merely grant that its place as *last* link in the chain makes it the most *conspicuous* link; in real importance it has no advantage over any one of its predecessors.

Perhaps the most celebrated turning point recorded in history was the crossing of the Rubicon. Suetonius[1] says:

> Coming up with his troops on the banks of the Rubicon, he halted for a while, and, revolving in his mind the importance of the step he was on the point of taking, he turned to those about him and said, "We may still retreat; but if we pass this little bridge, nothing is left for us but to fight it out in arms."

This was a stupendously important moment. And all the incidents, big and little, of Caesar's previous life had been leading up to it, stage by stage, link by link. This was the *last* link — merely the last one, and no bigger than the others; but as we gaze back at it through the inflating mists of our imagination, it looks as big as the orbit of Neptune.[2]

You, the reader, have a *personal* interest in that link, and so have I; so has the rest of the human race. It was one of the links in your life-chain, and it was one of the links in mine. We may wait, now, with bated breath, while Caesar reflects. Your fate and mine are involved in his decision.

While he was thus hesitating, the following incident occurred. A person remarked for his noble mien and graceful aspect appeared close at hand, sitting and playing upon a pipe. When not only the shepherds, but a number of soldiers also, flocked to listen to him, and some trumpeters among them, he snatched a trumpet from one of them, ran to the river with it, and, sounding the advance with a piercing blast, crossed to the other side. Upon this, Caesar exclaimed: "Let us go whither the omens of the gods and the iniquity of our enemies call us. *The die is cast.*"

So he crossed — and changed the future of the whole human race, for all time. But that stranger was a link in Caesar's life-chain, too; and a necessary one. We don't know his name, we never hear of him again; he was very casual; he acts like an accident; but he was no accident, he was there by compulsion of *his* life-chain, to blow the electrifying blast that was to make up Caesar's mind for him, and thence go piping down the aisles of history forever.

[1] **Suetonius:** Roman biographer and antiquarian.
[2] **Neptune:** fourth largest planet of the solar system.

If the stranger hadn't been there! But he *was*. And Caesar crossed. With such results! Such vast events — each a link in the *human race's* life-chain; each event producing the next one, and that one the next one, and so on: the destruction of the republic; the founding of the empire; the breaking up of the empire; the rise of Christianity upon its ruins; the spread of the religion to other lands — and so on: link by link took its appointed place at its appointed time, the discovery of America being one of them; our Revolution another; the inflow of English and other immigrants another; their drift westward (my ancestors among them) another; the settlement of certain of them in Missouri, which resulted in *me*. For I was one of the unavoidable results of the crossing of the Rubicon. If the stranger, with his trumpet blast, had stayed away (which he *couldn't,* for he was an appointed link) Caesar would not have crossed. What would have happened, in that case, we can never guess. We only know that the things that did happen would not have happened. They might have been replaced by equally prodigious things, of course, but their nature and results are beyond our guessing. But the matter that interests me personally is that I would not be *here* now, but somewhere else; and probably black — there is no telling. Very well, I am glad he crossed. And very really and thankfully glad, too, though I never cared anything about it before.

II

To me, the most important feature of my life is its literary feature. I have been professionally literary something more than forty years. There have been many turning points in my life, but the one that was the last link in the chain appointed to conduct me to the literary guild is the most *conspicuous* link in that chain. *Because* it was the last one. It was not any more important than its predecessors. All the other links have an inconspicuous look, except the crossing of the Rubicon; but as factors in making me literary they are all of the one size, the crossing of the Rubicon included.

I know how I came to be literary, and I will tell the steps that led up to it and brought it about.

The crossing of the Rubicon was not the first one, it was hardly even a recent one; I should have to go back ages before Caesar's day to find the first one. To save space I will go back only a couple of generations and start with an incident of my boyhood. When I was twelve and a half years old, my father died. It was in the spring. The summer came, and brought with it an epidemic of measles. For a time, a child died almost every day. The village was paralyzed with fright, distress, despair. Children that were not smitten with the disease were imprisoned in their homes to save them from the infection. In the homes there were no cheerful faces, there was no music, there was no singing but of solemn hymns, no voice but of prayer, no romping was allowed, no noise, no laughter, the family moved spectrally about on tiptoe, in a ghostly hush. I was a prisoner. My soul was steeped in this awful dreariness — and in fear. At some time or other every day and every night a sudden shiver shook me to the marrow, and I said to myself, "There, I've got it! and I shall die." Life on these miserable terms was not worth living, and at last I made up my mind to get the disease and have it over, one way or the other. I escaped from the house and went to the house of a neighbor where a playmate of mine was very ill with the malady. When the chance offered I crept into his room and got into bed with him. I was discovered by his mother and sent back into captivity. But I had the disease; they could not take that from me. I came near to dying. The whole village was interested, and anxious, and sent for news of me every day; and not only once a day, but several times. Everybody believed I would die; but on the fourteenth day a change came for the worse and they were disappointed.

This was a turning point of my life. (Link number one.) For when I got well my mother closed my school career and apprenticed me to a printer. She was tired of trying to keep me out of mischief, and the adventure of the measles decided her to put me into more masterful hands than hers.

I became a printer, and began to add one link after another to the chain which was to lead me into the literary profession. A long road, but I could not know that; and as I did not know what its goal was, or even that it had one, I was indifferent. Also contented.

A young printer wanders around a good deal, seeking and finding work; and seeking again, when necessity commands. N. B. Necessity is a *Circumstance;* Circumstance is man's master — and when Circumstance commands, he must obey; he may argue the matter — that is his privilege, just as it is the honorable privilege of a falling body to argue with the attraction of gravitation — but it won't do any good, he must *obey*. I wandered for ten years, under the guidance and dictatorship of Circumstance, and finally arrived in a city of Iowa, where I worked several months. Among the books that interested me in those days was one about the Amazon. The traveler told an alluring tale of his long voyage up the great river from Para to the sources of the Madeira, through the heart of an enchanted land, a land wastefully rich in tropical wonders, a romantic land where all the birds and flowers and animals were of the museum varieties, and where the alligator and the crocodile and the monkey seemed as much at home as if they were in the Zoo. Also, he told an astonishing tale about *coca,* a vegetable product of miraculous powers, asserting that it was so nourishing and so strength-giving that the native of the mountains of the Madeira region would tramp up hill and down all day on a pinch of powdered coca and require no other sustenance.

I was fired with a longing to ascend the Amazon. Also with a longing to open up a trade in coca with all the world. During months I dreamed that dream, and tried to contrive ways to get to Para and spring that splendid enterprise upon an unsuspecting planet. But all in vain. A person may *plan* as much as he wants to, but nothing of consequence is likely to come of it until the magician *Circumstance* steps in and takes the matter off his hands. At last Circumstance came to my help. It was in this way. Circumstance, to help or hurt another man, made him lose a fifty-dollar bill in the street; and to help or hurt me, made me find it. I advertised the find, and left for the Amazon the same day. This was another turning point, another link.

Could Circumstance have ordered another dweller in that town to go to the Amazon and open up a world trade in coca on a fifty-dollar basis and been obeyed? No, I was the only one. There were other fools there — shoals and shoals of them — but they were not of my kind. I was the only one of my kind.

Circumstance is powerful, but it cannot work alone; it has to have a partner. Its partner is man's *temperament* — his natural disposition. His temperament is not his invention, it is *born* in him, and he has no authority over it, neither is he responsible for its acts. He cannot change it, nothing can change it, nothing can modify it — except temporarily. But it won't stay modified. It is permanent, like the color of the man's eyes and the shape of his ears. Blue eyes are gray in certain unusual lights; but they resume their natural color when that stress is removed.

A Circumstance that will coerce one man will have no effect upon a man of a different temperament. If Circumstance had thrown the bank note in Caesar's way, his temperament would not have made him start for the Amazon. His temperament would have compelled him to do something with the money, but not that. It might have made him advertise the note—and *wait*. We can't tell. Also, it might have made him go to New York and buy into the Government, with results that would leave Tweed[3] nothing to learn when it came his turn.

Very well, Circumstance furnished the capital, and my temperament told me what to do with it. Sometimes a temperament is an ass. When that is the case the owner of it is an ass, too, and is going to remain one. Training, experience, association, can temporarily so polish him, improve him, exalt him that people will think he is a mule, but they will be mistaken. Artificially he *is* a mule, for the time being, but at bottom he is an ass yet, and will remain one.

By temperament I was the kind of person that *does* things. Does them, and reflects afterward. So I started for the Amazon without reflecting and without asking any questions. That was more than fifty years ago. In all that time my temperament has not changed, by even a shade. I have been punished many and many a time, and bitterly, for doing things and reflecting afterward, but these tortures have been of no value to me: I still do the thing commanded by Circumstance and Temperament, and reflect afterward. Always violently. When I am reflecting, on those occasions, even deaf persons can hear me think.

I went by the way of Cincinnati, and down the Ohio and Mississippi. My idea was to take ship, at New Orleans, for Para. In New Orleans I inquired, and found there was no ship leaving for Para. Also, that there never had *been* one leaving for Para. I reflected. A policeman came and asked me what I was doing, and I told him. He made me move on, and said if he caught me reflecting in the public street again he would run me in.

After a few days I was out of money. Then Circumstance arrived, with another turning point of my life—a new link. On my

---

[3] **Tweed:** Political boss of New York City's Tammany Hall around 1870. He was involved in the misappropriation of millions of dollars.

way down, I had made the acquaintance of a pilot. I begged him to teach me the river, and he consented. I became a pilot.

By and by Circumstance came again—introducing the Civil War, this time, in order to push me ahead another stage or two toward the literary profession. The boats stopped running, my livelihood was gone.

Circumstance came to the rescue with a new turning point and a fresh link. My brother was appointed secretary to the new Territory of Nevada, and he invited me to go with him and help him in his office. I accepted.

In Nevada, Circumstance furnished me the silver fever and I went into the mines to make a fortune, as I supposed; but that was not the idea. The idea was to advance me another step toward literature. For amusement I scribbled things for the Virginia City *Enterprise*. One isn't a printer ten years without setting up acres of good and bad literature, and learning—unconsciously at first, consciously later—to discriminate between the two, within his mental limitations; and meantime he is unconsciously acquiring what is called a "style." One of my efforts attracted attention, and the *Enterprise* sent for me and put me on its staff.

And so I became a journalist—another link. By and by Circumstance and the Sacramento *Union* sent me to the Sandwich Islands for five or six months, to write up sugar. I did it; and threw in a good deal of extraneous matter that hadn't anything to do with sugar. But it was this extraneous matter that helped me to another link.

It made me notorious, and San Francisco invited me to lecture. Which I did. And profitably. I had long had a desire to travel and see the world, and now Circumstance had most kindly and unexpectedly hurled me upon the platform and furnished me the means. So I joined the "Quaker City Excursion."

When I returned to America, Circumstance was waiting on the pier—with the *last* link—the conspicuous, the consummating, the victorious link: I was asked to *write a book,* and I did it, and called it *The Innocents Abroad.* Thus I became at last a member of the literary guild. That was forty-two years ago, and I have been a member ever since. Leaving the Rubicon incident away back where it belongs, I can say with truth that the reason I am in the literary profession is because I had the measles when I was twelve years old.

INTERPRETATION

1. Discuss Twain's re-definition of the subject in the first paragraph. Do you agree with his conception of a turning point? What is the purpose of the illustration of Caesar's crossing of the Rubicon? How does it help develop the essay?
2. Discuss Twain's idea of *necessity, circumstance,* and *temperament.* What does he mean by each of these terms? Do you think he means to say that the individual has little control of events that shape his life? Discuss the possibility that he is making fun of the whole idea of "The Turning Point of My Life."

STYLE AND METHOD

1. Review the essay for examples of Twain's use of exaggeration. How does Twain's humor compare with Thurber's in "The Human Being and the Dinosaur"? How do diction* and use of illustrations further characterize Twain's style?
2. Twain's essay treats in chronological order the events that led the author to his literary life. Why did Twain choose this method? Would any other approach have been as effective?

FOR WRITING

1. Can you remember events in your own past which you believe have had some effect on your life? Try writing an essay in which you discuss the influence of events that have had most to do with making you what you are.
2. Humorous writing is a very demanding kind of writing for most people, but there is usually a humorous side to every situation in life. Choose some serious situation from your own experience and write a paper which treats it humorously.

Stevenson's title alludes to a legendary golden city which was supposed to have existed somewhere in South America and was the goal of many an explorer's fruitless quest. Early in the history of this legend, the term came to be synonymous with any impossible quest or impractical goal. Sometimes the men who labored mightily for their "El Dorado" were ridiculed for their efforts, but they were fired with such hope and anticipation that even their failures were sometimes magnificent feats. In this essay, written over 100 years ago, Stevenson explores a question pertinent to the Space Age: the value of pursuing unreachable destinations.

El Dorado

ROBERT LOUIS STEVENSON

It seems as if a great deal were attainable in a world where there are so many marriages and decisive battles, and where we all, at certain hours of the day, and with great gusto and dispatch, stow a portion of victuals finally and irretrievably into the bag which contains us. And it would seem also, on a hasty view, that the attainment of as much as possible was the one goal of man's contentious life. And yet, as regards the spirit, this is but a semblance. We live in an ascending scale when we live happily, one thing leading to another in an endless series. There is always a new horizon for onward-looking men, and although we dwell on a small planet, immersed in petty business and not enduring beyond a brief period of years, we are so constituted that our hopes are inaccessible, like stars, and the term of hoping is prolonged until the term of life.

To be truly happy is a question of how we begin and not of how we end, of what we want and not of what we have. An aspiration is a joy forever, a possession as solid as a landed estate, a fortune which we can never exhaust and which gives us year by year a revenue of pleasurable activity. To have many of these is to be spiritually rich. Life is only a very dull and ill-directed theater unless we have some interests in the piece; and to those who have neither art nor science, the world is a mere arrangement of colors, or a rough footway where they may very well break their shins. It is in virtue of his own desires and curiosities that any man continues to exist with even patience, that he is charmed by the look of things and people, and that he wakens every morning with a renewed appetite for work and pleasure. Desire and curiosity are the two eyes through which he sees the world in the most enchanted colors; it is they that make women beautiful or fossils interesting; and the man may squander his estate and come to beggary, but if he keeps these two amulets, he is still rich in the possibilities of pleasure. Suppose he could take one meal so compact and comprehensive that he should never hunger any more; suppose him, at a glance, to take in all the features of the world and allay the desire for knowledge; suppose him to do the like in any province of experience — would not that man be in a poor way for amusement ever after?

One who goes touring on foot with a single volume in his knapsack reads with circumspection, pausing often to reflect, and often laying the book down to contemplate the landscape or the prints in the inn parlor; for he fears to come to an end of his entertainment and be left companionless on the last stages of his journey. A young fellow recently finished the works of Thomas Carlyle, winding up, if we remember aright, with the ten notebooks upon Frederick the Great.[1] "What!" cried the young fellow, in consternation, "is there no more Carlyle? Am I left to the daily papers?" A more celebrated instance is that of Alexander, who wept bitterly because he had no more worlds to subdue. And when Gibbon had finished the *Decline and Fall*,[2] he had only a few moments of joy; and it was with a "sober melancholy" that he parted from his labors.

Happily we shoot at the moon with ineffectual arrows; our hopes are set on inaccessible El Dorado; we come to an end of nothing here below. Interests are only plucked up to sow themselves again, like mustard. You would think, when the child was born, there would be an end to trouble; and yet it is only the

[1] **Frederick the Great:** a Prussian King (1712-1786) who, through enlightened policies promoting economic development and the impartial administration of justice, established Prussia as a strong national state.
[2] **Decline and Fall:** Gibbon's many-volumed classic dealing with the causes of the decline of the Roman Empire.

beginning of fresh anxieties; and when you have seen it through its teething and its education, and at last its marriage, alas! it is only to have new fears, new quivering sensibilities, with every day; and the health of your children's children grows as touching a concern as that of your own. Again, when you have married your wife, you would think you were got upon a hilltop and might begin to go downward by an easy slope. But you have only ended courting to begin marriage. Falling in love and winning love are often difficult tasks to overbearing and rebellious spirits; but to keep in love is also a business of some importance, to which both man and wife must bring kindness and good will. The true love story commences at the altar, when there lies before the married pair a most beautiful contest of wisdom and generosity, and a lifelong struggle toward an unattainable ideal. Unattainable? Aye, surely unattainable, from the very fact that they are two instead of one.

"Of making books there is no end," complained the Preacher,[3] and did not perceive how highly he was praising letters[4] as an occupation. There is no end, indeed, to making books or experiments, or to travel, or to gathering wealth. Problem gives rise to problem. We may study forever, and we are never as learned as we would. We have never made a statue worthy of our dreams. And when we have discovered a continent, or crossed a chain of mountains, it is only to find another ocean or another plain upon the farther side. In the infinite universe there is room for our swiftest diligence and to spare. It is not like the works of Carlyle, which can be read to an end. Even in a corner of it, in a private park, or in the neighborhood of a single hamlet, the weather and the seasons keep so deftly changing that although we walk there for a lifetime there will be always something new to startle and delight us.

There is only one wish realizable on the earth; only one thing that can be perfectly attained — death. And from a variety of circumstances we have no one to tell us whether it be worth attaining.

A strange picture we make on our way to our chimeras,[5] ceaselessly marching, grudging ourselves the time for rest; in-

[3] **"Of making books"** . . . **Preacher:** Ecclesiastes, chapter 12. The useless and vain pursuits of man constitute the Preacher's theme in this biblical book.
[4] **letters:** the writing of books; archaic term.
[5] **chimeras:** (ki mer' az) frightful, vain, or foolish fancies.

defatigable, adventurous pioneers. It is true that we shall never reach the goal; it is even more probable that there is no such place; and if we lived for centuries and were endowed with the powers of a god, we should find ourselves not much nearer what we wanted at the end. O toiling hands of mortals! O unwearied feet, traveling ye know not whither! Soon, soon, it seems to you, you must come forth on some conspicuous hilltop, and but a little way farther, against the setting sun, descry the spires of El Dorado. Little do ye know your own blessedness; for to travel hopefully is a better thing than to arrive, and the true success is to labor.

INTERPRETATION

1. Can you agree with Stevenson's last sentence? What examples from your own experience could you use to support, or refute, his basic theme?
2. If Stevenson were alive today, what would be his attitude about the exploration of space? What examples from his essay could be used today in arguing for space exploration? How would Stevenson comment about modern technology and industry? Discuss.

STYLE AND METHOD

1. Stevenson's language and many of his examples are from the Victorian period of the last century. How many of his allusions* are familiar to you? Are all his examples valid today? Explain. How is Stevenson's personality reflected in his style?
2. There are seven paragraphs in this essay. What is the function of each in the organization and development of the theme*? How is paragraph two different from paragraph three or four? Is the last paragraph a climax? Explain.
3. Read several paragraphs aloud for their rhythm. How many sentences are built up from a triad of clauses or phrases? What purposes, other than variety, are served by the short sentences?

FOR WRITING

1. Describe an experience in which you achieved a long-desired goal. What were your feelings both before and after you had attained it?
2. Pick one of Stevenson's examples or generalizations and expand it into an essay. Make your attitude both clear and consistent by your choice of details and illustrations. Example: "To be truly happy is a question of how we begin and not of how we end. . . ."

The personal essay invites the reader to go with the writer on an excursion — usually metaphorical but sometimes literal as well. The excursion may lead anywhere and discover a fascinating variety of attitudes, ideas, people, or places, but always it is the writer who is the guide, letting you see the things that are significant to him. He may start by telling you where the trip will take you and then carefully lead you there, or he may start with a discovery of his own and then explore it with all the excitement of a man who has stumbled on a new world. In "The Magic Lantern" the author explores the curious phenomenon of images — the personality a person presents to the world — and ponders the question, how do we know that others see what we expect them to see?

The Magic Lantern

ROBERT HENDERSON

One late fall Sunday not long ago, after a late breakfast, while the smell of toast still hung like a blessing in the air, I went to my room to put my image on. Not that I was aware that I was doing so, but there I was, in less than half an hour, the image of a shaved, combed man dressed in slightly baggy slacks and a weathered jacket, no fashion plate, to be sure, but still not precisely seedy, not old, not young, not tall, not short — an intermediate man, prepared to enjoy his leisure by taking a stroll in comfortable clothes on a fine fall Sunday. And if I was not aware, at the moment, that I had taken on an image, at least I had been suspecting for some time that I needed one. The word "image" skulks all around us, nowadays — in the newspapers, on the air, issuing from friend, advertisement, and stranger — and I could no longer shun the conclusion that an image is the one thing that all of us must have.

And what an autumn it had been for the *projecting* of images! God's teeth! Statesmen the world over, as fitful as chameleons, had projected image after image. Halloween had come and gone and so had an election. Goblins, new broomsticks, improbable faces, tricks and treats. An image is no good unless you project it. True, there had been peripheral talk of images unprojected and better so. George Washington, one paper noted, might have had no picnic running for President today; his face was a makeup man's nightmare, full of pocks. Thomas Jefferson's hands and feet were much too big for him — an asymmetrical image. James Madison was five feet four, and a hundred pounds — a scanty one. Who could have dreamed they would name an avenue for *him?* But, on the whole, the projectors of images seemed to have things in hand. Some margarine people even projected a non-image on television. It was butter, and they spoke of it anonymously, absent-mindedly, as "the — what do they call it? — the seventy-cent spread."

So I put on my hat that afternoon, and set out for a walk, considering what my image ought to be. Certainly it was not a thing to be left to chance. From what I had gathered, one made a sampling and then conceived an image, created it, established it, enlarged it, firmed it, improved it, *maximized* it (one has to do so many things with an image!), and off, projected, it went. Communicated. I was walking south toward Washington Square. The sun was high, but the breeze was cool in the shadows. On Fourteenth Street, I passed a lonely chestnut vender, a twisted man in a brown coat, rubbing his brown hands in the smoke from his cart and looking disgusted — a man who clearly viewed life as a whole with aversion. I thought that *he* could do with a better, brighter image. Sales would climb. But then I reflected that to find a good image and work it up might be something you couldn't do on just any stray Sunday.

Of course, people have always made images of themselves (I thought, crossing the street, sniffing the smoke of the chestnuts over my shoulder), but it used to seem simpler. You didn't go through so much. You just acted as if you were what you wished you were, and hoped for the best. Sometimes it worked, sometimes not.

As a sample, in college I knew a girl who wanted to be an image of worldliness. This was toward the end of prohibition.[1]

---

[1] **prohibition:** the period between 1920 and 1933 when the manufacture, sale, and transportation of intoxicating beverages was prohibited by the Eighteenth Amendment.

She was a dark girl with a tense, long-legged stride. She hung out in the campus bookstore, and smoked through a holder, in the shape of a tiny green snake, which she was always flicking here and there, to one side of her or the other, patting it with her fore-finger and scattering ashes and *dégagé*[2] remarks. She wore a leopard coat, which may have contributed to the report that she was a tiger woman. She was seldom around on Saturday night, when everyone else went to dances, but on Monday she would be back at the store, patting the snake and talking about cocktail parties. I don't think she was a tiger woman, or even a tiger girl. I think nobody saw her at dances because nobody asked her to them. Most boys were scared of her. If they drank, they drank out of bottles or flasks. Few of them knew quite what a cocktail was, but neither did she. In the end, that cracked her image. She overprojected. She borrowed someone's minuscule flat and invited the bookstore crowd to a cocktail party. When the respectful guests had gathered, she went to the kitchen, poured gin, grape juice, and ginger ale into a big cocktail shaker, and returned shaking it with practiced vigor, the snake between her teeth, and the mixture blew the top off the shaker and stippled[3] the guests deep purple. She never entirely recovered her aplomb. I don't suppose she knew, precisely, that she was trying to project an image, and in fact she may only have been trying to get to a dance. But plainly she did have an image. She conceived it and enlarged it, but she didn't firm it right, and I resolved, as I came to Twelfth Street and University Place, that I would not fall into her error.

I turned west on Twelfth. Other images from other days swam back and forth in my head. One was an image taken on by a haunted actor. He was haunted by the Count of Monte Cristo. He came from West Virginia, and he made a fair living out of just being ugly — a sober, gentle, thrifty man, with a face that was in demand for small criminal parts in modest plays. What he wanted more than anything else in the world was to take his adaptation of "Monte Cristo" on the road. He was wild to be James O'Neill. The road was languishing, and he believed that the time had come for him to save it. However, he knew that his face would never do. He took what money he had saved, disappeared for a long time, and came back with his face rebuilt.

[2] **dégagé** (dā gȧ zhā′): free and easy in manner.
[3] **stippled:** speckled or dappled with light and shadow.

He got pretty good parts at first — at least, he was hired for them — but he also kept being let go. The trouble was, his face wouldn't cross the footlights. Nothing discernible happened in it; it hadn't been broken in. He hadn't lived in it long enough to refine it and communicate it. I lost track of him after a while. I was told he had gone. home to West Virginia. Perhaps. He was very perplexed. All I know is he disappeared, and no new Monte Cristo took to the road.

I remembered also a girl who married very young, to the intense titillation of her friends. She was a round, soft, funny girl full of robust jokes and a popping wit — the humorist of her circle, which considered itself adult. This meant that it felt obliged to make adult quips about brides, but it found that it was doing so to no purpose. The bride's roundness grew matronly as the ring went on her finger. She became, on the instant, the image of corseted dignity. The married lady could understand no robust jokes for the life of her. Innuendo[4] was quite beyond her. She established the image resolutely, and maximized it thereafter, but she lost her status with the group, which is not at all what an image is meant to do.

I came to Fifth Avenue and turned south toward the Square, worrying. These were images, all right, but what help were they to me? They were scarcely the kind of images I was looking for. They belonged to people who wanted to *be* some way or other. *I* wanted to *seem*. After all, without an image I was only I, walking around on a Sunday afternoon. That was no image. Or was it? I thought that I ought to make another sampling. I began to look about me, and there were images on all sides. At the corner of Eleventh Street was a blind beggar with a tin cup. As I passed, I saw a tall man in a camel's-hair coat drop a penny into the cup. Image of charity. The blind man blessed him. The donor saw me watching, and scowled at me. At Tenth Street, an image of two lovers in blue jeans stood paralyzed by a kiss. I tried not to seem to notice, but they were more or less in the way. They parted as I circled them, and reproached me with forgiving eyes. Maybe I had projected a starchy, prudish image. I, in my carefree, rumpled slacks and all but rakish jacket!

At Eighth Street, a thin-faced woman strode across my path heading east. Her lips were set. She wore a dark-red beret with a

---

[4] **innuendo:** insinuation or suggestion.

big silver brooch on the front of it, tawny corduroy trousers, a faded trench coat, and a somehow warlike squint. Field-Marshal Montgomery.[5] She may not have meant to project him, but she did.

At Waverly Place, a chubby elderly man wearing a long green muffler came toward me bouncing gently on his toes. His hair stood up all over his head, and his hat rode it dangerously, like a skiff in a gray surf. He looked at me. I do not say he twinkled, but the word did come to mind, along with the thought that it might also have occurred to him. He was carrying four or five books and a bunch of mixed flowers, and he looked like a metropolitan gnome—a man who would like to be on a Christmas card. I thought he must have a firm Dickensian image of himself, and I had no doubt that he saw in me, and my indifference to dress, a bookish fellow who would spot it.

Coming out of the Square was a tiny man with a pair of Great Danes. They were leading him. He was putting up a good fight, though—checking them imperiously when they surged too fast, looking grim, looking as powerful as possible, barking at them. His voice was deep and explosive. He, himself, was predominantly pink—pink face, pink hair, small waxed pink mustache. He wore a Tyrolean hat[6] and carried a riding crop. He seemed to think he knew me, for he nodded as he swept past. "Great!" he said. "Great! Absolutely!" Then he was gone.

Gone where? To some sprawling, turreted house where he was—well, master? Groom? But where was there a sprawling, turreted house around the Village? Perhaps he was bound for some enormous apartment, the urban equivalent, where he lived with his two huge dogs. One could see them lying like statues on either side of him as he sat before his fire sipping brandy, cracking nuts, admiring his image. On the other hand, perhaps he lived cooped up in a couple of rooms, dogs and all, too poor to afford his image anywhere but out-of-doors. I tried to think what could have been great, absolutely. The day? Himself? The dogs? Me? If he thought he knew me (and supposed that I would know what it was he felt was great), just whom did he think he knew? What image did he see passing?

[5] **Field-Marshal Montgomery:** commander of the British tank forces in North Africa during World War II, a determined soldier and a brilliant strategist.
[6] **Tyrolean hat:** style of soft Alpine hat worn by men in western Austria and northern Italy, usually with a colored plume on one side.

For that matter, I was beginning to wonder what images some other people had seen. If the chestnut vender had seen a prospective client who passed him by, then maybe he was viewing *me*, not just life as a whole, with aversion. The man in the camel's-hair coat might have seen a censorious image, or a prying one. And what, after all, had *I* seen, looking at him? Perhaps it was his habit of years to give all his pennies to beggars. That could mount up. It occurred to me that the bouncing gnome might not dream that he belonged in *Martin Chuzzlewit*. Very likely he saw himself as a serious, cerebral man; very likely he had more astigmatism than twinkle. It was possible that only I had seen the images I had seen. How was I sure that they were the ones their projectors meant to project?

The sun had gone behind the Judson Memorial Church. Washington Square was cold. The folk singers (images borrowed from old grazing lands, and from mountains the singers had not climbed) were packing away their guitars and going home. I was beginning to think I was out on a wild-goose chase. How could I possibly create a dependable image, badly as I might need one to be in the swim? Suddenly I remembered all my dozen-odd middle initials. As it happens, I really have none — not a single one — but people keep trying to give them to me. Lately I got a note from an old friend. He had never before written my name with a middle initial, but now he supplied me with "M." Well, I thought, who am I? Matthew? And if I am, how does he feel about *him?* Matthew would certainly never resemble, say, Marshall. Am I Marshall? Is he nice?

I left the Square and walked back up Fifth Avenue, reflecting that the one who sees the image is, of course, the one who creates it. He makes it up to suit himself, depending on the color of the sky, the weather of his childhood, and the side of the bed he got out of in the morning, and it is never exactly the one that was projected. A change has come over it. It has gone through a lens; it is seen in his special light.

Something about all this was remotely familiar. It had to do with the very idea of projection, and, walking east on Fourteenth Street (where I was hoping I could buy some roasted chestnuts), I got it. When I was a child, I had a magic lantern. I loved it. I liked most of the pictures it projected, though I saw them in my own way. I had a few sets of slides called "Wonders of Nature,"

"Little Folks," "Scenes of American Life"—things like that. One scene of American life showed a whale upsetting a boatload of frenzied men. They were New Englanders, but not in my book. The whale, I knew, was out to swallow the harpooner, who was flying through the air. The harpooner was Jonah. He still is. In another slide, Little Folks were frolicking in snow. One of them was washing another's face in it. To some, this might look jolly, but it wasn't. The one being washed was going to catch a cold. He would be put to bed and have his temperature taken. He would have to eat junket. The snow—all snow—would melt. I never cared much for that slide. There was also Captain John Smith. I was jealous of him, for I was in love with Pocahontas, who was beautiful. I refused to believe that she was pleading for him. She wanted me. But, after all, the supply of slides was limited, and I soon got to know them too well. What never did cease to entrance me was something else: When you put a picture into a magic lantern right side up, it never fails to get itself projected upside down.

INTERPRETATION

1. Is the author's conclusion at the end of the first paragraph intended to be taken seriously? How can you tell? Why are Washington, Jefferson, and Madison mentioned in the second paragraph? What is the tone* of that paragraph?
2. In earlier times, the author recalls, "You just acted as if you were what you wished you were. . . ." Contrast that with the formula given for image-making today. Which seems more honest?
3. As he goes on, how does the author clarify what he means by "image"? How does the last paragraph seem to sum up what he has discovered, or re-discovered? Explain the significance of the last sentence of the essay.
4. Does the visual appearance of a person give you a complete image of his personality? Discuss what other kinds of information you might need before you had a clear picture of him. What image have you acquired of Mr. Henderson?

STYLE AND METHOD

1. The author uses many proper nouns and adjectives—for example, *Fifth Avenue, West Virginia, Washington Square, the Village,* and *Tyrolean.* What do these allusions* add to the essay? What images do they evoke for you? What connotations*? Are these the same for everyone in the class?

2. The personal quality of the essay depends in part on the manner in which the author seems to ramble from observations of himself through reflections about people he has known, people he meets on the street, and specific mention of the streets where he is walking. Retrace the thread of the author's thought and find out how the transitions were made. Is the essay unified? Does the thought really ramble?

FOR WRITING

1. What images do the people around you project? Pick out a few people and write a reflective report of your excursion through a day, recording the images of the people you meet. What information do you use? What do you ignore? Why?

2. Describe the image you have of some personality known to the entire class. Compare your description with that of others. Are there significant differences? If so, try to account for them in terms of the essay you have just read.

III

Exposition

Exposition

The purpose of exposition is to explain; the author attempts to make clear his understanding of a subject to an audience. Exposition may attempt to explain a process or a situation or tell how to do something; it may define a term or an idea, or analyze the qualities of a person, place, or thing; it may even attempt to explain how something happened. The writer of exposition is free to draw upon such modes of expression as narration and description, provided the larger purpose is fulfilled — to make clear the subject to the reader. In this section, for example, a contemporary biographer tells the story of how Dickens came to write *A Christmas Carol,* and a Scottish visitor to the States describes the beauty of three mountain states. But more typically, a scientist describes the scientific method of thought, an American novelist analyzes the character of Americans, and a former employer explains "how to be an employee." In exposition, the range of subject is as broad as the interests of man; the only characteristic common to all exposition is its purpose — to present a clear view of a subject.

What are the qualities of good expository writing? Clarity and precision should come first, of course. In exposition, no amount of flair or metaphor can improve a set of garbled directions or clarify a fuzzy idea. Second, organization is important since it is the visible evidence of the logical relationships among the parts of the subject. Huxley's "Method of Scientific Investigation," for example, demonstrates the value of clear organization in the exposition of even the most abstract ideas. It also illustrates the importance of a third quality of good expository writing, documentation — the presentation of particulars or details in support of a generalization. Finally, it may be said that prose that follows all these precepts will have the quality of objective thought. Good exposition reminds us that although much of life may seem irrational, there is a common ground of reasonableness that unites us man with man.

In this excerpt from his book *Death at an Early Age,* which
describes the author's experience teaching in a ghetto school,
Jonathan Kozol tells how he took over a class that had not had a
regular teacher all year, but only a long series of drifters and
incompetents. His account might be called *narrative exposition.*
The author relates the events factually as they happened, but he
also provides two other kinds of information: his personal
reactions to the situation and his appraisal of its overall meaning.
In this kind of writing the personality of the author is a strong
element because it is *his* story, of *his* experience; but it still
may be called exposition because the emphasis is on the clear
presentation of the situation and the experience. If you are
persuaded to accept the author's judgments, it is because his
evidence is so strong that you must.

A Class in Writing

JONATHAN KOZOL

I had a difficult time with that class of children for the first four
or five days. It was almost as confusing and chaotic as the first
days I had spent in the discipline school. Some of those morn-
ings, I thought of myself as a rowboat going under in mid-ocean,
the ocean being noise and cries and movements on all sides of me
and all at almost the same time. During those days, I am sure I
must have yelled and shouted at the children in that room as much
as any teacher had ever done before and I probably scared some
of them more than I should have. The point, though, is that I
really did survive with them, and that I survived, in the end, in
what I know now to have been the only good way: by which I
mean that I saw the *class* survive and saw them not merely calm
down but genuinely come to life again. I know, moreover, that it
was not creating fear and shouting which did it, although that may
have helped me to get through those first few days, but that it was
something far more continuous and more important. The real

reason that I was able to get on with those children in the state in which I found them is that I came into that room knowing myself to be absolutely on their side. I did not go in there with even the littlest suggestion that what had been going on that year was even one-fiftieth their fault. If I had done that, I am convinced that things would have been hopeless. I went in there, on the contrary, and in a manner that they soon detected, with loyalty only to them for their nerve and for their defiance and with an obvious and openly expressed dissatisfaction with the stupidity of a school system that had cheated them.

The first writing assignment that they passed in emphasized what many of those children were thinking and feeling. The assignment was to describe the way they felt about their school. As an alternative I said that, if they wanted, they could write about the street they lived on or about the whole neighborhood or about any other part of town. Because of the miserable state their writing was in, and out of a fear that they might not write anything at all if they felt they were going to be lambasted, I said that I wouldn't be looking at grammar or spelling or syntax in the beginning but that I would be looking for two things: (1) the richness and specificity of details and (2) the openness and courage with which they would put their own most private feelings down. Although I have taught all kinds of writing classes since then, I don't think that I ever again will receive such a trusting and wide-open response.

"In my school," began a paper that was handed back to me a few days later, "I see dirty boards and I see papers on the floor. I see an old browken window with a sign on it saying, Do not unlock this window are browken. And I see cracks in the walls and I see old books with ink poured all over them and I see old painting hanging on the walls. I see old alfurbet letter hanging on one nail on the wall. I see a dirty fire exit I see a old closet with supplys for the class. I see pigons flying all over the school. I see old freght trains throgh the fence of the school yard. I see pictures of contryies hanging on the wall and I see desks with wrighting all over the top of the desks and insited of the desk."

Another paper that was passed in to me said this: "There is a torn up house I live near and the stairs are broken down. The windows are boarded up too. One day I saw a little boy and his dog on the third floor. I don't know how they got up there but they were. The doors are pushed in and there is trash in the house dirt for it hasn't been clean for a long time. Everything is boarded up. The railing on the porch looks like it is going to fall off. One of the steps are about to fall off. Some children even go into the yard and on the porch of the house. The yard has glass, paper, rocks, broken pens and pencils, a torn dress, some pants, in it. It is the junkiest yard Ive ever seen. There is always a black cat in the yard too I never go near it though. I don't go into the yard but I look over my fence and I look into the house and yard."

Another child told me this: "I see lots of thinings in this room. I see new teachers omots every day. I can see flowers and children books and others things. I like the 100 papers I like allso cabnets. I don't like the drity windows. And the dusty window shallvalls . . . ."

A little girl wrote this: "I can see old cars with gas in it and there is always people lighting fires old refrigartor an wood glass that comes from the old cars old trees and trash old weeds and people put there old chairs in there an flat tires and one thing there is up there is wood that you can make dog houses and there are beautiful flowers and there are dead dogs and cats . . . On some of the cars the weel is of and wisey bottles beer cans car seats are all out cars are all tip over and just the other day there was a fire and it was just blasting and whew in the back there is a big open space where Girl Scouts could mabe cook . . . this feild was a gas staition and the light pole is still up."

This was one more: "I see pictures in my school. I see pictures of Spain and a pictures of Portofino and a pictures of Chicago. I see arithmetic paper a spellings paper. I see a star chart. I see the flag of our Amerrica. The room is dirty . . . The auditorium dirty the seats are dusty. The light in the auditorium is brok. The curtains in the auditorium are ragged they took the curtains down because they was so ragged. The bathroom is dirty sometime the toilet is very hard. The cellar is dirty the hold school is dirty sometime . . . The flowers are dry every thing in my school is so so dirty."

When these essays were passed in, I showed one of them to the Reading Teacher. She became very angry. Her first reaction, which was expressed soon after I had handed her the essay, was to accuse me of having somehow concocted or coaxed this writing out of the child, whoever it was, who had composed it. "You must have induced it," she said, or "suggested it" or "invited it" or something like that, which was a way of disqualifying totally the independent intelligence and perception of the child who did the writing, at the same time that it discredited the impartiality and honesty of the teacher who could have allowed such thoughts to find their way to paper. What she said to me, essentially, was that I must have planted such gloomy word-pictures in the minds of the children or else they could not conceivably have written such things down. I was, on the contrary, very happy and quite proud of the children's essays because they were so direct and open and also so much filled with details. It was, I suppose, correct that in a sense I *had* induced this writing by telling the class to really go out and look at things and not write about their neighborhood or their school or about anything as if it were identical with the ingredients of the world or neighborhood that was often depicted in the pictures of their books. The Reading Teacher also was probably correct in saying that the children wouldn't have written those essays if I hadn't said what I did because, as I have already shown, the great majority had been thoroughly disciplined into the same kind of pretense which the teachers themselves had adopted for self-comfort; and this was a pretense which did not allow for broken cars and boarded windows. Another of the children's essays just started off and announced that in September they had begun with such and such a teacher and then had had so and so, and then so and so, and then so and so, and right on through a list of about eight or nine teachers ending up finally with me. It was cold-blooded, factual, showed a good memory and was shatteringly effective simply by rattling off almost the entire list without making any pointed comments. This again she may or may not have done if she hadn't been told she *could* do it, because the general atmosphere at school militated against a photographic frankness of that sort.

The Reading Teacher was upset by this, by whichever of the essays it was that I showed her, but rather than coming to terms with it by moving toward the center of the problem and by asking how the curriculum and tone of the school program fitted in with such a picture of this child's life, the Reading Teacher instead was able to handle the child's honesty by pointing out to me that I had probably angled for this, or induced it or coaxed it or had been looking for it anyway—the last of which charges possibly held a grain of truth but did not have a thing to do with the problems that the essays posed for her. The crux of it, I suppose, is that this woman, like many other teachers, had worked hard to develop and to solidify a set of optimistic values. To perpetrate the same views upon her pupils therefore was not to lie to them (for her), at least not consciously, but to extend to them, to attempt really to "sell" to them, her own hard-earned hopes about the world. During a long career she had had a great deal of apparent success in inducing the children she taught to write cheery and pastel little letters and stories and book reports to correspond to her own views. The reason the essays written by my pupils were bound to be disturbing to her was that she either deeply knew, or at least faintly feared, that they were true.

There was another example of something like this at one point a little earlier in the year. On one wall of the section of the auditorium where the Reading Teacher took her pupils, there was a list which I once took the time to copy down. What the list amounted to was a collection of suggested adjectives for the children to try to use when they were doing book reports. I remember that I studied the list and later discussed it with the Reading Teacher because there was something quite remarkable about it: All of the adjectives were laudatory. Everything that they implied was something nice. "Humorous" and "interesting" and "comical" and "adventurous" were typical of the words which were recommended to the children by virtue of being included in this list. There wasn't one that left room for even partial criticism. As these were the adjectives which the children were being asked to use, the consequence, except in the case of a rare intellectual accident, would have had to be a book report that spoke only in terms of various kinds of "good." Since we know that not all books are good, and in fact that many books are bad, and since we know in particular that many of the books at school were poor, that some were really rotten and that only a handful, probably only a very slim minority were books of any real quality at all, and since, beyond that (and this seems much more important) even a book that seems good to one person, to a teacher or to one pupil, may very likely seem poor to another pupil, and be poor for him, and for some very good reason, too — for all of these reasons I was curious about the effect of this list of laudatory adjectives which had faded upon the wall from what I believe to have been many years of use.

I remember a day when I was reading in the auditorium with a small group of children. We were reading, out of the phonics book *Wide Doors Open,* a story which none of them seemed to like very much and several were yawning the whole while. The Reading Teacher's manner of handling this would have been to attempt to "sell" it to the children, to call it wonderful and to sweep over them with a wave of persuasive enthusiasm in order to make up for their resistance to the work. I did not see why I ought to do this or why I ought to try to force upon them an appreciation of a type of story which they did not like. The story that we were reading was for some good reason of no importance to them and I was not going to try to persuade them it was terrific when they did not feel it. When we were done with the story I asked them whether they had liked it, and the thing that astonished me was that almost every one of them pretended that he *had*. I said: "What did you think of it? How would you describe it? What kind of story was it?" The answers came back: "Interesting" – "humorous" – "colorful" – "adventurous" – and all of the rest of the words on the Reading Teacher's list.

I twisted my head and I looked up at the list in the back of the room. There they all were. The words that they had given me were all up in neat order on the permissible list. They had not even begun thinking. They had not even started responding. They had simply assumed that, because I had asked the question, one of those words must be the right answer. The terrible thought that there *was* a right answer and that I already *knew* it and that it remained only for them to *guess* it was most disheartening of all. I remember that when they suggested each adjective it was not in a voice which said "I think it was humorous" – or "I think it was adventurous" – or "I think it was interesting" – or any other kind of definitive assertion of opinion. Rather, it was all phrased as a kind of guessing-game to which there was one answer: "Humorous?" "Adventurous?" "Interesting?" "Comical?" It was all in the interrogative and the effort was all to find out what I, their teacher, had already decided to be true. Finally, irritated and a little angry, I asked them flatly: "What are you telling me? You've all been yawning and twisting. Why didn't you pay attention if all of those wonderful things were so?"

One boy answered me simply, as if there were no contradiction between this and the use of the other words: "Because it was so babyish." Then how on earth could they have used all of the words on the Reading Teacher's list? Another boy said: "It was so boring." So there the real answer was. It seemed obvious why they had lied to me in the beginning. The Reading Teacher had taught them that those were the only things you were supposed to say about a book. One of them, one of those adjectives, was "correct" and the only problem for them was to find out which one it was. The word, all too clearly, had been divorced from the world, and the application of the correct pat adjective need have nothing in particular to do with the child's idea about the book.

I felt troubled enough about this to relate it later to the Reading Teacher. Just as with the essays by the children that I had shown her, I felt she was immediately disturbed by what she was hearing but I also recognized that she was very quick to cancel it out. She seemed troubled for a moment but then, instead of saying that it was a pity, or that it was funny but regrettable, or too bad that they had reacted in such a manner, or anything else at all that might have brought her doubt or pause, she said only this:

"At least it shows that they know the words on the list."

What I felt when she said that, was that knowing all those big words on the list would not be of any use. It would not be of any use because they could not work with them but could only "supply" them, fetch them out literally from their place on the list, in much the same manner that a young dog fetches a thrown stick. By reassuring herself that at least the children had gotten down those big words for future use, the Reading Teacher was able to rise above the painful matter that she had effectively taught them to be good liars and in fact had equipped them with a set of tools to keep themselves at as far as possible a distance from the truth.

Rather than learn those ten-dollar words, the introduction of which into their book reports might win them such rewards as gold stars and extra points, the children would have gained greatly from having been invited to search their own barrel of modifiers, containing such words as "boring," "horrible," "terrible," "great," "pathetic," "idiotic," "terrific," "marvelous" or "dumb." These are the kinds of strong words which are looked for by good college English instructors in their efforts at erasing the use of the kinds of cliché terms listed above. But what process of education is it which would inculcate these very unnatural "cultured words" at the age of ten only to have to define their artificiality and point up their lack of vitality and attempt in many cases to root them out only ten years later?

I remember the Reading Teacher on one occasion asking a child for the antonym of "fat" and getting "skinny." The Reading Teacher's response was something on this order: "Oh, let's see if we can't find a nicer word than skinny"—and getting "thin" and "slender" in its place. A decade later, if that child made it to college, I thought, her English teacher would work his heart out to get "skinny" back again.

At one point later in the spring, the Deputy Superintendent, Miss _____, went on record as indicating that she held it a key goal of the _____ Public Schools to break the children of what she called their "speech patterns." There is no way to be absolutely certain of what she intended, but if the Deputy Superintendent meant by this process the replacement of words like "skinny" by such a word as "thin" or "slender," then I think she may very well succeed in enabling some of the children to speak more like herself but I do not believe that she will have helped them toward expressing themselves richly or with any kind of honesty or strength. Honest writing and private feeling seem to me to be the only possible starting-points for everything else in teaching English and one of the first places where the world outside and the word within the classroom ought to eloquently coexist. To bring about this kind of a meeting would not be easy in much of the present _____ school system, but it would be education.

INTERPRETATION

1. Explain what is meant by the "cheery and pastel" letters and stories the Reading Teacher had taught the students to write. What attitude toward education in general do they represent? What different attitude underlies Kozol's writing assignment?
2. The author states that the real reason he succeeded with his students was that he felt himself "absolutely on their side." Do his actions testify to the truth of this statement? Do you think Kozol helped his students? Explain.

STYLE AND METHOD

1. What proportion of the essay is taken up with illustrative incident? (What is the effect of leaving the children's letters just as they were

written by the children?) What general statements are illustrated by each of the incidents? Is the evidence persuasive?
2. At what point in his account does Kozol make his summary statement about the proper relation of writing to experience? Is it effectively placed there? Explain.
3. How successful do you think the author was in subordinating his private feelings to fact and reason?

FOR WRITING

Describe the way you feel about *your* school — or neighborhood or city. Your paper will be judged on the richness and specificity of details and on the candor with which it is written.

"Americans seem to live and breathe and function by paradox,"
says John Steinbeck, and to prove his point he pairs off just about
all the generalizations that can be made about American life
and shows them to be contradictions. In the process, he goes a
long way toward defining the American character. You probably
will find something of yourself or your family in some of these
paradoxes*. You may even be able to explain some of them, or to
define "the American Way of Life," which Steinbeck says defies
definition. But in any case this article will stimulate you to try to
grasp that elusive notion of what it means to be an American.

Paradox and Dream

JOHN STEINBECK

One of the generalities most often noted about Americans is
that we are a restless, a dissatisfied, a searching people. We bridle
and buck under failure, and we go mad with dissatisfaction in the
face of success. We spend our time searching for security, and
hate it when we get it. For the most part we are an intemperate
people: we eat too much when we can, drink too much, indulge
our senses too much. Even in our so-called virtues we are intemperate: a teetotaler is not content not to drink—he must stop
all the drinking in the world; a vegetarian among us would outlaw
the eating of meat. We work too hard, and many die under the
strain; and then to make up for that we play with a violence as
suicidal.

The result is that we seem to be in a state of turmoil all the
time, both physically and mentally. We are able to believe that
our government is weak, stupid, overbearing, dishonest, and
inefficient, and at the same time we are deeply convinced that it
is the best government in the world, and we would like to impose
it upon everyone else. We speak of the American Way of Life as
though it involved the ground rules for the governance of heaven.
A man hungry and unemployed through his own stupidity and

that of others, a man beaten by a brutal policeman, a woman forced into prostitution by her own laziness, high prices, availability, and despair—all bow with reverence toward the American Way of Life, although each one would look puzzled and angry if he were asked to define it. We scramble and scrabble up the stony path toward the pot of gold we have taken to mean security. We trample friends, relatives, and strangers who get in the way of our achieving it; and once we get it we shower it on psychoanalysts to try to find out why we are unhappy, and finally—if we have enough of the gold—we contribute it back to the nation in the form of foundations and charities.

We fight our way in, and try to buy our way out. We are alert, curious, hopeful, and we take more drugs designed to make us unaware than any other people. We are self-reliant and at the same time completely dependent. We are aggressive, and defenseless. Americans overindulge their children and do not like them; the children in turn are overly dependent and full of hate for their parents. We are complacent in our possessions, in our houses, in our education; but it is hard to find a man or woman who does not want something better for the next generation. Americans are remarkably kind and hospitable and open with both guests and strangers; and yet they will make a wide circle around the man dying on the pavement. Fortunes are spent getting cats out of trees and dogs out of sewer pipes; but a girl screaming for help in the street draws only slammed doors, closed windows, and silence.

Now there is a set of generalities for you, each one of them canceled out by another generality. Americans seem to live and breathe and function by paradox; but in nothing are we so paradoxical as in our passionate belief in our own myths. We truly believe ourselves to be natural-born mechanics and do-it-your-self-ers. We spend our lives in motor cars, yet most of us—a great many of us at least—do not know enough about a car to look in the gas tank when the motor fails. Our lives as we live them would not function without electricity, but it is a rare man or woman who, when the power goes off, knows how to look for a burned-out fuse and replace it. We believe implicitly that we are the heirs of the pioneers; that we have inherited self-sufficiency and the ability to take care of ourselves, particularly in relation to nature. There isn't a man among us in ten thousand who knows how to butcher a cow or a pig and cut it up for eating, let alone a wild animal. By natural endowment, we are great rifle shots and great hunters—but when hunting season opens there is a slaughter of farm animals and humans by men and women who couldn't hit a real target if they could see it. Americans treasure the knowledge that they live close to nature, but fewer and fewer farmers feed more and more people; and as soon as we can afford to we eat out of cans, buy frozen TV dinners, and haunt the delicatessens. Affluence means moving to the suburbs, but the American suburbanite sees, if anything, less of the country than the city apartment dweller with his window boxes and his African violets carefully tended under lights. In no country are more seeds and plants and equipment purchased, and less vegetables and flowers raised.

The paradoxes are everywhere: We shout that we are a nation of laws, not men—and then proceed to break every law we can if we can get away with it. We proudly insist that we base our political positions on the issues—and we will vote against a man because of his religion, his name, or the shape of his nose.

Sometimes we seem to be a nation of public puritans and private profligates. There surely can be no excesses like those committed by good family men away from home at a convention. We believe in the manliness of our men and the womanliness of our women, but we go to extremes of expense and discomfort to cover any natural evidence that we are either. From puberty we are preoccupied with sex; but our courts, our counselors, and our psychiatrists are dealing constantly with cases of sexual failure or charges of frigidity or impotence. A small failure in business can quite normally make a man sexually impotent.

We fancy ourselves as hard-headed realists, but we will buy anything we see advertised, particularly on television; and we buy it not with reference to the quality or the value of the product, but directly as a result of the number of times we have heard it mentioned. The most arrant nonsense about a product is never questioned. We are afraid to be awake, afraid to be alone, afraid to be a moment without the noise and confusion we call entertainment. We boast of our dislike of highbrow art and music, and we have more and better-attended symphonies, art galleries, and theaters than any country in the world. We detest abstract art and produce more of it than all the rest of the world put together.

One of the characteristics most puzzling to a foreign observer is the strong and imperishable dream the American carries. On inspection, it is found that the dream has little to do with reality in American life. Consider the dream of and the hunger for home. The very word can reduce nearly all of my compatriots to tears. Builders and developers never build houses—they build homes. The dream home is either in a small town or in a suburban area where grass and trees simulate the country. This dream home is a permanent seat, not rented but owned. It is a center where a man and his wife grow graciously old, warmed by the radiance of well-washed children and grandchildren. Many thousands of these homes are built every year; built, planted, advertised, and sold— and yet, the American family rarely stays in one place for more than five years. The home and its equipment are purchased on time and are heavily mortgaged. The earning power of the father is almost always overextended, so that after a few years he is not able to keep up the payments on his loans. That is on the losing side. But suppose the earner is successful and his income increases. Right away the house is not big enough, or in the proper neighborhood. Or perhaps suburban life palls, and the family moves to the city, where excitement and convenience beckon.

Some of these movements back and forth seem to me a result of just pure restlessness, pure nervousness. We do hear, of course, of people who keep the same job for twenty years, or thirty years, or forty years, and get a gold watch for it; but the numbers of these old and faithful employees are decreasing all the time. Part of the movement has to do with the nature of business itself. Work in factories, in supermarkets, for contractors on the construction of houses, bridges, public buildings, or more factories is often temporary; the job gets done, or local taxes or wage increases or falling sales may cause a place of business to move to a new area. In addition, many of the great corporations have a policy of moving employees from one of their many branches to another. The employee with the home dream finds that with every removal he loses money. The sellers of homes make their profit on the down payment and on the interest on the loan; but the private owner who wants to turn over his dream home and move on to another finds that he always takes a loss. However, the dream does not die—it just takes another form.

Today, with the ancient American tendency to look for greener pastures still very much alive, the mobile home has become the new dream. It is not a trailer; it is a house, long and narrow in shape, and equipped with wheels so that it can, if necessary, be transported over the highway to a new area. In a mobile home, a man doesn't have to take a loss when he moves; his home goes with him. Until recently, when the local authorities have set about finding means of making Mr. Mobile pay his way, a mobile home owner living in a rented space in a trailer park could avoid local taxes and local duties while making use of the public schools and all the other facilities American towns set up for their people. The mobile way of life is not a new thing in the world, of course. It is more than probable that humans lived this way for hundreds of thousands of years before they ever conceived of settling down—the herdsmen followed the herds, the hunters followed the game, and everybody ran from the weather. The Tartars moved whole villages on wheels, and the die-hard gypsies have never left their caravans. No, people go back to mobility with enthusiasm for something they recognize, and if they can double the dream—have a symbol home and mobility at the same time—they have it made. And now there are huge settlements of these metal houses clustered on the edges of our cities. Plots of grass and shrubs are planted, awnings stretched out, and garden chairs appear. A community life soon springs up—a life having all the signs of status, the standards of success or failure that exist elsewhere in America.

There is no question that American life is in the process of changing, but, as always in human history, it carries some of the past along with it; and the mobile home has one old trap built into it. Automobile manufacturers discovered and developed the American yearning for status. By changing the appliances and gadgetry on each new model, they could make the car owner feel that his perfectly good automobile was old-fashioned and therefore undesirable. His children were afraid to be seen in it; and, since a family's image of success in the world, or status, is to a certain extent dependent on the kind of a car the man drives, he was forced to buy a new one whether he needed it or not. Outdated mobile homes carry the same stigma. Every year new models appear, costing from five thousand to fifty thousand dollars, with new fixtures, colors—new, and therefore desirable. A family with an old model, no matter how comfortable and sound, soon feels *déclassé*. Thus the turnover in mobile houses is enormous, and thus the social strata re-establish themselves:

the top people have the newest models, and lesser folk buy the used homes turned in as down payments on the newer ones. And the trailer cities have neighborhoods as fiendishly snobbish as have any other suburban developments—each one has its Sugar Hill, its upper-middle-class area, and its slums. The pattern has not changed; and none of this has in any way affected the American dream of home, which remains part Grandma Moses and part split-level ranch house in an area where to keep a cow or a pen of chickens is to break the law.

Of course, the home dream can be acted out almost anywhere. A number of years ago, when I lived on East 51st Street in New York City, I saw an instance of it every day on my morning walk, near Third Avenue, where great numbers of old red brick buildings were the small, walk-up cold-water flats in which so many New Yorkers lived. Every summer morning about nine o'clock a stout and benign-looking lady came down the stairs from her flat to the pavement carrying the great outdoors in her arms. She set out a canvas deck chair, and over it mounted a beach umbrella —one of the kind which has a little cocktail table around it—and then, smiling happily, this benign and robust woman rolled out a little lawn made of green raffia in front of her chair, set out two pots of red geraniums and an artificial palm, brought a little cabinet with cold drinks—Coca-Cola, Pepsi-Cola—in a small icebox; she laid her folded copy of the *Daily News* on the table, arranged her equipment, and sank back into the chair—and she was in the country. She nodded and smiled to everyone who went by, and somehow she conveyed her dream to everyone who saw her, and everyone who saw her was delighted with her. For some reason I was overwhelmed with a desire to contribute to this sylvan retreat, and so one day when she had stepped inside for a moment, I deposited on her table a potted fern and a little bowl with two goldfish; and the next morning, I was pleased to see that these had been added to the permanent equipment. Every day through that summer the fern and the goldfish were part of the scene.

The home dream is only one of the deepset American illusions which, since they can't be changed, function as cohesive principles to bind the nation together and make it different from all other nations. It occurs to me that all dreams, waking and sleeping, are powerful and prominent memories of something real, of something that really happened. I believe these memories — some of them, at least — can be inherited; our generalized dreams of water and warmth, of falling, of monsters, of danger and pre-monitions may have been pre-recorded on some kind of genetic tape in the species out of which we evolved or mutated, just as some of our organs which no longer function seem to be physical memories of other, earlier processes. The national dream of Americans is a whole pattern of thinking and feeling and may well be a historic memory surprisingly little distorted. Furthermore, the participators in the dream need not have descended physically from the people to whom the reality happened. This pattern of thought and conduct which is the national character is absorbed even by the children of immigrants born in America, but it never comes to the immigrants themselves, no matter how they may wish it; birth on American soil seems to be required.

I have spoken of the dream of home that persists in a time when home is neither required nor wanted. Until very recently home was a real word, and in the English tongue it is a magic word. The ancient root word *ham*, from which our word "home" came, meant the triangle where two rivers meet which, with a short wall, can be defended. At first the word "home" meant safety, then gradually comfort. In the immediate American past, the home meant just those two things; the log houses, even the sod houses, were havens of safety, of defense, warmth, food, and comfort. Outside were hostile Indians and dangerous animals, crippling cold and starvation. Many houses, including the one where President Johnson was born, built only a few generations back, have thick walls and gunslits for defense, a great hearth for cook-ing and for heat, a cellar under the floor and an attic for the storage of food, and sometimes even an interior well in case of siege. A home was a place where women and children could be reasonably safe, a place to which a man could return with joy and slough off his weariness and his fears. This symbol of safety and comfort is so recent in our history that it is no wonder that to all of us it remains dear and desirable.

It is an American dream that we are great hunters, trackers, woodsmen, deadshots with a rifle or a shotgun; and this dream is deeply held by Americans who have never fired a gun or hunted anything larger or more dangerous than a cockroach. But I wonder whether our deep connection with firearms is not indeed a national potential; not long ago we had to be good hunters or we starved, good shots or our lives were in danger. Can this have carried over? Early in World War II, I worked for the Training Command of the Air Force, and spent a good deal of time at the schools for aerial gunnery. The British, having been in the war for a long time, sent teams of instructors to teach our newly inducted men to handle the tail and ball-turret guns in our B-17 bombers, but the instruction began with small arms, since all shooting is pretty much the same. I remember an Englishman saying to me, "It is amazing how quickly these men learn. Some of them have never handled a weapon, and yet it seems to come to them as though they knew it; they pick it up much faster than the English lads do. Maybe they're just born with the knack."

I suggested, "Think of the time of Crécy and Agincourt,[1] when the longbow dominated battlefields. Now, the yew of the longbows was not English, it was Spanish. The French had access to the longbow and surely they knew its effectiveness, and still they never used it."

"That's right," he said. "Our lads had the knack, didn't they? But also they had practice and habit; the bow was in their blood. Maybe they were bowmen before they ever handled a bow, because it was expected of them. You may have genes of firearms in your systems."

The inventiveness once necessary for survival may also be a part of the national dream. Who among us has not bought for a song an ancient junked car, and with parts from other junked cars put together something that would run? This is not lost; American kids are still doing it. The dreams of a people either create folk literature or find their way into it; and folk literature, again, is always based on something that happened. Our most persistent folk tales — constantly retold in books, movies, and television shows — concern cowboys, gunslinging sheriffs, and Indian fighters. These folk figures existed — perhaps not quite as they are recalled nor in the numbers indicated, but they did exist; and this dream also persists. Even businessmen in Texas wear the high-heeled boots and big hats, though they ride in air-conditioned

---

[1] **Crécy and Agincourt:** towns in northern France; sites of English victories over French forces in 1346 and 1415 respectively. English yeomen, armed with longbows, cut down the French mounted knights, thus ending the era of cavalry supremacy.

Cadillacs and have forgotten the reason for the high heels. All our children play cowboy and Indian; the brave and honest sheriff who with courage and a six-gun brings law and order and civic virtue to a Western community is perhaps our most familiar hero, no doubt descended from the brave mailed knight of chivalry who battled and overcame evil with lance and sword. Even the recognition signals are the same: white hat, white armor—black hat, black shield. And in these moral tales, so deepset in us, virtue does not arise out of reason or orderly process of law—it is imposed and maintained by violence.

I wonder whether this folk wisdom is the story of our capability. Are these stories permanent because we know within ourselves that only the threat of violence makes it possible for us to live together in peace? I think that surviving folk tales are directly based on memory. There must have been a leader like King Arthur; although there is no historical record to prove it, the very strength of the story presumes his existence. We know there were gunslinging sheriffs—not many, but some; but if they had not existed, our need for them would have created them. It interests me that the youthful gangs in our cities, engaging in their "rumbles" which are really wars, and doing so in direct and overt disobedience of law and of all the pressures the police can apply—that these gangs take noble names, and within their organizations are said to maintain a code of behavior and responsibility toward one another and an obedience to their leaders very like that of the tight-knit chivalric code of feudal Europe; the very activities and attitudes which raise the hand of the law against these gangs would, if the nation needed them, be the diagnostics of heroes. And indeed, they must be heroes to themselves.

A national dream need not, indeed may not be clear-cut and exact. Consider the dream of France, based on a memory and fired in the furnace of defeat and occupation, followed by the frustration of a many-branched crossroads until Charles-*le-plus-Magne*[2] polished up the old word "glory" and made it shine. *La Gloire* brightened French eyes; defensive arrogance hardened and even the philosophically hopeless were glorious and possessive in their hopelessness, and the dark deposits of centuries were washed from the glorious buildings in Paris. When this in-

---

[2] **Charles-le-plus-Magne:** Charlemagne, king of Franks 768-814; emperor of the West as Charles I, 800-814; established Holy Roman Empire.

spired people looked for examples of glory they remembered the Sun King,[3] who left them bankrupt, and the Emperor Napoleon,[4] whose legacy was defeat and semi-anarchy; but glory was in both men and both times—and France needed it, for glory is a little like dignity: only those who do not have it feel the need for it.

For Americans, too, the wide and general dream has a name. It is called "the American Way of Life." No one can define it or point to any one person or group who lives it, but it is very real nevertheless, perhaps more real than that equally remote dream the Russians call Communism. These dreams describe our vague yearnings toward what we wish we were and hope we may be: wise, just, compassionate, and noble. The fact that we have this dream at all is perhaps an indication of its possibility.

INTERPRETATION

1. Look up *paradox* in the Glossary. Discuss Steinbeck's paradoxes. Can you find evidence to support them beyond that provided by Steinbeck?
2. What is the American Dream? How is the dream like a myth?
3. How does Steinbeck describe life in America today? How closely does it correspond to your idea of "the American Way of Life"? Is "the American Way of Life" just another dream?

STYLE AND METHOD

1. By making two lists, distinguish between the generalities and the concrete examples used by Steinbeck. Which does he use more of? Steinbeck assumes a firsthand knowledge of the particulars of American life on the part of his reader. Would the essay be stronger if the author had stopped to document* each of his statements? Explain.
2. Notice how the contrasting of ideas is reflected in the carefully balanced antithesis* of individual sentences—for example, "We fight our way in, and try to buy our way out." Do you find this style interesting? What do you imagine are its dangers?

---

[3] **Sun King:** Louis XIV, king of France 1643-1715.
[4] **Napoleon:** French military leader and conqueror; emperor of France 1804-1815 as Napoleon I.

FOR WRITING
1. Choose one paradox about which you feel strongly and either disagree with it or explain it.
2. Steinbeck says no one can define "the American Way of Life." Write your definition of what it means to you. Compare yours with those written by other members of the class.

It may be true that no two people are exactly alike, that each of us comes out in a single-copy edition. It may even be that no two personalities are alike, that each is unique. Still, unless a person has the skill to fully express his unique inner self, it can never be known to others or appreciated. But, as Mr. Lucas points out, our manner of expressing ourselves is precisely what we mean by *style*. What he is really concerned about, though, is *good* style, and if everyone has not the gift of being able to write really well, everyone can at least benefit from a few simple rules to improve his style. Why should one care about style? Because the person who cares about his expression, will, through his concern for language, become a better user of language and thereby a better person as well.

What Is Style?

F. L. LUCAS

When it was suggested to Walt Whitman that one of his works should be bound in vellum, he was outraged—"Pshaw!" he snorted, "—hangings, curtains, finger bowls, chinaware, Matthew Arnold!"[1] And he might have been equally irritated by talk of style; for he boasted of "my barbaric yawp"—he would *not* be literary; his readers should touch not a book but a man. Yet Whitman took the pains to rewrite *Leaves of Grass* four times, and his style is unmistakable. Samuel Butler maintained that writers who bothered about their style became unreadable but he bothered about his own. "Style" has got a bad name by growing associated with precious and superior persons who, like Oscar Wilde, spend a morning putting in a comma, and the afternoon (so he said) taking it out again. But such abuse of "style" is misuse of English. For the word means merely "a way of expressing oneself, in language, manner, or appearance"; or,

[1] **Matthew Arnold:** English poet, critic, and essayist.

secondly, "a *good* way of so expressing oneself"—as when one says, "Her behavior never lacked style."

Now there is no crime in expressing oneself (though to try to *im*press oneself on others easily grows revolting or ridiculous). Indeed one cannot help expressing oneself, unless one passes one's life in a cupboard. Even the most rigid Communist, or Organization-man, is compelled by Nature to have a unique voice, unique fingerprints, unique handwriting. Even the signatures of the letters on your breakfast table may reveal more than their writers guess. There are blustering signatures that swish across the page like cornstalks bowed before a tempest. There are cryptic signatures, like a scrabble of lightning across a cloud, suggesting that behind is a lofty divinity whom all must know, or an aloof divinity whom none is worthy to know (though, as this might be highly inconvenient, a docile typist sometimes interprets the mystery in a bracket underneath). There are impetuous squiggles implying that the author is a sort of strenuous Sputnik streaking round the globe every eighty minutes. There are florid signatures, all curlicues and danglements and flamboyance, like the youthful Disraeli (though these seem rather out of fashion). There are humble, humdrum signatures. And there are also, sometimes, signatures that are courteously clear, yet mindful of a certain simple grace and artistic economy—in short, of style.

Since, then, not one of us can put pen to paper, or even open his mouth, without giving something of himself away to shrewd observers, it seems mere common sense to give the matter a little thought. Yet it does not seem very common. Ladies may take infinite pains about having style in their clothes, but many of us remain curiously indifferent about having it in our words. How many women would dream of polishing not only their nails but also their tongues? They may play freely on that perilous little organ, but they cannot often be bothered to tune it. And how many men think of improving their talk as well as their golf handicap?

No doubt strong silent men, speaking only in gruff monosyllables, may despise "mere words." No doubt the world does suffer from an endemic plague of verbal dysentery. But that, precisely, is bad style. And consider the amazing power of mere words. Adolf Hitler was a bad artist, bad statesman, bad general, and bad man. But largely because he could tune his rant, with psychological nicety, to the exact wave length of his audiences and make millions quarrelsome-drunk all at the same time by his command of windy nonsense, skilled statesmen, soldiers, scientists were blown away like chaff, and he came near to rule the world. If Sir Winston Churchill had been a mere speechifier, we might well have lost the war; yet his speeches did quite a lot to win it.

No man was less of a literary aesthete than Benjamin Franklin; yet this tallow-chandler's son, who changed world history, regarded as "a principal means of my advancement" that pungent style which he acquired partly by working in youth over old *Spectators;* but mainly by being Benjamin Franklin. The squinting demagogue, John Wilkes,[2] as ugly as his many sins, had yet a tongue so winning that he asked only half an hour's start (to counteract his face) against any rival for a woman's favor. "Vote for you!" growled a surly elector in his constituency. "I'd sooner vote for the devil!" "But in case your friend should not stand . . . ?" Cleopatra, that ensnarer of world conquerors, owed less to the shape of her nose than to the charm of her tongue. Shakespeare himself has often poor plots and thin ideas; even his mastery of character has been questioned; what does remain unchallenged is his verbal magic. Men are often taken, like rabbits, by the ears. And though the tongue has no bones, it can sometimes break millions of them.

"But," the reader may grumble, "I am neither Hitler, Cleopatra, nor Shakespeare. What is all this to me?" Yet we all talk — often too much; we all have to write letters — often too many. We live not by bread alone but also by words. And not always with remarkable efficiency. Strikes, lawsuits, divorces, all sorts of public nuisance and private misery, often come just from the gaggling incompetence with which we express ourselves. Americans and British get at cross-purposes because they use the same words with different meanings. Men have been hanged on a comma in a statute. And in the valley of Balaclava[3] a mere verbal ambiguity,

[2] **John Wilkes:** English political reformer who led a dissolute life; he was expelled from the House of Commons, imprisoned, and fined; he championed Colonial rights in America and became the idol of the mob in England.

[3] **Valley of Balaclava:** in the SW Soviet Union on the Black Sea; scene of the "Charge of the Light Brigade" in the Crimean War, 1854.

about *which* guns were to be captured, sent the whole Light Brigade to futile annihilation.

Words can be more powerful, and more treacherous, than we sometimes suspect; communication more difficult than we may think. We are all serving life sentences of solitary confinement within our own bodies; like prisoners, we have, as it were, to tap in awkward code to our fellow men in their neighboring cells. Further, when A and B converse, there take part in their dialogue not two characters, as they suppose, but six. For there is A's real self — call it A_1; there is also A's picture of himself — A_2; there is also B's picture of A — A_3. And there are three corresponding personalities of B. With six characters involved even in a simple tête-à-tête, no wonder we fall into muddles and misunderstandings.

Perhaps, then, there are five main reasons for trying to gain some mastery of language:

We have no other way of understanding, informing, misinforming, or persuading one another.

Even alone, we think mainly in words; if our language is muddy, so will our thinking be.

By our handling of words we are often revealed and judged. "Has he written anything?" said Napoleon of a candidate for an appointment. "Let me see his *style*."

Without a feeling for language one remains half-blind and deaf to literature.

Our mother tongue is bettered or worsened by the way each generation uses it. Languages evolve like species. They can degenerate; just as oysters and barnacles have lost their heads. Compare ancient Greek with modern. A heavy responsibility, though often forgotten.

Why and how did I become interested in style? The main answer, I suppose, is that I was born that way. Then I was, till ten, an only child running loose in a house packed with books, and in a world (thank goodness) still undistracted by radio and television. So at three I groaned to my mother, "Oh, I *wish* I could read," and at four I read. Now travel among books is the best travel of all, and the easiest, and the cheapest. (Not that I belittle ordinary travel — which I regard as one of the three main pleasures in life.) One learns to write by reading good books, as one learns to talk by hearing good talkers. And if I have learned anything of writing, it is largely from writers like Montaigne, Dorothy Osborne, Horace Walpole, Johnson, Goldsmith, Montesquieu, Voltaire, Flaubert and Anatole France. Again, I was reared on Greek and Latin, and one can learn much from translating Homer or the Greek Anthology, Horace or Tacitus, if one is thrilled by the originals and tries, however vainly, to recapture some of that thrill in English.

But at Rugby I could *not* write English essays. I believe it stupid to torment boys to write on topics that they know and care nothing about. I used to rush to the school library and cram the subject, like a python swallowing rabbits; then, still replete as a postprandial[4] python, I would tie myself in clumsy knots to embrace those accursed themes. Bacon was wise in saying that reading makes a full man; talking, a ready one; writing, an exact one. But writing from an empty head is futile anguish.

At Cambridge, my head having grown a little fuller, I suddenly found I *could* write—not with enjoyment (it is always tearing oneself in pieces)—but fairly fluently. Then came the War of 1914-18; and though soldiers have other things than pens to handle, they learn painfully to be clear and brief. Then the late Sir Desmond MacCarthy[5] invited me to review for the *New Statesman;* it was a useful apprenticeship, and he was delightful to work for. But I think it was well after a few years to stop; reviewers remain essential, but there are too many books one *cannot* praise, and only the pugnacious enjoy amassing enemies. By then I was an ink-addict—not because writing is much pleasure, but because not to write is pain; just as some smokers do not so much enjoy tobacco as suffer without it. The positive happiness of writing comes, I think, from work when done—decently, one hopes, and not without use—and from the letters of readers which help to reassure, or delude, one that so it is.

But one of my most vivid lessons came, I think, from service in a war department during the Second War. Then, if the matter one sent out was too wordy, the communication channels might choke; yet if it was not absolutely clear, the results might be serious. So I emerged, after six years of it, with more passion than ever for clarity and brevity, more loathing than ever for the obscure and the verbose.

---

[4] **postprandial:** after-dinner. Here, it describes a python who has just eaten.
[5] **Sir Desmond MacCarthy:** British writer and critic.

For forty years at Cambridge I have tried to teach young men to write well, and have come to think it impossible. To write really well is a gift inborn; those who have it teach themselves; one can only try to help and hasten the process. After all, the uneducated sometimes express themselves far better than their "betters." In language, as in life, it is possible to be perfectly correct — and yet perfectly tedious, or odious. The illiterate last letter of the doomed Vanzetti[6] was more moving than most professional orators; 18th Century ladies, who should have been spanked for their spelling, could yet write far better letters than most professors of English; and the talk of Synge's[7] Irish peasants seems to me vastly more vivid than the later style of Henry James.[8] Yet Synge averred that his characters owed far less of their eloquence to what he invented for them than to what he had overheard in the cottages of Wicklow and Kerry:

"*Christy.* 'It's little you'll think if my love's a poacher's, or an earl's itself, when you'll feel my two hands stretched around you, and I squeezing kisses on your puckered lips, till I'd feel a kind of pity for the Lord God is all ages sitting lonesome in His golden chair.'

"*Pegeen.* 'That'll be right fun, Christy Mahon, and any girl would walk her heart out before she'd meet a young man was your like for eloquence, or talk at all.'"

Well she might! It's not like that they talk in universities — more's the pity.

But though one cannot teach people to write well, one can sometimes teach them to write rather better. One can give a certain number of hints, which often seem boringly obvious — only experience shows they are not.

One can say: Beware of pronouns — they are devils. Look at even Addison,[9] describing the type of pedant who chatters of style without having any: "Upon enquiry I found my learned friend had dined that day with Mr. Swan, the famous punster; and desiring *him* to give me some account of Mr. Swan's conver-

[6] **Vanzetti:** Italian political radical arrested with Nicola Sacco for the murder of a shoe-factory paymaster and guard at Braintree, Mass., and theft of payroll; doubt of guilt created world-wide protests, but both were electrocuted in 1927 after special committee found previous trial valid.

[7] **Synge:** Irish dramatist and promoter of Celtic revival of 1890's.

[8] **Henry James:** American novelist (1843-1916) who became a naturalized British citizen.

[9] **Addison:** English essayist, poet, and statesman; writer of social satire and literary criticism.

sation, *he* told me that *he* generally talked in the Paronomasia,[10]
that *he* sometimes gave in to the Ploce,[11] but that in *his* humble
opinion *he* shone most in the Antanaclasis."[12] What a sluttish
muddle of *he* and *him* and *his*! It all needs rewording. Far
better repeat a noun, or a name, than puzzle the reader, even for a
moment, with ambiguous pronouns. Thou shalt not puzzle thy
reader.

Or one can say: Avoid jingles. The B.B.C. news bulletins seem
compiled by earless persons, capable of crying round the globe:
"The enemy is re*port*ed to have seized this im*port*ant *port*, and
reinforcements are hurrying up in sup*port*." Any fool, once told,
can hear such things to be insupportable.

Or one can say: Be sparing with relative clauses. Don't string
them together like sausages, or jam them inside one another like
Chinese boxes or the receptacles of Buddha's tooth. Or one
can say: Don't flaunt jargon, like Addison's Mr. Swan, or the
type of modern critic who gurgles more technical terms in a page
than Johnson[13] used in all his *Lives* or Sainte-Beuve in thirty
volumes. But dozens of such snippety precepts, though they may
sometimes save people from writing badly, will help them little
toward writing well. Are there no general rules of a more positive
kind, and of more positive use?

Perhaps. There *are* certain basic principles which seem to me
observed by many authors I admire, which I think have served
me and which may serve others. I am not talking of geniuses,
who are a law to themselves (and do not always write a very good
style, either); nor of poetry, which has different laws from prose;
nor of poetic prose, like Sir Thomas Browne's or De Quincey's,
which is often more akin to poetry; but of the plain prose of
ordinary books and documents, letters and talk.

The writer should respect truth and himself; therefore honesty.
He should respect his readers; therefore courtesy. These are
two of the cornerstones of style. Confucius saw it, twenty-five
centuries ago: "The Master said, The gentleman is courteous,
but not pliable: common men are pliable, but not courteous."

First, honesty. In literature, as in life, one of the fundamentals

[10] **Paronomasia:** playing on words, punning.
[11] **Ploce:** emphatic repetition of a word with particular reference to its special
significance.
[12] **Antanaclasis:** repeating a word in a different or even contrary sense.
[13] **Johnson:** Samuel Johnson (1709-1784), British author and critic.

is to find, and be, one's true self. One's true self may indeed be unpleasant (though one can try to better it); but a false self, sooner or later, becomes disgusting—just as a nice plain woman, painted to the eyebrows, can become horrid. In writing, in the long run, pretense does not work. As the police put it, anything you say may be used as evidence against you. If handwriting reveals character, writing reveals it still more. You cannot fool *all* your judges *all* the time.

Most style is not honest enough. Easy to say, but hard to practice. A writer may take to long words, as young men to beards—to impress. But long words, like long beards, are often the badge of charlatans. Or a writer may cultivate the obscure, to seem profound. But even carefully muddied puddles are soon fathomed. Or he may cultivate eccentricity, to seem original. But really original people do not have to think about being original— they can no more help it than they can help breathing. They do not need to dye their hair green. The fame of Meredith, Wilde or Bernard Shaw[14] might now shine brighter, had they struggled less to be brilliant; whereas Johnson remains great, not merely because his gifts were formidable but also because, with all his prejudice and passion, he fought no less passionately to "clear his mind of cant."

Secondly, courtesy—respect for the reader. From this follow several other basic principles of style. Clarity is one. For it is boorish to make your reader rack his brains to understand. One should aim at being impossible to misunderstand—though men's capacity for misunderstanding approaches infinity. Hence Molière[15] and Po Chu-i[16] tried their work on their cooks; and Swift[17] his on his menservants—"which, if they did not comprehend, he would alter and amend, until they understood it perfectly." Our bureaucrats and pundits, unfortunately, are less considerate.

Brevity is another basic principle. For it is boorish, also, to waste your reader's time. People who would not dream of stealing a penny of one's money turn not a hair at stealing hours of one's life. But that does not make them less exasperating. There-

[14] **Meredith, Wilde, Bernard Shaw:** British authors.
[15] **Molière:** pseudonym of Jean Baptiste Poquelin, French actor and playwright.
[16] **Po Chu-i:** Chinese poet under T'ang dynasty whose lyric poems were engraved on stone tablets by imperial decree.
[17] **Swift:** English satirist whose articles and pamphlets guided public opinion in matters of politics.

fore there is no excuse for the sort of writer who takes as long as a marching army corps to pass a given point. Besides, brevity is often more effective; the half can say more than the whole, and to imply things may strike far deeper than to state them at length. And because one is particularly apt to waste words on preambles before coming to the substance, there was sense in the Scots professor who always asked his pupils—"Did ye remember to tear up that fir-r-st page?"

Here are some instances that would only lose by lengthening:

It is useless to go to bed to save the light, if the result is twins. (Chinese proverb.)

My barn is burnt down—

Nothing hides the moon. (Complete Japanese poem.)

Je me regrette. (Dying words of the gay Vicomtesse d'Houdetot.[18])

I have seen their backs before. (Wellington, when French marshals turned their backs on him at a reception.)

Continue until the tanks stop, then get out and.walk. (Patton to the Twelfth Corps, halted for fuel supplies at St. Dizier, 8/30/44.)

Or there is the most laconic diplomatic note on record: when Philip of Macedon wrote to the Spartans that, if he came within their borders, he would leave not one stone of their city, they wrote back the one word—"If."

Clarity comes before even brevity. But it is a fallacy that wordiness is necessarily clearer. Metternich[19] when he thought something he had written was obscure would simply go through it crossing out everything irrelevant. What remained, he found, often became clear. Wellington, asked to recommend three names for the post of Commander-in-Chief, India, took a piece of paper and wrote three times—"Napier."[20] Pages could not have been clearer—or as forcible. On the other hand the lectures, and the sentences, of Coleridge became at times bewildering because his mind was often "wiggle-waggle"; just as he could not even walk straight on a path.

[18] **Vicomtesse d'Houdetot:** French beauty known for her friendship with Rousseau.

[19] **Metternich:** Austrian statesman and diplomat, largely responsible for policy of stability of European governments from 1815-1830.

[20] **Napier:** Robert Napier, British army officer appointed commander in chief in India (1870).

But clarity and brevity, though a good beginning, are only a beginning. By themselves, they may remain bare and bleak. When Calvin Coolidge,[21] asked by his wife what the preacher had preached on, replied "Sin," and, asked what the preacher had said, replied, "He was against it," he was brief enough. But one hardly envies Mrs. Coolidge.

An attractive style requires, of course, all kinds of further gifts — such as variety, good humor, good sense, vitality, imagination. Variety means avoiding monotony of rhythm, of language, of mood. One needs to vary one's sentence length (this present article has too many short sentences; but so vast a subject grows here as cramped as a djin[22] in a bottle); to amplify one's vocabulary; to diversify one's tone. There are books that petrify one throughout, with the rigidly pompous solemnity of an owl perched on a leafless tree. But ceaseless facetiousness can be as bad; or perpetual irony. Even the smile of Voltaire can seem at times a fixed grin, a disagreeable wrinkle. Constant peevishness is far worse, as often in Swift; even on the stage too much irritable dialogue may irritate an audience, without its knowing why.

Still more are vitality, energy, imagination gifts that must be inborn before they can be cultivated. But under the head of imagination two common devices may be mentioned that have been the making of many a style — metaphor and simile. Why such magic power should reside in simply saying, or implying, that A is like B remains a little mysterious. But even our unconscious seems to love symbols; again, language often tends to lose itself in clouds of vaporous abstraction, and simile or metaphor can bring it back to concrete solidity; and, again, such imagery can gild the gray flats of prose with sudden sun-glints of poetry.

If a foreigner may for a moment be impertinent, I admire the native gift of Americans for imagery as much as I wince at their fondness for slang. (Slang seems to me a kind of linguistic fungus; as poisonous, and as short-lived, as toadstools.) When Matthew Arnold lectured in the United States, he was likened by one newspaper to "an elderly macaw pecking at a trellis of grapes"; he observed, very justly, "How lively journalistic fancy is among the Americans!" General Grant, again, unable to hear him,

---

[21] **Calvin Coolidge:** thirtieth president of the United States (1923-29).

[22] **djin:** supernatural spirit that can assume various forms.

remarked: "Well, wife, we've paid to see the British lion, but as we can't hear him roar, we'd better go home." By simile and metaphor, these two quotations bring before us the slightly pompous, fastidious, inaudible Arnold as no direct description could have done.

Or consider how language comes alive in the Chinese saying that lending to the feckless is "like pelting a stray dog with dumplings," or in the Arab proverb: "They came to shoe the pasha's horse, and the beetle stretched forth his leg"; in the Greek phrase for a perilous cape—"stepmother of ships"; or the Hebrew adage that "as the climbing up a sandy way is to the feet of the aged, so is a wife full of words to a quiet man"; in Shakespeare's phrase for a little England lost in the world's vastness—"in a great Poole, a Swan's-nest"; or Fuller's libel on tall men—"Ofttimes such who are built four stories high are observed to have little in their cockloft"; in Chateaubriand's "I go yawning my life"; or in Jules Renard's portrait of a cat, "well buttoned in her fur." Or, to take a modern instance, there is Churchill on dealings with Russia: "Trying to maintain good relations with a Communist is like wooing a crocodile. You do not know whether to tickle it under the chin or beat it over the head. When it opens its mouth, you cannot tell whether it is trying to smile or preparing to eat you up." What a miracle human speech can be, and how dull is most that one hears! Would one hold one's hearers, it is far less help, I suspect, to read manuals on style than to cultivate one's own imagination and imagery.

I will end with two remarks by two wise old women of the civilized 18th Century.

The first is from the blind Mme. du Deffand (the friend of Horace Walpole) to that Mlle. de Lespinasse with whom, alas, she was to quarrel so unwisely: "You must make up your mind, my queen, to live with me in the greatest truth and sincerity. You will be charming so long as you let yourself be natural, and remain without pretension and without artifice." The second is from Mme. de Charrière, the Zélide whom Boswell had once loved at Utrecht in vain, to a Swiss girl friend: "Lucinde, my clever Lucinde, while you wait for the Romeos to arrive, you have nothing better to do than become perfect. Have ideas that are clear, and expressions that are simple." (*"Ayez des idées nettes et des expressions simples.''*) More than half the bad writing in the world, I believe, comes from neglecting those two very simple pieces of advice.

In many ways, no doubt, our world grows more and more complex; sputniks cannot be simple; yet how many of our complexities remain futile, how many of our artificialities false. Simplicity too can be subtle—as the straight lines of a Greek temple, like the Parthenon at Athens, are delicately curved, in order to look straighter still.

INTERPRETATION

1. Discuss the five reasons Lucas gives for acquiring a good writing style. Are they all equally important?
2. Discuss Lucas' feeling about the prospect of teaching someone to write well. Does he think it is possible? What does he think is the relationship between teaching a person to write and his style?
3. Discuss Lucas' advice to writers in relation to Franklin's (page 225). According to Lucas' standards—honesty, courtesy, brevity, and clarity—was Franklin a good writer? Of the selections you have read, which would you rate highest by these tests?

STYLE AND METHOD

1. What devices does Lucas use to tell you what to do and what not to do? What is the place of "rules" in his directions for good writing?
2. How would you judge Lucas' own style? Is he ever wordy? pretentious? Does he get off the subject? Evaluate his writing by applying his own standards to it.

FOR WRITING

Evaluate one or more of the following selections, using Lucas' five general criteria for good writing—honesty, courtesy, brevity, clarity, and technical correctness: "A Letter from a Grandmother" (page 4); "The Magic Lantern" (page 83); "On Writing and Conversing" (page 222); "Paradox and Dream" (page 103).

Biography, at its best, brings its subject to life. But sometimes, if the biographer does not have a first hand acquaintance with the person he writes about, his writing, based on secondary sources, can be a lifeless recording of fact, uncorrected by personal observation. In the following short biographical sketch, Herbert Mitgang relies for his material on personal encounters he had with the poet and biographer, Carl Sandburg. The effect, more personal than what one usually expects of biography, provides a very intimate impression of Sandburg and of some of the salient qualities that made up his character.

Carl Sandburg

HERBERT MITGANG

Carl Sandburg wrote his autobiography in a series of books called *Always the Young Strangers; Chicago Poems; The People, Yes; The American Songbag; Abraham Lincoln: The Prairie Years;* and *Abraham Lincoln: The War Years.* Only the first of these was a formal autobiography and it took him only through his soldiering days as a private in the Sixth Infantry Regiment of Illinois Volunteers in the Spanish-American War. The rest of his life can best be discovered by reading his works — literally, for his life-style informed his poetry, biography, and history.

When he addressed a joint session of Congress on the 150th anniversary of Abraham Lincoln's birth, Sandburg ended by citing the letter Lincoln wrote about a proposed marble monument for a beloved friend, Representative Owen Lovejoy of Illinois, who died in the midst of the Civil War. And Sandburg quoted Lincoln: "Let him have the marble monument, along with the well-assured and more enduring one in the hearts of those who love liberty, unselfishly, for all men."

Before Carl Sandburg is enshrined in marble, a handful of living memories may be relevant from an honored, occasional companion. In the last line of *Always the Young Strangers,* Carl wrote: "If it can be done, it is not a bad practice for a man of many years to die with a boy heart." It was the boy heart that pumped bravely and freely through much of his life and writing. He was not as stiff-necked as some of his critics; he was willing to speak with candor though he wrote with great care; in a convivial mood he was one of the most joyous of men. He used that marvelous voice of his as an instrument — his friend, Andrés Segovia,[1] recently told me that Carl's pitch was musically sound — and he was interested in how others expressed themselves. To Tallulah Bankhead[2] he said, "I'd like to put your voice in my pocket."

We were walking around his *Prairie Years* country a few years ago, and he relaxed by throwing out two-liners:

"Am I the first girl you ever kissed?"
"No, but I want you to know that I'm a lot more particular than I used to be."

"Have you a criminal lawyer in this burg?"
"We think so but we haven't been able to prove it on him yet."

In Springfield, we passed a Walgreen's and he spotted a sign in the window saying $2.98 watches were reduced to $1.89. "Let's get us a couple of watches and clocks," he said. We also got some jackknives, which he loved. He used them to cut his cigars in half and, where some dudes carry handkerchiefs, he stuffed cigar butts. When he got to the end of the butt, he took out a pocket knife, jabbed it neatly into the tobacco, and used it as a handle for the last half-inch. He called this, grinning, a hobo way of "sucking the nick-o-teen."

The commonplace in the streets he made uncommon, vulgar, and sometimes hilarious. A sign said: CARS LOVE SHELL. He expanded on this: CARS WORSHIP SHELL . . . CARS ARE JUST PASSIONATE ABOUT SHELL.

The language of advertising offended him, and he despised and mocked commercials on television. At dinner he used a gadget to cut them off. "Here comes a woman who *inhales*," he said. "Click, click." As we ate, he parodied TV commercials with an

---

[1] **Andrés Segovia:** Spanish guitarist who developed new guitar technique permitting wide range of music.
[2] **Tallulah Bankhead:** American actress known for both dramatic and comic roles.

old jingle before he swallowed: "Through the lips and over the tongue — Look out, guts! Here I come!" That, he explained, came from the old fad of "Fletcherizing" — tasting all the food.

His system of bestowing autographs in restaurants and on the street had a certain logic. If a youngster came over with a napkin to sign, he usually did. If an adult male came, he would quiz him on how many of his books he had read; if the answer was satisfactory, he might sign or ask him to return with one of the books. If an adult female asked, chances would increase based on the degree of pulchritude. A well-thumbed Sandburg book always helped. Waitresses, shoeshine boys, and airline hostesses usually got his firm block signature, but respectable-looking stuffed shirts rarely.

He could blast politicians, especially Republicans. One evening after dinner we walked into the Illinois State Capitol building. He mentioned that he knew the Governor's father when the latter served as a Chicago alderman. A Republican publicist handed Sandburg some political literature, which he accepted; but then the publicist added, "This literature is given to you courtesy of the Secretary of State." Sandburg exploded, "You can tell the Secretary of State to go to hell!" Later I asked him why he had jumped on the poor fellow, and Sandburg softly explained, "The Statehouse is no place to give out political literature."

In his hometown of Galesburg, we stood in front of "Old Main" on the Knox College campus, where Lincoln had debated Douglas in 1858. As a youth delivering milk, Carl had cut across the campus many times and read the plaque with Lincoln's phrase that "they are blowing out the moral lights around us," referring to slave owners. Here Sandburg could not resist striking out at some favorite targets. "I would say to those who are known in this hour in our country as Birchers," he said, sneering, "I would say that those who propose to impeach a Chief Justice of the Supreme Court of the United States, without saying what evidence they have — they are hoping that they blow out moral lights around us." And, warming up in front of the Knox students, he continued, "The Birch Society is secret, like the Nazis. Those who want to impeach Chief Justice Warren don't know America. Richard Milhous Nixon," he added, sarcastically, somehow making the pronunciation sound evil.

"General Eisenhower, he was silent during the McCarthy era. Why?" This was Adlai Stevenson territory, and Sandburg, as an old friend and campaigner for the Governor and Presidential candidate, was feeling his political oats.

An owl-eyed student from the college paper tried to get a rise out of Sandburg, and succeeded, by asking him what he thought of the poetry of Robert Frost. Sandburg snarled, "How many of my poems and his have you read?" The student mumbled in shock, mentioned a few, and then retreated. I was interested in the answer (many people asked him this) myself.

Later that night in his hotel room, we sat around drinking his favorite black-label Jack Daniel's. First we had some with soda. Then we drank it with water. Finally, when we got close to the bottom of the bottle, we found the proper formula—neat, over ice. At this point, I felt emboldened to ask him the question, too:

"Carl, what *do* you think of Frost's stuff?"

"Robert Frost is a fine poet, but . . . ," he said, without a trace of malice and more in sorrow, ". . . But what can you expect from him? He's a Re-pub-lican."

We headed the next day for 331 East Third Street, where he was born January 6, 1878. It is a three-room frame house, the second house east of the Chicago, Burlington & Quincy tracks. He began to sing. "Mama, mama, mama, have you heard the news? Daddy got killed on the C-B-and-Q's." The house is lovingly preserved by the Carl Sandburg Association. "My father swung a hammer and sledge at the railway blacksmith shop," Sandburg said. "He used an X to sign his name. There ought to be an organization made up of people whose fathers couldn't write their signatures—it might tell a little bit more about this country than some of the so-called super-patriot organizations."

Here in this Swedish pioneer's cottage, with little more protection against the elements than a log cabin, Carl was born on a cornhusk mattress. One of his great prairie poems, from *Cornhuskers,* came to the surface:

> I was born on the prairie and the milk
> of its wheat, the
> red of its clover, the eyes of its women,
> gave me a song and a slogan.

Through Galesburg the trains of many railroads run—the

CB&Q, the Burlington, the Santa Fe. Long ago the night whistles had summoned Sandburg on the road to Chicago and thence across America. Now, too, he heard Chicago calling. But first he checked in by phone with his brilliant, warm wife, Paula, at the farm in Flat Rock, North Carolina, to tell her he was on his way home. He read her a newspaper editorial about his visit to Galesburg.

"Paula," he said, "did you know what you're married to? It says here that I'm a 'white-thatched octogenarian.'"[3] And, perhaps recalling the days early in this century when both were Social-Democratic Party organizers, she said, "You've been called worse things, buddy."

No train was fast enough to get out of the home town. Saying goodbye to an old friend, Max Goodsill of Knox College, he said, "Shake the hand that shook the hand of Elvis Presley." Then we caught a two-engine feeder plane on a one-slice-of-chewing-gum airline. Sandburg tried to settle back comfortably in the narrow seat. The plane shook and shuddered into the sky. When the chewing gum arrived, Carl opened his eyes, reached for a slice and put it in his jacket pocket next to the cut cigar butts, and asked the blushing hostess her name. "You're not what's wrong with this airline," he said, and, settling back, he took out a bandana, placed it across his eyes, and dreamed his way to Chicago.

INTERPRETATION

1. What kind of person was Carl Sandburg? When you finish the article, do you feel as if you know him? Do you like him? Mention specifics which account for your feeling.
2. What characteristic, according to Mitgang, was the basic ingredient in Sandburg's personality? What do some of Sandburg's own comments contribute to this image?

STYLE AND METHOD

1. How does Mitgang help you come to know Sandburg? Does he describe him directly? What kind of information are you given?
2. Do you think the author was or was not fond of Sandburg? Why? How does he let his feelings show?

---

[3] **octogenarian:** person between the ages of eighty and ninety.

FOR WRITING

1. Choose one of the anecdotes in the article and explain what it revealed to you about the character of Sandburg.
2. Describe someone you know, using only things that the person says or does, not your own description, to develop the character of the person.

How much do you see when you travel? How do you describe it? interpret it? Most people have difficulty describing a trip to the grocery store, let alone their impressions of a continent. Is it because we do not truly see? Alan Sharp's description of a tour through three states will make you look at everything more carefully, for he has the gift of making word images. They communicate what he has seen with clarity, depth, and dimension. What he creates is more than a verbal picture — it becomes an exhilarating experience.

Colorado, Utah, and Montana

ALAN SHARP

By the time you get to Colorado the size of America has been made quite unmistakably clear. Kansas is the living demonstration of a basic geometric proposition gone insane — that of a straight line being the shortest distance between two points. Not in Kansas it's not. As an argument for the vastness of America it takes some beating, this landscape of block color and infinite lines and hard-edge shapes. One longs for a more rhetorical utterance, for overstatement and flamboyance, for the essential gaudiness of poetry. The few people we spoke to in Kansas were understandably laconic. In the face of such unrelieved acreage, terseness was an inevitable idiom.

In choosing to travel in America at all, and in further choosing to travel by car, the intention was to absorb certain experiences which are not to be found elsewhere. Certainly not in Europe where there is a scaled down quality about the landscape that is both its bane and its beauty. I was seeking to assault a sensibility reared on patchwork fields and hand carved hamlets with a broadside of American gargantua. Not simply area but mass, volume and density. My trinity of giants was Colorado, Utah, and Montana and I approached them in ignorance, scarcely witting that they constituted a virtual continent of their own, offering more than the eye could reasonably focus or the mind comprehend. If Kansas proved one thing, then these proved something else again, something different in kind rather than degree. There are, it seems to me, countless Americas, all distinctive, all genuine. I think—from somewhat limited experience admittedly—few can be more American than these three mountain states.

The approach to Colorado is marked by a gradual elevation. Nothing spectacular, just a drift upwards that the car took without protest or qualm, moving down the miles in its upper sixties. We came in on Highway 96, deliberately rather low, meaning to drive through southern Colorado and swing up north once in Utah. It was a route which missed Denver and the Rocky Mountain National Park but since our object was to catch the flavor of a landscape rather than list the major attractions, it had its advantages.

So it was as we slugged Cokes at a filling station close to the Colorado-Kansas state line, the man who sidled around the car, wiping off the windshield, checking the oil and the battery, was unmoved by our sense of distance.

"It's a big country," we told him.

"Ain't small," he said, his apothegm made the more pithy by a feeling that he thought we were talking about Kansas.

Across the state line the first Colorado town is Towner. We were in and through before it had time to register almost. All I remember of Towner is a boy and a dog on the outskirts, walking away from the town, the dog brisk and curious, the boy with his hands in his pockets. We'd have stopped but he didn't seem to want a lift. The boy had straight, corn-blond hair and the dog had black patches on its flank. They were heading west when last seen and I am fairly certain the boy was Brandon de Wilde.[1]

About 20 odd miles further on we crossed the Big Sandy River and came to Chivington, named doubtless for Colonel John M. of Sand Creek Massacre fame. It came as a shock to move from the world of movie romanticism to the more prosaic monuments of history. Chivington is much like Towner but we stopped and put

---

[1] **Brandon de Wilde:** American movie actor.

gas in, trying in an aimless sort of way to sense the century-old aura of tension and fear and reprisal. Maybe it's just a question of some forms of history being more real than others; I'd never have thought to summon up the shades of the Tower of London, but here, in the dry Colorado afternoon it all seemed close and probable.

When we drove on, the final torpor of that unflinching Kansas highway was gone and we were in the West, savoring the heady brew which fact and fiction, intermingling, creates.

Going south on 287 were a cluster of reservoirs, water atolls in a dry sea, spangled with innumerable gauds of sunlight, cool on the eye as green islands to ocean voyagers. We were starting to feel Colorado's size and texture now. The land was dusty-looking between the sinews of its rivers; the air, as befitted 5,000 feet, was devoid of damp and gave the distances a clarity which destroyed perspective. We discarded both the 50 and the 350 in favor of the narrower, more direct 10 and took off into the steadily rising uplands towards Walsenburg. This gave us our first real sight of the mountains, the spinal column of a continent, the huge watershed that is both goal and obstacle to the westward traveler.

We were running towards the Sangre de Cristo Range, curving their great crescent down into New Mexico, receiving the fall of the sun on their high snows in tints of rose and pink, blood blushes above the sombre purple of the lower slopes. As we approached, the sun accelerated in its descent so that we seemed engaged in a race, in pursuit of the day itself. Between twin sentinel buttes, the Rattlesnakes, and on into the very shadow of the mountains. The sun, cooling now to orange red, hung a moment above the ragged edge of the range, and the sky blanched in expectation of its exit. Then, like a piece of theater, like sublime melodrama it sank, the peaks catching spotlights, the sky descending like a curtain and a band of intense ochre light rimming the horizon.

We stayed overnight at Walsenburg and were gone early, up into the mountains, up and up into the thin crystal air, cleansing the eye and thinning the mixture. The car wouldn't look at sixty and we let it crawl up and sent sight ranging ahead. Mountains are one of the great dreamscapes; the mind responds to them as to few other natural events. We drove through the La Veta Pass at almost 10,000 feet and beyond and above us the peaks aspired to heaven, whose air was rarest, unflawed that early by clouds. There was a kind of breathlessness, an awe that is oddly painful to the nonreligious mind. In the face of such one wishes to invoke ideas of God and metaphysics. The inability to do so is frustrating, the hollowness of finding church litany beautiful without subscribing to the convictions contained therein.

So to begin descent again was a kind of relief, to mind and carburetor both. The ice goes gradually out of the air and the eye is returned to vistas of ambiguity from those empty upper certitudes. This ambiguity is made most exquisitely manifest in the Great Sand Dunes National Monument, which seduces the eye at some 20 miles distance. Its shapes, all curvature and mound, tremble on the eye, like a mirage, like a longing. Colors haunt rather than inhabit these forms. There is a diaphanous quality, of flesh seen through silk, an ocular eroticism that conjures images of bosom and thigh out of seraglios[2] of the imagination. Seen through binoculars there are flanks and haunches of exquisite smoothness and running across them, wind-honed edges keen enough to make the sight flinch, like the thought of razored flesh.

There is no escaping the mountains for long, however. Through Alamosa and running alongside the high reaches of the Rio Grande the San Juan Range begins to rise up out of the foothills. We dodged it for a time by taking the arrow-straight 385 north to Saguache across the plain, but after that it was up into the mountains and again it was the rare, taut air and a chill that came through the vents and anesthetized the legs, and a general disemboweled feeling about the engine. One is gradually taken over by the landscape; the easy prose of the flat lands is broken and the mind absorbs the reckless oratory of peaks and gorges, of summit and chasm. This is the landscape of fundamentalism, of good and evil, of incompatible polarity. Only a mind steeped on Old Testamental certitude could view it without being shrunk to merest iota. *The mind hath mountains, cliffs of fall, sheer, no man fathomed!* The writer of those words never saw Colorado but had he, it would have been with a recognition born of spiritual empathy. This country is for birds, visionaries, and cars with variable altitude carburetion.

Its awesomeness is brought to finale by the Black Canyon of the Gunnison River. Here, such is the power of the landscape that the mind is totally inverted, its most basic tenets overthrown. Looking down into this gorge, such is its velocity and depth that

[2] **seraglios:** portions of Moslem houses reserved for wives and concubines; harems.

one sees it as a mountain, an upside-down mountain range, intaglio[3] rather than cameo,[4] the dim white spume of its waters a high snow line. One is dizzied by this reversal of spatial location, the feeling of looking up into the depths of the earth. The paradox stupifies and exhilarates. Later, when driving, there is a curious residual uncertainty as to which hand down will take us round a left bend. Our day's drive of some 350 miles had quite exhausted us, across such terrain and susceptible, constantly, to such stimulus. We cleared Grand Junction and stayed the night at Fruita, sleeping dark rushing sleeps, laced with vertigo and unscalable gradients.

In the morning Utah awaited us, bone bare in the yellow-white sunlight. We drove through on 70 and dropped south, crossed the Green River after an hour or so and then took 24 down into canyon country. This was something else again. If we had just come from the spiritual landscape of Gothic Christianity we were now in the landscape of ascetic mysticism. The earth and rocks are tortured into a fantastica of shapes, stained with the colors of artifice, gray blues and coral reds, lemons and ivories, all of a pigment so arid, so essentially febrile as to torment the mind with disbelief. An area such as this brings into focus the archetypal significance of those savannahs of the heart's desiring, with their connotations of fruitfulness and ease, that haunt the minds of men. Here is the physical metaphor of a mind deranged, tortured by its own longings for verity. It is the landscape of the wilderness paintings of the Middle Ages, peopled by penitents and gaunt wild-eyed prophets making straight the ways of their Lord.

Escarpments rose above us that seemed devoid of anything but their own existence. Nothing grew, nothing moved, no hint was there that anything had ever grown or moved. Bared to sun and wind and rain, in aeon-old immolation, they engendered in the traveler a wish for trees and grass beneath and a stream to float towers on.

We had a coffee in Hanksville and thought on Butch Cassidy and the Wild Bunch,[5] a little more witting of what elements they

---

[3] **intaglio:** sunken or incised carving.
[4] **cameo:** design carved in relief with other layers as background.
[5] **Butch Cassidy and the Wild Bunch:** a colorful group of bank and train robbers including Butch Cassidy, Harry Longbaugh (the Sundance Kid), and Etta Place, who operated in the early years of the century throughout the Old West.

had absorbed in the rabid granulation of their characters. The interaction of landscape and character is an imprecise science and one admitting of much poetic speculation. Yet to pass through such terrain as this and not imagine those exposed to it would be in some measure affected, is to put very little emphasis on the responsiveness of the human imagination.

Beyond Hanksville the road climbs steadily through a continuing area of rocks, buttes, mesas and gorges, with everywhere bands and layers of coloring that seem almost human in their brilliance and incongruity. Through the Capitol Reef National Monument, almost 20 miles of cliff line the roadside until the coating of the eye is rubbed raw by the abrasion of looking. With something akin to relief we climb up through Torrey and into the beautiful high valley at the upper reaches of the Fremont River. There are trees again and the eye perches in the cool of their branches, among the trembling tinsel of aspen, on the firm twigs of silver birch and under the conifers' gloom.

High on the Awapa Plateau, a wind joining forces with 8,000 odd feet of altitude to make things hard for the Chevy, we pushed on towards the 70 and the northward run to Salt Lake City. On the far side of the Wasatch Range we could see its barren uplands stretching west in fold and furrow, baked brown and tawny, like the heaped hides of leviathans.[6] A land like this aches in the mind; the barriers it presents to mere survival affect even those who will pass the night in motels watching the movies of yesteryear.

We had decided against spending time in Salt Lake City partially because cities take time and we had a long drive north to Montana ahead, and also because cities, all but a few, are at variance with the landscapes they inhabit, and our concern was primarily with the land, the parts people may only come in pilgrimage to, but may not dwell in. So it was we were gone from Salt Lake without having seen its tabernacles and shrines, even though in some ways they gave expression to our theories of man and his environment. We preferred the fact rather than the artifact, with no disparagement intended.

The Great Salt Lake and the subsequent Salt Flats are pure, unaided hallucination. Rather than go straight north on 91 we looped left, round the bottom of the lake and out across the flats. It was early in the morning and the road was quiet. Ten miles or

---

[6] **leviathans:** enormous creatures.

so out of Salt Lake City the taut straight of the 40 slacks left, and on the starboard side appears the vision of the Great Salt Lake. The road does not run beside it for long, or at any rate not for long enough. One can only try to keep from mounting the shoulder with disbelief. Jade green and lapis lazuli[7] with cinnamon shores this inland sea, a breeze pewters the surface, small surf like scrolls of palest green trace the edge. Overhead, lead-bottomed clouds galleon south, their shadows blooming upon the surface of the lake in great purple flowers, in spreading stains of indigo, turning the shores to sienna sand, to terra-cotta pavings. The colors interplay, shifting through a spectrum more marine than lunar, a landscape drowned in oceanic pastels where the sun is sieved into particles of light the size of fish eggs. It is the delicacy of shading which is ultimately the grandest magic, no demarcations or abrupt transitions, only gradations of imperceptible hues unifying the whole exquisite terrain.

As for inhabitants none could be seen and few guessed at. Only a pavilion on the fabled shore gave an intimation of what beings might dwell there. It stood, solitary and without warning, the way fairy tale palaces do, its walls rust-red brick, its turrets and cupolas apple-green, Byzantine, mosque-like. Within, doubtless, were rooms skeined in gossamer web, thick with dust and accumulated silences, and on a catafalque[8] in the high hall, cameo-faced, a thralled maid.

We watched the shore for signs of her knight, come a long dolorous way across the salt wastes, his horse drooping tail and neck in weary unison, rust on his shield, a white rime in his beard. But none came that morning. Less fleeting, but scarcely less magical was the Great Salt Lake Desert. Here too the dominant sense was not of land but of sea. The ranges of hills on either side drifted on the billows of mirage and we sailed at a serene 70 m.p.h. through their archipelagoes. The road wake[9] straight and the silence hypnotic, the sibilance of our wheels like the unheeded noises of a ship under sail. The American continental experience is in its moments of purest poetry not terrestrial but pelagic.[10] Here on the blind bright plains of desiccated sea, The

[7] **lapis lazuli:** bluish violet color named for semi-precious stone of same hue.
[8] **catafalque:** structure supporting coffin during a funeral.
[9] **wake:** track left by a vessel passing through water.
[10] **pelagic:** oceanic; pertaining to the open sea as distinguished from coastal waters.

White Whale and Ahab seem fitting metaphors. This is part of the American sense of space; his land oceans are sufficiently chartless, even yet, to make mariners of the most mundane travelers.

Once across the Salt Flats and beginning the ascent towards Nevada there is one last long look at them, a-quiver with heat and light, bisected by the road. Along that road are frequent signs warning drivers against going to sleep. It would be pointless asking them not to dream. More than any other landscape I know, the 90 miles from Salt Lake City are the stuff of which dreams are constructed.

As you leave Idaho the foothills come at you inexorably and beyond them the big battalions wait. From Monida Pass, which is nearly 7,000 feet up, you wind along the valley roads between the ramparts of rock and their dark jacketings of fir and pine and tamarack. It's cold and when you step outside it's like you'd been sucking peppermints. Perhaps there is not Colorado's grandeur or Utah's spectacular contrasts, but Montana has a bulging, muscle-thick quality about it. These mountains go on and on and on for as far as you care to drive north.

We went off the wide, interstate 15 at Dillon and started an eastward drift, aiming to come out below Butte and go due east on 90. It's quiet on the 41 and traffic doesn't exactly pile up. Our thoughts were not now of religion or metaphysics. There was a concreteness, a this-is-the-way-things-are-ness about the country that is relaxing. The road runs ahead and you follow it, the sky holds a few far clouds in its steely blue vaults, the air is winy with tree sap and polishes the lining of your lungs to a silvery sheen.

As you drive you know that on the far side there are plains whose extent and regularity equal those of Kansas. One sees remotest glimpses of the Jefferson River winding shallow along its course. Across Twin Bridges and through Silver Star, remembering Gary Cooper was born in Helena, Montana, and, oddly enough, so was Myrna Loy. By the roadside they have grass the color of that boy's hair, corn-blond, bleached yellow. Is he still heading westward, towards the mountains?

Once on the 90, we speed up a bit and start to thin out the highlands. Bozeman is less than 5,000 feet, virtually subterranean, but then it's up again to take the Bozeman pass before starting the long descension to the plains, along with the great snake of the Yellowstone.

As we leave the haunts of the Mountain Men, those most atavistic[11] of Americans, it's only to enter on what in its way is probably the most romanticized landscape of American history, scene of some of the few pitched U.S. Cavalry battles against the Indians, including the most famous and the most traumatic of all, Custer's defeat at the hands of the Sioux and Cheyenne. Around this event, miniscule by modern standards in terms of mortalities and numbers involved, hangs an aura of conjecture and speculation that amounts to a mystique.

Partially it is the defeat of United States arms, an unfamiliar experience even to the present day, and of course partly it is the somewhat superficial enigma of Custer himself. We took the turn off the Custer Battlefield National Monument beyond Billings. The mountains had by now given way to rolling uplands, hollowed by the water courses, and beyond, eastward, the tawny haze of the Great Plains. There is necessarily a certain disorientation when the Monument is reached; it is a battleground one has fairly vivid notions about, unlike Austerlitz, say. It all seems more open, less dramatic than the imagination would have it. But the somber block of the Custer memorial and the poignant terseness of the white headstones takes hold and the eminence on which the 7th Cavalry achieved immortality becomes somehow right in the context of the rest of this ample, undulant country.

They were not swept over by a surf of savages, nor did they knot themselves into a pyramid of resolute defiance, but spread out on this knoll they succumbed as seashore castles succumb to the inexorable encroachments of the tide, piecemeal, in hand to hand bitterness, their rifles jamming, their hand guns emptying and the realization growing that this was indeed a finale.

The Little Big Horn travels indifferently to join its larger relative, and in union they go to join the Yellowstone. The wind gnaws on the headstones and here and there grow tufts of yellow, corn, blond grass. The Indians called Custer "Yellow Hair," one recalls, and the chance poetry of things moves the mind with the fragility of its coincidence.

---

[11] **atavistic:** reverting to an earlier or primitive type.

History is only another aspect of landscape, the acts of humans achieving the form of natural events. Whether Custer's last stand was hubris[12] or Nemesis[13] is not clear. Its vibrations are still to be felt, however, coming up from a hundred years ago, and his fate still exercises the imagination in ways that mightier destinies cannot.

From now on Montana is rolling level, a respite after the summits and depths. It stretches ahead and one's senses are lulled on the black and gold checker of its prairie. There is in the land a vast emptiness, purer, less constraining than its Kansas counterpart. There are occasional islands on this main, a grove of cotton woods spill blue umbrage[14] beside a river or a sudden patch of irrigated green and once, in a backyard, unattended, an oil pump pecked patiently at the earth.

The mountains are rubbed smooth by the pumice of distance, their ragged edges becoming a smooth blue scroll. Eastward, the world might well terminate, for all the hint these opaque featureless horizons offer. We are sailing into eternities of space, the light lying long and flat on the land. We catch countless insects on our screen, the ochre explosions of butterflies and the small green beads of some unknown, luckless flier. As the light goes, so the whole world seems to run ever so slightly downhill. It is an illusion of free fall and, having come so far, we allow it to take hold the plummet towards night. The mind contracts before the concept of such space. The sky puts forth its countless stars; rhomboids and trapeziums, eternal triangles and empty squares. The stars define location without area more exquisitely than any text, trembling dust-like on the very verge of sight. The sky of Montana is almost as large as Montana itself. In the dark it seems even bigger than before and we leave as we entered, swallowed whole by this leviathan of a continent and dimly longing, in the whale's belly,[15] for some sight of the pigmy hedgerows of a lesser land.

---

[12] **hubris:** arrogance resulting from overbearing pride or passion.
[13] **Nemesis:** retributive justice or vengeance.
[14] **umbrage:** that which gives shade, as a leafy tree.
[15] allusion to Jonah in the belly of the whale.

INTERPRETATION

1. Discuss the central purpose of the article. Is it to make you want to travel? to make you appreciate America? to provide geological information?
2. How does the article make you feel? What part is most impressive? Which passages do you find most striking? Do they contain interpretation as well as description?

STYLE AND METHOD

1. How does the author organize the article? Would you have done it any differently? Why? Why is there no conclusion?
2. Here are three examples of Sharp's descriptive imagery. What is really happening in each situation he describes?

    a. "The sun, cooling now to orange red, hung a moment above the ragged edge of the range, and the sky blanched in expectation of its exit."

    b. "One is gradually taken over by the landscape; the easy prose of the flat lands is broken and the mind absorbs the reckless oratory of peaks and gorges, of summit and chasm."

    c. "It's cold and when you step outside it's like you'd been sucking peppermints."

FOR WRITING

1. Write a literal* description of a scene or action. Then write an imaginative account of the same subject.
2. Compare the style of Sharp's descriptive writing with that in Orwell's "Shooting an Elephant" (page 52) or with E. B. White's "Afternoon of an American Boy" (page 61). How do they differ? Which is most figurative? How do the differences reflect the differing purposes of these writers?

The following story appeared in the *Los Angeles Times* a few days
after the death of Senator Robert Kennedy. It is not the usual
"straight news" story: it has a by-line (the reporter's name) and it
does not have the standard five *w*'s first paragraph. Articles like
this one are called "human interest" features. This one is a
poignant story of a person who was accidentally involved in a
tragic situation. His life has been changed and he has learned
something about life which many people never come to
understand—that life is made up of good and bad; that they can
exist together and even flow from each other. Thackrey captures
the meaning of the experience in a manner not possible in a news
story, yet without departing from objective reporting.

All Part of Life

TED THACKREY, JR.

Sometimes it is hard for a man to know whether to be happy or
sad.

Juan Romero is just 17, but already this problem troubles him
because of things that have happened since the night he worked
overtime as a busboy at the Ambassador to get a chance to shake
hands with Sen. Robert F. Kennedy.

A moment after that handshake there was a burst of gunfire.

Juan found himself on his knees beside the wounded Senator.
He did his best to comfort his hero, and pressed a rosary into the
dying man's hands.

"I haven't cried since I was a baby," he recalled. "But I was
crying . . . ."

The next day, Juan dropped out of his ROTC class at Roosevelt High School because "I don't like guns anymore," and told
himself that in his world "everything is different now."

But that was only the beginning.

"The Good, the Bad . . . All Part of Life, Young Juan Learns," by Ted Thackrey, from *The Times*,
June 20, 1968. Copyright, 1968, by the *Los Angeles Times*. Reprinted by permission.

"I always liked people," he said, "and I thought they were good. But then I wonder, 'If people are good, how can such a thing happen to such a man?' And this made me very sad."

Juan's father, Flavio Romero, was worried about the boy.

"My father doesn't say much," Juan smiled. "He doesn't show what he feels. But I see him looking at me, sometimes. And he tells me, 'Do not think of this. Do not make a show. It will seem different, later.'"

But Juan could not help thinking. His friends at school wanted him to talk about it, but he couldn't. "I didn't have it straight in my own mind, so how could I tell them?"

Then he received a letter — the first of many.

A picture of Juan, kneeling beside the Senator, had appeared in several newspapers and magazines throughout the world. And suddenly he discovered that he had a world of friends.

"The people who wrote," he said. "They were very nice, the things they said. Three sent me a rosary — for the one that went with Mr. Kennedy.

"And people said that I was good, and that they liked me, just because I was there with him when he was hurt. Here at the hotel, people smile at me who never noticed me before.

"And at home, my mother tells me she is proud of me, and my sister she keeps a scrapbook of stories about me and letters and even a ten-dollar bill someone sent to me.

"It is hard to understand. I did nothing. It just happened. Mr. Kennedy was there and he needed someone with him, that's all."

One letter especially puzzled Juan.

"A lady in Ohio, she said it was good that it was me, a Mexican-American, who was with the Senator," he said. "She said she thought he would have liked that. But, why?"

Juan took a few days off from his job — he works an average of six hours a day, during summer vacation — to try and think it out.

"But it didn't help much," he said. "People smile at me and say nice things about me, and this makes me happy. But it is all because Mr. Kennedy was shot, and this is very bad.

"Some people wrote the hotel and said they wanted to send some money so I could go to trade school and learn to make a good living, and this was nice. I would like to do that.

"But I would be a busboy all my life rather than have such a thing happen to such a good man. I ask my father, but he says I must understand it myself. No one can understand for me, or tell me."

Juan nodded. "So, this is what I think:

"I think you can be happy and be sad all at the same time. I think maybe everyone who grows up is this way. I think that is how you know that you have grown up, because you can be that way.

"And I think maybe now I will grow up, too."

INTERPRETATION

1. What irony does Juan see in the attitude of others toward the incident— his mother, his father, the people who write letters to him?
2. What has Juan Romero learned about life? How does he define being grown-up? Do you agree with his definition?

STYLE AND METHOD

1. Who tells Juan's story, Juan or Thackrey? Whose voice is heard more in the article?
2. How does Thackrey tie together Juan's words? What purpose do Thackrey's words serve in the article?

FOR WRITING

1. Rewrite this incident as straight news.
2. Many writers have based whole novels on incidents as brief as this one. If you like to write, try writing a short story based on this article about Juan Romero.

If biography is the story of a man's life, how are we to understand the sub-title "Biography of a Classic"? Probably as preparing us for the history or origin of a great piece of writing. But in this case, Edgar Johnson may be implying even more — that the life of Charles Dickens and that of *A Christmas Carol* were in some way closely related. Did the author give life to the story or did the story give life to the author? Both were true, as Mr. Johnson points out. But as he also makes clear, Scrooge and the other characters of the *Carol* were conceived with such fierce life and energy that they caused a rebirth of concern for the luckless victims of nineteenth-century English industrialism.

A Christmas Carol:
Biography of a Classic

EDGAR JOHNSON

For Charles Dickens, 1843 was full of vexations. Angry Americans kept writing him scurrilous letters about *American Notes.* His new novel, *Martin Chuzzlewit,* was not selling well — fewer than half the 40,000 to 50,000 copies of each monthly number that *Pickwick* and *Nicholas Nickleby* had sold. Even after he had taken his hero to America and started lambasting the American eagle, sales edged up only another 3,000. His perennially improvident father and his voracious brothers were again hounding him for money. His fine new residence in Devonshire Terrace was expensive to run. He had four small children and another on the way. His publishers, Chapman and Hall — "the scaly-headed vultures" — had infuriated him by suggesting that, due to limping sales, his monthly drawing account be reduced from £ 200 to £ 150.

"A Christmas Carol: Biography of a Classic," from *A Christmas Carol* by Charles Dickens, a facsimile of the first edition with an introduction and a bibliographical note by Edgar Johnson, published by University Microfilms, a Xerox company.

Suddenly, early in October, while he was making a speech on public education at the Manchester Athenaeum, from a platform on which sat Disraeli[1] and Cobden,[2] a way out of his difficulties flashed into his mind. Something in "the bright eyes and beaming faces" of his audience — in contrast to the gloomy economic philosophy of the industrial Midlands — gave him the idea for a glowing, cheerful, heart-moving Christmas story. It would be brought out in time for the holidays; it would sell enormously — he knew it would; he would make at least £ 1,000, and his troubles would be over! Thus was the origin of *A Christmas Carol,* with its vigorous protest against the greed of gain, incongruously entangled with the need of gain — the images of Scrooge and his three Spirits rising to exorcise the tyranny by which Dickens felt enslaved.

Certainly none of his books more utterly seized possession of him. Beginning on his return from Manchester, he lived the story; it poured itself out of him with such fury that it was completed in little more than six weeks. Over it, he said, he "wept and laughed, and wept again, and excited himself in a most extraordinary manner," feverishly pacing "about the black streets of London 15 and 20 miles many a night when all sober folks had gone to bed." And when it was finished and through the press, he "broke out like a madman." His spirits imperiously demanded release. "Such dinings, such dancings, such conjurings, such blind-man's buffings, such theater-goings, such kissings-out of old years and kissings-in of new ones never took place in these parts before."

The *Carol* was unquestionably intended to make money. But at the same time, the manuscript, scored with corrections and deletions, with balloons swelling out of the text into the margin, and with entire redrafts of many pages (all to a degree highly unusual with Dickens at this stage of his career), bears witness to the loving care with which the book was composed, the fury of creative artistry that drove him. And although it was published on commission, with Dickens paying all the publication costs, and was to sell at the low price of 5 shillings, he insisted on an elaborate and expensively decorative format, with gilt edges, colored end-pages, a title page in two colors, and four hand-

---

[1] **Disraeli:** English statesman and novelist; British prime minister in 1868 and 1874-80.
[2] **Cobden:** English statesman and political economist; advocator of free trade.

colored engravings. Financial problems were forgotten in a passion for perfection.

Nor was its success with the public less than Dickens had hoped. The sixth thousand was roaring through the presses by December 24; 2,000 of the second and third editions were speedily taken by the trade. Critics and fellow authors were no less enthusiastic. "You have done more good," exclaimed the critic, Francis Jeffrey, "by this little publication . . . than can be traced to all the pulpits and confessionals in Christendom since Christmas 1842." "It seems to me," Thackeray burst out vehemently, "a national benefit, and to every man or woman who reads it a personal kindness." Since then, *A Christmas Carol* has pierced its way into the hearts of half the world.

But *A Christmas Carol* is more than a celebration of punch, plum puddings, kissing games, and warmth of heart. It is the core of Dickens's philosophy and a burning assault on the economic cruelties he saw around him in society. The Peace on Earth the *Carol* sings is not for those who make the world a battlefield of greed and who war on love itself. The story is an attack on the business rapacity that was making nineteenth-century England into a wasteland of satanic mills and industrial slums, and a blast against the rationalization of the political economists who defended a heartless system.

Both goods and services, the economists said, were subject only to the laws of supply and demand. There was no just price; businessmen bought in the cheapest market and sold in the dearest. There was no just wage; employers paid what competition decreed under the "iron law of wage." Men must take what they could get, and if their numbers drove down the wage, or if they were unskilled, ill, or aged, they must try or go to the workhouse. "Cash-nexus"[3] was the sole bond between man and man. The supreme embodiment of this economic theory was the concept of "the economic man," whose every action was dictated by the demands of monetary gain. Scrooge, in the *Christmas Carol,* is the personification of the economic man.

"Humbug!" he snarls at the ideas of generosity, kindness, sentiment, tenderness. Imagination he dismisses as a species of mental indigestion. His life is limited to his ledgers, cash boxes, and bills of sale. He systematically bullies his clerk, Bob Cratchit,

---

[3] **cash-nexus:** bond or tie of money.

and pays him the lowest possible wage. He feels that he discharges his full duty to society in paying his share of the taxes that keep the jails and workhouses going, and he bitterly resents having his pockets picked to support even these gloomy bastilles. The unemployed and the ill, for him, are merely idle and useless; they had better die, he echoes Malthus,[4] and decrease the surplus population. So wholly does Scrooge exemplify the economic man that his cupidity has no purpose beyond itself. He has no pleasures, eats meagerly, lives parsimoniously.

His business philosophy and his way of life have crushed all natural affection, deformed and stunted all the warmer impulses of humanity that even he once knew. The lonely boy he used to be, weeping in school, the tender brother, the disinterested young man who once fell in love with a dowerless girl — all have shrunk into a mere moneymaking machine, as hard and sharp as flint, as frozen as the internal ice that clutches his shriveled heart. Misled by a false conception of self-interest, Scrooge has crippled himself into bleak sterility.

But worse, his fallacy is the fallacy of organized society. In the course of its development it, too, has gone astray and then hardened itself in the obdurate error of a heartless economic theory. It neglects the poor; it denies them education; it gives them no protection from greedy employers; it lets them be thrown out of work; it confines them in filthy slums; it allows misery to goad them into crime and then punishes them ferociously. The deepening evils of the times all demonstrated that laissez-faire business enterprise represented the most disastrous social shortsightedness.

This is what the Ghost of Christmas Present means in the story when it shows Scrooge the two ragged and wolfish children glaring from beneath its robes. "They are Man's," says the spirit. "And they cling to me appealing from their fathers. This boy is Ignorance. This girl is Want. Beware them both, and all of their degree, but most of all beware this boy, for on his brow I see that written which is Doom, unless the writing be erased." And when Scrooge asks if they have no refuge, the spirit ironically quotes his own words: "Are there no prisons? Are there no workhouses?"

[4] **Malthus:** English political economist and clergyman known for the theory that population tends to increase faster than food supply, and poverty and war must naturally restrict the increase unless birth is controlled.

Coldhearted arrogance and injustice storing up a dangerous heritage of ignorance, poverty, and rebellion — such is Dickens's judgment of the economic system Scrooge exemplifies. In making himself into an economic machine, in degrading his victims into snarling and ferocious beasts, Scrooge has accomplished the dehumanization of man.

A Christmas Carol is thus an allegory, a seriocomic parable of social redemption. Marley's Ghost is the symbol of divine grace. The three Christmas Spirits are the working of that grace through the agencies of memory, example, and fear. And Scrooge is more than a solitary man. He is the embodiment of all the concentration upon material gain and heartless indifference to the welfare of human beings that the economists had built into a system, that businessmen were pursuing relentlessly, and that society in its blindness was taking for granted as inevitable. Scrooge's conversion is an image of the change of heart in mankind for which Dickens hoped.

INTERPRETATION

1. What incident inspired Dickens to write *A Christmas Carol?* What personal difficulties were troubling Dickens at the time? What irony* does Johnson find in the situation?
2. Why does Johnson include this historical information? What does it have to do with Dickens's character? With *A Christmas Carol?* With the society to which it was addressed? How does Johnson suggest that the story is an allegory*?

STYLE AND METHOD

1. Does Johnson's method help justify calling the article a biography? How does the author combine elements of history, literary analysis, and biography? Which element do you think predominates?
2. Why does Johnson begin with the anecdote about Dickens? What difference would it have made if he had reversed the order of the information?

FOR WRITING

1. What evidence does the article furnish that Dickens was a humanitarian? Define the term and write a paper showing how Dickens fits the definition.
2. If you have read *A Christmas Carol,* comment on how effectively it criticizes some of the "dehumanizing" effects of an industrial society.

In the first section of this book, S. I. Hayakawa introduces the
basic idea of theoretical semantics: words are symbols. Now,
Stuart Chase, who has written extensively about man's problems
with communications, gives an illustration of a critical problem of
semantics in practice: what is the meaning (or what is the range
of meanings) of a word? The "meaning" of a term should depend
on its *referent* — that is, on the object, or action, or situation to
which the word refers; but when the meaning of the word is
obscured by emotion, the word will serve only to arouse approval
or resentment. The term *fascism* has less impact today than in
1937, but Chase's survey still gives clear evidence of how we can
be tyrannized by our language.

The Semantic Discipline

STUART CHASE

The young semanticist will realize that he cannot acquire useful
concepts by thinking alone. Most concepts also demand doing.
It is perfectly hopeless to sit down and think about "money,"
"credit," "democracy," "love," "internationalism." The cortex
turns into a merry-go-round. No, if he wants more knowledge,
he must go outside his mind and observe things in action, take
measurements and records, inspect the results of those who have
observed and recorded. He knows that if a concept is incon-
structible and unworkable in the real world, it is meaningless.
And from time to time he remembers Stefansson's account of the
ostrich in *The Standardization of Error*. The ostrich, by popular
accord and definition, is a bird which buries its head in the sand
at the approach of danger. Actual or biological ostriches, however, run like hell.

His mind will be open for exciting discoveries in the real
world — inventions, new ways of employing energy, new sorts of
atoms, finer observations in medicine and physiology, but espe-

cially verifiable knowledge about political and social affairs. He will tend to be at peace with his environment, content with the understanding that this is his world and he is a part of it, and not yearning for other worlds whose locations, dates, and compositions cannot be determined.

Pursuit of "fascism." As a specific illustration, let us inquire into the term "fascism" from the semantic point of view. Ever since Mussolini popularized it soon after the World War, the word has been finding its way into conversations and printed matter, until now one can hardly go out to dinner, open a newspaper, turn on the radio, without encountering it. It is constantly employed as a weighty test for affairs in Spain, for affairs in Europe, for affairs all over the world. Sinclair Lewis tells us that it can happen here. His wife, Dorothy Thompson, never tires of drawing deadly parallels between European fascism and incipient fascism in America. If you call a professional communist a fascist, he turns pale with anger. If you call yourself a fascist, as does Lawrence Dennis, friends begin to avoid you as though you had the plague.

In ancient Rome, fasces were carried by lictors[1] in imperial processions and ceremonies. They were bundles of birch rods, fastened together by a red strap, from which the head of an ax projected. The fasces were symbols of authority, first used by the Roman kings, then by the consuls, then by the emperors. A victorious general, saluted as "Imperator" by his soldiers, had his fasces crowned with laurel.

Mussolini picked up the word to symbolize the unity in a squad of his black-shirted followers. It was also helpful as propaganda to identify Italy in 1920 with the glories of imperial Rome. The program of the early fascists was derived in part from the nationalist movement of 1910, and from syndicalism. The fascist squadrons fought the communist squadrons up and down Italy in a series of riots and disturbances, and vanquished them. Labor unions were broken up and crushed.

People outside of Italy who favored labor unions, especially socialists, began to hate fascism. In due time Hitler appeared in Germany with his brand of National Socialism, but he too crushed labor unions, and so he was called a fascist. (Note the confusion caused by the appearance of Hitler's "socialism" among the more

[1] **lictors:** officers who precede the Roman magistrates in procession and bear the fasces as insignia.

orthodox brands.) By this time radicals had begun to label any-one they did not like as a fascist. I have been called a "social fascist" by the left press because I have ideas of my own. Mean-while, if the test of fascism is breaking up labor unions, certain American communists should be presented with fasces crowned with laurel.

Well, what does "fascism" mean? Obviously the term by itself means nothing. In one context it has some meaning as a tag for Mussolini, his political party, and his activities in Italy. In another context it might be used as a tag for Hitler, his party, and his political activities in Germany. The two contexts are clearly not identical, and if they are to be used one ought to speak of the Italian and German varieties of fascism$_1$, and fascism$_2$.

More important than trying to find meaning in a vague abstrac-tion is an analysis of what people believe it means. Do they agree? Are they thinking about the same referent when they hear the term or use it? I collected nearly a hundred reactions from friends and chance acquaintances during the early summer of 1937. I did not ask for a definition, but asked them to tell me what "fascism" meant to them, what kind of a picture came into their minds when they heard the term. Here are sample reactions:

Schoolteacher: A dictator suppressing all opposition.
Author: One-party government. "Outs" unrepresented.
Governess: Obtaining one's desires by sacrifice of human lives.
Lawyer: A state where the individual has no rights, hope, or
    future.
College student: Hitler and Mussolini.
United States senator: Deception, duplicity, and professing to do
    what one is not doing.
Schoolboy: War. Concentration camps. Bad treatment of work-
    ers. Something that's got to be licked.
Lawyer: A coercive capitalistic state.
Teacher: A government where you can live comfortably if you
    never disagree with it.
Lawyer: I don't know.
Musician: Empiricism, forced control, quackery.
Editor: Domination of big business hiding behind Hitler and
    Mussolini.
Short-story writer: A form of government where socialism is
    used to perpetuate capitalism.

Housewife: Dictatorship by a man not always intelligent.

Taxi-driver: What Hitler's trying to put over. I don't like it.

Housewife: Same thing as communism.

College student: Exaggerated nationalism. The creation of artificial hatreds.

Housewife: A large Florida rattlesnake in summer.

Author: I can only answer in cuss words.

Housewife: The corporate state. Against women and workers.

Librarian: They overturn things.

Farmer: Lawlessness.

Italian hairdresser: A bunch, all together.

Elevator starter: I never heard of it.

Businessman: The equivalent of the NRA.

Stenographer: Terrorism, religious intolerance, bigotry.

Social worker: Government in the interest of the majority for the purpose of accomplishing things democracy cannot do.

Businessman: Egotism. One person thinks he can run everything.

Clerk: Il Duce. Oneness. Ugh!

Clerk: Mussolini's racket. All business not making money taken over by the state.

Secretary: Black shirts. I don't like it.

Author: A totalitarian state which does not pretend to aim at equalization of wealth.

Housewife: Oppression. No worse than communism.

Author: An all-powerful police force to hold up a decaying society.

Housewife: Dictatorship. President Roosevelt is a dictator, but he's not a fascist.

Journalist: Undesired government of masses by a self-seeking, fanatical minority.

Clerk: Me, one and only, and a lot of blind sheep following.

Sculptor: Chauvinism[2] made into a religious cult and the consequent suppression of other races and religions.

Artist: An attitude toward life which I hate as violently as anything I know. Why? Because it destroys everything in life I value.

Lawyer: A group which does not believe in government interference, and will overthrow the government if necessary.

Journalist: A left-wing group prepared to use force.

[2] **chauvinism:** blind, unreasoning devotion to one's country, race, religion, sex, etc.

Advertising man: A governmental form which regards the individual as the property of the state.

Further comment is really unnecessary. It is safe to say that kindred abstractions, such as "democracy," "communism," "totalitarianism," would show a like reaction. The persons interviewed showed a dislike of "fascism," but there was little agreement as to what it meant. A number skipped the description level and jumped to the inference level, thus indicating that they did not know what they were disliking. Some specific referents were provided when Hitler and Mussolini were mentioned. The Italian hairdresser went back to the bundle of birch rods in imperial Rome.

There are at least fifteen distinguishable concepts in the answers quoted. The ideas of "dictatorship" and "repression" are in evidence but by no means uniform. It is easy to lump these answers in one's mind because of a dangerous illusion of agreement. If one is opposed to fascism, he feels that because these answers indicate people also opposed, then all agree. Observe that the agreement, such as it is, is on the *inference* level, with little or no agreement on the *objective* level. The abstract phrases given are loose and hazy enough to fit our loose and hazy conceptions interchangeably. Notice also how readily a collection like this can be classified by abstract concepts; how neatly the pigeonholes hold answers tying fascism up with capitalism, with communism, with oppressive laws, or with lawlessness. Multiply the sample by ten million and picture if you can the aggregate mental chaos. Yet this is the word which is soberly treated as a definite thing by newspapers, authors, orators, statesmen, talkers, the world around.

INTERPRETATION
1. What does Chase's article demonstrate about the way words acquire their meanings? About the way they can lose their usefulness?
2. A word which appeals exclusively or primarily to our emotions of approval or disapproval is called a "loaded word" or a "label." What loaded words are current among your group of friends? in our national life today?

STYLE AND METHOD
1. What purpose is served by printing the interview responses? Could the point have been made as effectively in any other way? (If so, how? If not, why not?)

2. What audience do you think Chase was writing for, scholars or the general public? How is this fact reflected in his tone and diction? Be specific.

FOR WRITING
1. Conduct your own semantic research project, using a word of your own choosing. Report on the results. Discuss the results with your class.
2. Write what the word "communism" means to you. Discuss the word and the meaning people give to the word. Where do the meanings come from?

From Shakespeare's day to the present, there has always been a market for the manual that tells how to do something: tie fishing flies, learn a foreign language, repair a car, or make a barnful of money—all in a few simple steps. At first glance this essay might appear to be the same kind of thing. Mr. Drucker, however, goes deeper than his title implies. There are the components to know and master, and there are some steps to take, but there is much more, too. There are things to know about yourself, as well as about the operation of business, that may hold the key to your happiness and success as an employee.

How to Be an Employee

PETER F. DRUCKER

Most of you graduating today will be employees all your working life, working for somebody else and for a paycheck. And so will most, if not all, of the thousands of other young Americans graduating this year in all the other schools and colleges across the country.

Ours has become a society of employees. A hundred years or so ago only one out of every five Americans at work was employed, i.e., worked for somebody else. Today only one out of five is not employed but working for himself. And where fifty years ago "being employed" meant working as a factory laborer or as a farmhand, the employee of today is increasingly a middle-class person with a substantial formal education, holding a professional or management job requiring intellectual and technical skills. Indeed, two things have characterized American society during these last fifty years: the middle and upper classes have become employees; and middle-class and upper-class employees have been the fastest-growing groups in our working population—

growing so fast that the industrial worker, that oldest child of the Industrial Revolution, has been losing in numerical importance despite the expansion of industrial production.

This is one of the most profound social changes any country has ever undergone. It is, however, a perhaps even greater change for the individual young man about to start. Whatever he does, in all likelihood he will do it as an employee; wherever he aims, he will have to try to reach it through being an employee.

Yet you will find little if anything written on what it is to be an employee. You can find a great deal of very dubious advice on how to get a job or how to get a promotion. You can also find a good deal on work in a chosen field, whether it be metallurgy or salesmanship, the machinist's trade or bookkeeping. Every one of these trades requires different skills, sets different standards, and requires a different preparation. Yet they all have employeeship in common. And increasingly, especially in the large business or in government, employeeship is more important to success than the special professional knowledge or skill. Certainly more people fail because they do not know the requirements of being an employee than because they do not adequately possess the skills of their trade; the higher you climb the ladder, the more you get into administrative or executive work, the greater the emphasis on ability to work within the organization rather than on technical competence or professional knowledge.

Being an employee is thus the one common characteristic of most careers today. The special profession or skill is visible and clearly defined; and a well-laid-out sequence of courses, degrees, and jobs leads into it. But being an employee is the foundation. And it is much more difficult to prepare for it. Yet there is no recorded information on the art of being an employee.

The Basic Skill

The first question we might ask is: what can you learn in college that will help you in being an employee? The schools teach a great many things of value to the future accountant, the future doctor, or the future electrician. Do they also teach anything of value to the future employee? The answer is: "Yes — they teach the one thing that it is perhaps most valuable for the future employee to know. But very few students bother to learn it."

This one basic skill is the ability to organize and express ideas in writing and in speaking.

As an employee you work with and through other people. This means that your success as an employee—and I am talking of much more here than getting promoted—will depend on your ability to communicate with people and to present your own thoughts and ideas to them so they will both understand what you are driving at and be persuaded. The letter, the report or memorandum, the ten-minute spoken "presentation" to a committee are basic tools of the employee.

If you work as a soda jerker you will, of course, not need much skill in expressing yourself to be effective. If you work on a machine your ability to express yourself will be of little importance. But as soon as you move one step up from the bottom, your effectiveness depends on your ability to reach others through the spoken or the written word. And the further away your job is from manual work, the larger the organization of which you are an employee, the more important it will be that you know how to convey your thoughts in writing or speaking. In the very large organization, whether it is the government, the large business corporation, or the Army, this ability to express oneself is perhaps the most important of all the skills a man can possess.

Of course, skill in expression is not enough by itself. You must have something to say in the first place. The popular picture of the engineer, for instance, is that of a man who works with a slide rule, T square, and compass. And engineering students reflect this picture in their attitude toward the written word as something quite irrelevant to their jobs. But the effectiveness of the engineer—and with it his usefulness—depends as much on his ability to make other people understand his work as it does on the quality of the work itself.

Expressing one's thoughts is one skill that the school can really teach, especially to people born without natural writing or speaking talent. Many other skills can be learned later—in this country there are literally thousands of places that offer training to adult people at work. But the foundations for skill in expression have to be laid early: an interest in and an ear for language; experience in organizing ideas and data, in brushing aside the irrelevant, in wedding outward form and inner content into one structure; and above all, the habit of verbal expression. If you do not lay these foundations during your school years, you may never have an opportunity again.

If you were to ask me what strictly vocational courses there are in the typical college curriculum, my answer — now that the good old habit of the "theme a day" has virtually disappeared — would be: the writing of poetry and the writing of short stories. Not that I expect many of you to become poets or short-story writers — far from it. But these two courses offer the easiest way to obtain some skill in expression. They force one to be economical with language. They force one to organize thought. They demand of one that he give meaning to every word. They train the ear for language, its meaning, its precision, its overtones — and its pitfalls. Above all they force one to write.

I know very well that the typical employer does not understand this as yet, and that he may look with suspicion on a young college graduate who has majored, let us say, in short-story writing. But the same employer will complain — and with good reason — that the young men whom he hires when they get out of college do not know how to write a simple report, do not know how to tell a simple story, and are in fact virtually illiterate. And he will conclude — rightly — that the young men are not really effective, and certainly not employees who are likely to go very far.

The next question to ask is: what kind of employee should you be? Pay no attention to what other people tell you. This is one question only you can answer. It involves a choice in four areas — a choice you alone can make, and one you cannot easily duck. But to make the choice you must first have tested yourself in the world of jobs for some time.

Here are the four decisions — first in brief outline, then in more detail:

1. Do you belong in a job calling primarily for faithfulness in the performance of routine work and promising security? Or do you belong in a job that offers a challenge to imagination and ingenuity — with the attendant penalty for failure?

2. Do you belong in a large organization or in a small organization? Do you work better through channels or through direct contacts? Do you enjoy more being a small cog in a big and powerful machine or a big wheel in a small machine?

3. Should you start at the bottom and try to work your way up, or should you try to start near the top? On the lowest rung of

the promotional ladder, with its solid and safe footing but also
with a very long climb ahead? Or on the aerial trapeze of "a
management trainee," or some other staff position close to
management?

4. Finally, are you going to be more effective and happy as a
specialist or as a "generalist," that is, in an administrative job?

Let me spell out what each of these four decisions involves:

The decision between secure routine work and insecure work
challenging the imagination and ingenuity is the one decision
most people find easiest to make. You know very soon what kind
of person you are. Do you find real satisfaction in the precision,
order, and system of a clearly laid-out job? Do you prefer the
security not only of knowing what your work is today and what it
is going to be tomorrow, but also security in your job, in your
relationship to the people above, below, and next to you, and
economic security? Or are you one of those people who tend to
grow impatient with anything that looks like a "routine" job?
These people are usually able to live in a confused situation in
which their relations to the people around them are neither clear
nor stable. And they tend to pay less attention to economic
security, find it not too upsetting to change jobs, etc.

There is, of course, no such black-and-white distinction between people. The man who can do only painstaking detail work
and has no imagination is not much good for anything. Neither
is the self-styled "genius" who has nothing but grandiose ideas
and no capacity for rigorous application to detail. But in practically everybody I have ever met there is a decided leaning one
way or the other.

The difference is one of basic personality. It is not too much
affected by a man's experiences; for he is likely to be born with
the one or the other. The need for economic security is often as
not an outgrowth of a need for psychological security rather than
a phenomenon of its own. But precisely because the difference is
one of basic temperament, the analysis of what kind of temperament you possess is so vital. A man might be happy in work for
which he has little *aptitude;* he might be quite successful in it.
But he can be neither happy nor successful in a job for which he
is *temperamentally* unfitted.

You hear a great many complaints today about the excessive
security-consciousness of our young people. My complaint is

the opposite: in the large organizations especially, there are not enough job opportunities for those young people who need challenge and risk. Jobs in which there is greater emphasis on conscientious performance of well-organized duties rather than on imagination—especially for the beginner—are to be found, for instance, in the inside jobs in banking or insurance, which normally offer great job security but not rapid promotion or large pay. The same is true of most government work, of the railroad industry, particularly in the clerical and engineering branches, and of most public utilities. The bookkeeping and accounting areas, especially in the larger companies, are generally of this type, too—though a successful comptroller is an accountant with great management and business imagination.

At the other extreme are such areas as buying, selling, and advertising, in which the emphasis is on adaptability, on imagination, and on a desire to do new and different things. In those areas, by and large, there is little security, either personal or economic. The rewards, however, are high and come more rapidly. Major premium on imagination—though of a different kind and coupled with dogged persistence on details—prevails in most research and engineering work. Jobs in production, as supervisor or executive, also demand much adaptability and imagination.

Contrary to popular belief, very small business requires, above all, close attention to daily routine. Running a neighborhood drugstore or a small grocery, or being a toy jobber, is largely attention to details. But in very small business there is also room for quite a few people of the other personality type—the innovator or imaginer. If successful, a man of this type soon ceases to be in a very small business. For the real innovator there is, still, no more promising opportunity in this country than that of building a large out of a very small business.

Big Company or Small?

Almost as important is the decision between working for a large and for a small organization. The difference is perhaps not so great as that between the secure, routine job and the insecure, imaginative job; but the wrong decision can be equally serious.

There are two basic differences between the large and the small enterprise. In the small enterprise you operate primarily through personal contacts. In the large enterprise you have established "policies," "channels" of organization, and fairly rigid procedures. In the small enterprise you have, moreover, immediate effectiveness in a very small area. You can see the effect of your work and of your decisions right away, once you are a little bit above the ground floor. In the large enterprise even the man at the top is only a cog in a big machine. To be sure, his actions affect a much greater area than the actions and decisions of the man in the small organization, but his effectiveness is remote, indirect, and elusive. In a small and even in a middle-sized business you are normally exposed to all kinds of experiences, and expected to do a great many things without too much help or guidance. In the large organization you are normally taught one thing thoroughly. In the small one the danger is of becoming a jack-of-all-trades and master of none. In the large one it is of becoming the man who knows more and more about less and less.

There is one other important thing to consider: do you derive a deep sense of satisfaction from being a member of a well-known organization — General Motors, the Bell Telephone System, the government? Or is it more important to you to be a well-known and important figure within your own small pond? There is a basic difference between the satisfaction that comes from being a member of a large, powerful, and generally known organization, and the one that comes from being a member of a family, between impersonal grandeur and personal — often much too personal — intimacy; between life in a small cubicle on the top floor of a skyscraper and life in a crossroads gas station.

Start at the Bottom, Or ... ?

You may well think it absurd to say that anyone has a choice between beginning at the bottom and beginning near the top. And indeed I do not mean that you have any choice between beginners' jobs and, let us say, a vice-presidency at General Electric. But you do have a choice between a position at the bottom of the hierarchy and a staff position that is outside the hierarchy but in view of the top. It is an important choice.

In every organization, even the smallest, there are positions that, while subordinate, modestly paid, and usually filled with young and beginning employees, nonetheless are not at the bottom. There are positions as assistant to one of the bosses; there are positions as private secretary; there are liaison positions for various departments; and there are positions in staff capacities, in industrial engineering, in cost accounting, in personnel, etc. Every one of these gives a view of the whole rather than of only one small area. Every one of them normally brings the holder into the deliberations and discussions of the people at the top, if only as a silent audience or perhaps only as an errand boy. Every one of these positions is a position "near the top," however humble and badly paid it may be.

On the other hand, the great majority of beginners' jobs are at the bottom, where you begin in a department or in a line of work in the lowest-paid and simplest function, and where you are expected to work your way up as you acquire more skill and more judgment.

Different people belong in these two kinds of jobs. In the first place, the job "near the top" is insecure. You are exposed to public view. Your position is ambiguous; by yourself you are a nobody—but you reflect the boss's status; in a relatively short time you may even speak for the boss. You may have real power and influence. In today's business and government organization the hand that writes the memo rules the committee; and the young staff man usually writes the memos, or at least the first draft. But for that very reason everybody is jealous of you. You are a youngster who has been admitted to the company of his betters, and is therefore expected to show unusual ability and above all unusual discretion and judgment. Good performance in such a position is often the key to rapid advancement. But to fall down may mean the end of all hopes of ever getting anywhere within the organization.

At the bottom, on the other hand, there are very few opportunities for making serious mistakes. You are amply protected by the whole apparatus of authority. The job itself is normally simple, requiring little judgment, discretion, or initiative. Even excellent performance in such a job is unlikely to speed promotion. But one also has to fall down in a rather spectacular fashion for it to be noticed by anyone but one's immediate superior.

Specialist or "Generalist"?

There are a great many careers in which the increasing emphasis is on specialization. You find these careers in engineering and in accounting, in production, in statistical work, and in teaching. But there is an increasing demand for people who are able to take in a great area at a glance, people who perhaps do not know too much about any one field — though one should always have one area of real competence. There is, in other words, a demand for people who are capable of seeing the forest rather than the trees, of making over-all judgments. And these "generalists" are particularly needed for administrative positions, where it is their job to see that other people do the work, where they have to plan for other people, to organize other people's work, to initiate it and appraise it.

The specialist understands one field; his concern is with technique, tools, media. He is a "trained" man; and his educational background is properly technical or professional. The generalist — and especially the administrator — deals with people; his concern is with leadership, with planning, with direction-giving, and with coordination. He is an "educated" man; and the humanities are his strongest foundation. Very rarely is a specialist capable of being an administrator. And very rarely is a good generalist also a good specialist in a particular field. Any organization needs both kinds of people, though different organizations need them in different ratios. It is your job to find out, during your apprenticeship, into which of those two job categories you fit, and to plan your career accordingly.

Your first job may turn out to be the right job for you — but this is pure accident. Certainly you should not change jobs constantly or people will become suspicious — rightly — of your ability to hold any job. At the same time you must not look upon the first job as the final job; it is primarily a training job, an opportunity to analyze yourself and your fitness for being an employee.

The Importance of Being Fired

In fact there is a great deal to be said for being fired from the first job. One reason is that it is rarely an advantage to have started as an office boy in the organization; far too many people will still consider you a "green kid" after you have been there for twenty-five years. But the major reason is that getting fired from the first job is the least painful and the least damaging way to learn how to take a setback. And whom the Lord loveth he teacheth early how to take a setback.

Nobody has ever lived, I daresay, who has not gone through a period when everything seemed to have collapsed and when years of work and life seemed to have gone up in smoke. No one can be spared this experience; but one can be prepared for it. The man who has been through earlier setbacks has learned that the world has not come to an end because he lost his job—not even in a depression. He has learned that he will somehow survive. He has learned, above all, that the way to behave in such a setback is not to collapse, himself. But the man who comes up against it for the first time when he is forty-five is quite likely to collapse for good. For the things that people are apt to do when they receive the first nasty blow may destroy a mature man with a family, whereas a youth of twenty-five bounces right back.

Obviously you cannot contrive to get yourself fired. But you can always quit. And it is perhaps even more important to have quit once than to have been fired once. The man who walks out on his own volition acquires an inner independence that he will never quite lose.

When to Quit

To know when to quit is therefore one of the most important things—particularly for the beginner. For on the whole, young people have a tendency to hang on to the first job long beyond the time when they should have quit for their own good.

One should quit when self-analysis shows that the job is the wrong job—that, say, it does not give the security and routine one requires, that it is a small-company rather than a big-organization job, that it is at the bottom rather than near the top, a specialist's rather than a generalist's job, etc. One should quit if the job demands behavior one considers morally indefensible, or if the whole atmosphere of the place is morally corrupting—if, for instance, only yes men and flatterers are tolerated.

One should also quit if the job does not offer the training one needs either in a specialty or in administration and the view of the whole. The beginner not only has a right to expect training from his first five or ten years in a job; he has an obligation to get as much training as possible. A job in which young people are not given real training—though, of course, the training need not be a formal "training program"—does not measure up to what they have a right and a duty to expect.

But the most common reason why one should quit is the absence of promotional opportunities in the organization. That is a compelling reason.

I do not believe that chance of a promotion is the essence of a job. In fact there is no surer way to kill a job and one's own usefulness in it than to consider it as but one rung in the promotional ladder rather than as a job in itself that deserves serious effort and will return satisfaction, a sense of accomplishment, and pride. And one can be an important and respected member of an organization without ever having received a promotion; there are such people in practically every office. But the organization itself must offer fair promotional opportunities. Otherwise it stagnates, becomes corrupted, and in turn corrupts. The absence of promotional opportunities is demoralizing. And the sooner one gets out of a demoralizing situation, the better. There are three situations to watch out for:

The entire group may be so young that for years there will be no vacancies. That was a fairly common situation in business a few years back, as a result of the depression. Middle and lower management ranks in many companies were solidly filled with men in their forties and early fifties—men who were far too young to be retired but who had grown too old, during the bleak days of the Thirties, to be promotable themselves. As a result the people under them were bottled up; for it is a rare organization that will promote a young man around his older superior. If you find yourself caught in such a situation, get out fast. If you wait it will defeat you.

Another situation without promotional opportunities is one in which the group ahead of you is uniformly old—so old that it will have to be replaced long before you will be considered ready to move up. Stay away from organizations that have a uniform age structure throughout their executive group—old or young. The only organization that offers fair promotional opportunities is one in which there is a balance of ages.

Who Gets Promoted?

And finally there is the situation in which all promotions go to members of a particular group—to which you do not belong. Some chemical companies, for instance, require a master's degree in chemistry for just about any job above sweeper. Some

companies promote only engineering graduates, some government agencies only people who majored in economics, some railroads only male stenographers, some British insurance companies only members of the actuaries' association. Or all the
good jobs may be reserved for members of the family. There may
be adequate promotional opportunities in such an organization—
but not for you.

On the whole there are proportionately more opportunities in
the big organization than in the small one. But there is very real
danger of getting lost in the big organization—whereas you are
always visible in the small one. A young man should therefore
stay in a large organization only if it has a definite promotional
program which ensures that he will be considered and looked at.
This may take several forms: it may be a formal appraisal and
development program; it may be automatic promotion by senior-
ity as in the prewar Army; it may be an organization structure
that actually makes out of the one big enterprise a number of
small organizations in which everybody is again clearly visible
(the technical term for this is "decentralization").

But techniques do not concern us here. What matters is that
there should be both adequate opportunities and fair assurance
that you will be eligible and considered for promotion. Let me
repeat: to be promoted is not essential, either to happiness or to
usefulness. To be considered for promotion is.

Your Life Off the Job

I have only one more thing to say: to be an employee it is not
enough that the job be right and that you be right for the job. It
is also necessary that you have a meaningful life outside the job.

I am talking of having a genuine interest in something in which
you, on your own, can be, if not a master, at least an amateur
expert. This something may be botany, or the history of your
county, or chamber music, cabinetmaking, Christmas-tree growing, or a thousand other things. But it is important in this "employee society" of ours to have a genuine interest outside of the
job and to be serious about it.

I am not, as you might suspect, thinking of something that will
keep you alive and interested during your retirement. I am speaking of keeping yourself alive, interested, and happy during your

working life, and of a permanent source of self-respect and standing in the community outside and beyond your job. You will need such an interest when you hit the forties, that period in which most of us come to realize that we will never reach the goals we have set ourselves when younger—whether these are goals of achievement or of worldly success. You will need it because you should have one area in which you yourself impose standards of performance on your own work. Finally, you need it because you will find recognition and acceptance by other people working in the field, whether professional or amateur, as individuals rather than as members of an organization and as employees.

This is heretical philosophy these days when so many companies believe that the best employee is the man who lives, drinks, eats, and sleeps job and company. In actual experience those people who have no life outside their jobs are not the really successful people, not even from the viewpoint of the company. I have seen far too many of them shoot up like a rocket, because they had no interests except the job; but they also come down like the rocket's burned-out stick. The man who will make the greatest contribution to his company is the mature person—and you cannot have maturity if you have no life or interest outside the job. Our large companies are beginning to understand this. That so many of them encourage people to have "outside interests" or to develop "hobbies" as a preparation for retirement is the first sign of a change toward a more intelligent attitude. But quite apart from the self-interest of the employer, your own interest as an employee demands that you develop a major outside interest. It will make you happier, it will make you more effective, it will give you resistance against the setbacks and the blows that are the lot of everyone; and it will make you a more effective, a more successful, and a more mature employee.

You have no doubt realized that I have not really talked about how to be an employee. I have talked about what to know before becoming an employee—which is something quite different. Perhaps "how to be an employee" can be learned only by being one. But one thing can be said. Being an employee means working with people; it means living and working in a society. Intelligence, in the last analysis, is therefore not the most important quality. What is decisive is character and integrity. If you work on your own, intelligence and ability may be sufficient. If you work with people, you are going to fail unless you also have basic integrity. And integrity—character—is the one thing most, if not all, employers consider first.

There are many skills you might learn to be an employee, many abilities that are required. But fundamentally the one quality demanded of you will not be skill, knowledge, or talent, but character.

INTERPRETATION

1. Is Drucker's essay really about "how to be an employee"? What does he say the essay is really about? Where does he say it? Does that make a difference in your understanding the essay?
2. According to the author, why are writing and organizing information and ideas so important? Under what circumstances is this general ability or skill *un*important? Do you agree? Why? What general qualification does Drucker think is of crucial importance to *all* employees?
3. What four areas of occupational choice does Drucker think a person must consider? What does he say a person must have done before the choice can be made? In your opinion, what is the most important factor he asks you to consider?

STYLE AND METHOD

1. When Drucker talks about the skill of writing or speaking, he points out some standards. Do you think his own writing lives up to the standards? How would Lucas (page 114) rate Drucker's essay? Is the organization of this essay effective?
2. How much of Drucker's advice is good common sense, and how much is idealistic speculation? Give some examples to support your view.

FOR WRITING

1. Choose any major idea mentioned in the essay and explain why you agree or disagree with it.
2. Write a paper in which you explain what you think Drucker means by "character." Then make any additions or qualifications you think are necessary.

If you are taking a science course which includes laboratory experiments, you may be following procedures that were first developed and taught by the author of this lecture. Thomas Huxley, the nineteenth-century British biologist, believed in the value of science as a way of getting at the truth of nature. He fought for the establishment of scientific exploration and frequently took opportunities to speak and write about science. The following lecture demonstrates his ability to make clear even the most abstract principles of scientific method to the general public.

The Method of Scientific Investigation

THOMAS HUXLEY

You have heard it repeated, I dare say, that men of science work by means of induction and deduction and that, by the help of these operations, they wring from nature certain other things (which are called natural laws and causes), and that out of these, by some cunning skill of their own, they build up hypotheses and theories. And it is imagined by many that the operations of the common mind can be by no means compared with these processes. To hear all these large words, you would think that the mind of a man of science must be constituted differently from that of his fellow men. But if you will not be frightened by terms, you will discover that you are quite wrong, and that all these terrible apparatus are being used by yourself every day of your life.

A very trivial circumstance will serve to exemplify this. Suppose you go into a fruiterer's shop, wanting an apple. You take up one, and, on biting it, you find it is sour. You look at it and see that it is hard and green. You take up another one, and that too is hard, green, and sour. The shopman offers you a third; but, before biting it, you examine it and find that it is hard and green, and you immediately say that you will not have it, as it must be sour, like those you have already tried.

Nothing can be more simple than that, you think; but if you will take the trouble to analyze what has been done by your mind, you will be greatly surprised. In the first place, you have performed the operation of induction. You found that, in two experiences, hardness and greenness in apples went together with sourness. It was so in the first case, and it was confirmed by the second. True, it is a very small basis,[1] but still it is enough to make an induction from; you generalize the facts, and you expect to find sourness in apples when you get hardness and greenness. You found upon that a general law — that all hard and green apples are sour; and this, so far as it goes, is a perfect induction.

Well, having got your natural law in this way, when you are offered another apple which you find is hard and green, you say, "All hard and green apples are sour; this apple is hard and green; therefore this apple is sour." That train of reasoning is what we call a syllogism, and has all its various parts and terms — its major premise, its minor premise, and its conclusion — and, by the help of further reasoning, you arrive at your final determination, "I will not have that apple." You see, you have, in the first place, established a law by induction, and upon that you have founded a deduction and reasoned out the special conclusion of the particular case.

Well now, suppose, having got your law, that at some time afterward you are discussing the qualities of apples with a friend. You say to him, "It is a very curious thing, but I find that all hard and green apples are sour!" Your friend says to you, "But how do you know that?" You at once reply, "Oh, because I have tried them over and over again, and have always found them to be so." Well, if we were talking science instead of common sense, we should call that an experimental verification. And, if still opposed, you go further and say, "I have heard from the people in Somersetshire and Devonshire, where a large number of apples are grown, that they have observed the same thing. It is also found to be the case in Normandy and in North America. In short, I find it to be the universal experience of mankind wherever attention has been directed to the subject." Whereupon your friend, unless he is a very unreasonable man, agrees with you and is convinced that

[1] **. . . it is a very small basis:** it is based on very few examples.

you are quite right in the conclusion you have drawn. He sees that the experiment has been tried under all sorts of conditions as to time, place, and people, with the same results; and he says with you, therefore, that the law you have laid down must be a good one and that he must believe it.

In science we do the same, though in a much more delicate manner. In scientific inquiry it becomes a matter of duty to expose a supposed law to every possible kind of verification and to take care, moreover, that this is done intentionally and not left to a mere accident, as in the case of the apples. And in science, as in common life, our confidence in a law is in exact proportion to the absence of variation in the result of our experimental verifications. For instance, if you let go your grasp of an article that you may have in your hand, it will immediately fall to the ground. This is a very common verification of one of the best established laws of nature — that of gravitation. The method by which men of science establish the existence of that law is exactly the same as that by which we have established the trivial proposition about the sourness of hard and green apples. But we believe it in such an extensive, thorough, and unhesitating manner because the universal experience of mankind verifies it, and we can verify it ourselves at any time; and that is the strongest possible foundation on which any natural law can rest.

So much, then, by way of proof that the method of establishing laws in science is exactly the same as that pursued in common life. Let us now turn to another matter (though really it is but another phase of the same question), and that is, the method by which, from the relations of certain phenomena, we prove that some of these phenomena stand in the position of causes toward the other.

I want to put the case clearly before you, and will therefore show you what I mean by another familiar example. I will suppose that you, on coming down in the morning to the parlor of your house, find that a teapot and some spoons which had been left in the room on the previous evening are gone. The window is open and you observe the mark of a dirty hand on the window frame; and perhaps you notice the impress of a hobnailed shoe on the gravel outside. All these phenomena have struck your attention instantly, and before two seconds have passed you say, "Oh, somebody has broken open the window, entered the room, and run off with the spoons and the teapot!" That speech is out of your mouth in a moment. And you will probably add, "I know; I am quite sure of it!" You mean to say exactly what you know; but in reality you are giving expression to what is an hypothesis. You do not *know* it at all; it is nothing but an hypothesis rapidly founded on a long train of inductions and deductions.

What are those inductions and deductions, and how have you got at this hypothesis? You have observed, in the first place, that the window is open. But by a train of reasoning involving many inductions and deductions, you have probably arrived long before at the general law—and a very good one it is—that windows do not open of themselves; and you conclude that something has opened the window. A second general law that you have arrived at in the same way is this: that teapots and spoons do not go out of a window spontaneously; and you are satisfied that, since the teapot and the spoons are not now where you left them, they have been removed. In the third place, you look at the marks on the window sill and the shoe marks outside, and you say that in all previous experience the former kind of mark has never been produced by anything else but the hand of a human being; and the same experience shows that no other animal but man at present wears shoes with hobnails in them such as would produce the marks in the gravel.

You next reach the conclusion that, as these kinds of marks have not been left by any other animal than man, nor are liable to be formed in any other way than by a man's hand and shoe, the marks in question have been formed by a man in that way. You have, further, a general law, founded on observation and experience—that some men are thieves—and you assume at once from all these premises that the man who made the marks outside and on the window sill opened the window, got into the room, and stole your teapot and spoons. You have now arrived at a *vera causa;* you have assumed a cause which, it is plain, is competent to produce all the phenomena you have observed. You can explain all these phenomena only by the hypothesis of a thief. But that is a hypothetical conclusion, of the justice of which you have no absolute proof at all; it is only rendered highly probable by a series of inductive and deductive reasonings.

I suppose your first action, assuming that you have established this hypothesis to your own satisfaction, will very likely be to go off for the police and set them on the track of the burglar, with the view to recovering your property. But just as you are starting with this object, some person comes in and, on learning what you are about, says, "My good friend, you are going on a great deal too fast. How do you know that the man who really made the marks took the spoons? It might have been a monkey that took them, and the man may have merely looked in afterward."

You would probably reply, "Well, that is all very well, but you see it is contrary to all experience of the way teapots and spoons are abstracted; so that, at any rate, your hypothesis is less probable than mine."

While you are talking the thing over in this way, another friend arrives, and he might say, "Oh, my dear sir, you are certainly going on a great deal too fast. You are most presumptuous. You admit that all these occurrences took place when you were fast asleep, at a time when you could not possibly have known anything about what was taking place. How do you know that the laws of nature are not suspended during the night? It may be that there has been some kind of supernatural interference in this case." In point of fact, he declares that your hypothesis is one of which you cannot at all demonstrate the truth.

Well, now, you cannot at the moment answer that kind of reasoning. You feel that your worthy friend has you somewhat at a disadvantage. You will feel perfectly convinced in your own mind, however, that you are quite right, and you say to him, "My good friend, I can be guided only by the natural probabilities of the case, and if you will be kind enough to step aside and permit me to pass, I will go and fetch the police." Well, we will suppose that your journey is successful and that by good luck you meet with a policeman, that eventually the burglar is found with your property on his person, and that the marks correspond to his hand and to his boots. Probably any jury would consider those facts a very good experimental verification of your hypothesis and would act accordingly.

Now, in this supposed case, I have taken phenomena of a very common kind, in order that you might see what are the different steps in an ordinary process of reasoning. All the operations I have described, you will see, are involved in the mind of any man of sense in leading him to a conclusion as to the course he should take in order to make good a robbery and punish the offender.

I say that you are led, in that case, to your conclusion by exactly the same train of reasoning as that which a man of science pursues when he is endeavoring to discover the origin and laws of the most occult phenomena. The process is, and always must be, the same. Precisely the same mode of reasoning was employed by Newton and Laplace in their endeavors to discover and define the causes of the movements of the heavenly bodies as you, with your own common sense, would employ to detect a burglar. The only difference is this: that the nature of the inquiry being more abstruse, every step has to be most carefully watched, so that there may not be a single crack or flaw in your hypothesis. A flaw or crack in many of the hypotheses of daily life may be of little or no moment as affecting the general correctness of the conclusion at which we may arrive; but, in a scientific inquiry, a fallacy, great or small, is always of importance and is sure to be, in the long run, productive of mischievous, if not fatal, results.

Do not allow yourself to be misled by the common notion that any hypothesis is untrustworthy simply because it is an hypothesis. It is often urged, in respect to some scientific conclusion, that, after all, it is only an hypothesis. But what more have we to guide us in nine-tenths of the most important affairs of daily life than hypotheses, and often very ill-based ones? Therefore, in science, where the evidence of an hypothesis is subjected to the most rigid examination, we may rightly pursue the same course. Every great step in our progress in discovering causes has been made in exactly the same way as that which I have detailed to you. When we observe the occurrence of certain facts and phenomena, we ask, naturally enough, "What process, what kind of operation known to occur in nature will, when applied to a particular case, unravel and explain the mystery?" Hence you have the scientific hypothesis; and its value will be proportionate to the care and completeness with which its basis has been tested and verified. It is as true in these matters as in the commonest affairs of practical life: the guess of the fool will be folly, while the guess of the wise man will contain wisdom. In all cases you see that the value of the result depends on the patience and faithfulness with which the investigator applies to his hypothesis every possible kind of verification.

INTERPRETATION

1. What is the scientific method? How many basic steps are there in the investigative process? What are some instances where you might have occasion to use the method?
2. What does Huxley mean by "induction"? What does he mean by "deduction"? Mention examples that Huxley uses.
3. According to Huxley, what is that most essential quality an investigator must have in order to be successful?

STYLE AND METHOD

1. How does Huxley attempt to prove the point he wants to make? Why is this method a natural one for a scientific-minded writer to use?
2. How does Huxley utilize common experience to demonstrate the validity of the scientific method? Discuss his examples and the tone he uses in communicating them to his audience. Refer to specific passages.

FOR WRITING

1. Write an essay in which you demonstrate that you employ the scientific method in at least three kinds of situations in your daily life.
2. You are an astronaut on the moon. You have discovered a rock wall with what appear to be chisel marks on it. What hypotheses can you make that could help explain their presence?

Some expositions — like the abortive attempt of this father to explain the "new math" to an unwilling son — can end in tatters. Russell Baker's sketch, however, is a neat, well-controlled piece of exposition. By adopting a dramatic presentation, he makes wonderfully clear the dilemma of one generation in trying to communicate with another. And whether the author himself ever lived through the exact experience he describes is less important than the *persona** he adopts in order to dramatize the problem he presents.

Night Life in America

BY RUSSELL BAKER

(Here comes Peter.) "What do you mean you don't understand the arithmetic, Peter?" *(You'd think that out of eight kids we'd have at least one who could understand arithmetic.)*

"Look, all they ask you to do is convert 234 base 5 to base 10. Didn't the teacher show you how to do that?" *(Fat chance.)*

"All right. Give daddy the book and I'll explain it to you." *(This is insane. It says when you get five x's you draw a blue line around them and call it 10, and when you get five groups of five x's with blue lines around all of them you draw a red line around the whole bunch and call it 100. The kid will think I've flipped if I try to tell him that.)*

"Look, Peter, it's perfectly simple." *(Oh, boy!)* "In base five the second number to the left of the number on the right end tells you how many fives you've got and the number on the right end tells you how many ones you have left over." *(He's gone absolutely blank.)*

"Now, if we want to change 7 base 10 into base 5, what have we got? One 5 and a 2 left over, so we simply write a 1 and a 2 and we have our answer: 7 base ten equals 12 base five." *(When, for heaven's sake, would you have ever to do something as ridiculous as that?)*

"You don't understand why you have to learn base five? That's a silly question, Peter. If men were born with five fingers instead of ten, we'd probably be using base five all the time. Listen, suppose the dollar had only fifty cents instead of a hundred—" *(I'm talking like an idiot. Why couldn't just one of them understand arithmetic?)*

"Now see here, Mister, it doesn't matter whether you think base 5 is stupid or not. I happen to think income tax Form 1040 is stupid, but I have to learn how to do it anyhow because that's the way life is."

"What is Form 1040? There's modern education for you! They teach you to convert base 5 to base 10 before they show you how to recognize a capital-gain advantage." *(Steady! Neither Internal Revenue nor new math was the boy's idea.)*

"No, you may not turn on 'Every Night at the Movies' until you convert 234 base 5 to base 10. Now get on it. *(Better get on it myself so I can figure it out while he's still confused. Let's see: 234 base five means we have 4 ones left over plus three blue-lined boxes, each of which contains 5 x's, giving us a total of 19. The 2 means we have two red-lined boxes, each containing five sets of blue-lined boxes, which of course contain 5 x's giving us a total of 50 in the red-lined boxes. Adding the 19 gives a total of 69. The answer is 234 in base 5 equals 69 in base 10.)*

"No, Peter, the answer is not 468." *(Watch it! He's ready to cry. Explain with quiet charm and beautiful logic the simplicity of what he is doing.)*

"Pete, old boy, the beauty of the new math is its logic. We start on the right with the ones. They flow with beautiful simplicity into blue boxes which, in turn, flow into red boxes filled with blue ones." *(Well, it must have seemed logical to Einstein.)*

"How do I know what color boxes come after the red boxes? I'm not a mathematician! I don't design the boxes! I'm just an unbeautiful, illogical, complicated—." *(Well, that cuts it. Here she comes.)*

"No, darling, of course I am not screaming at Peter. I am merely trying to explain the difference between base 5 and base 10." *(If you don't like the noise, why don't you come out here and try it yourself?)*

"Peter, stop crying and let's forget all about the boxes. Okay? With the boxes we're getting way ahead of ourselves and if we go on with the boxes *(my ulcer is going to perforate)* we're not going to get anywhere." *(No wonder everybody in the country needs a psychiatrist. They'll diagnose the kid as a "new schizophrenic" with overt base 5 hostility.)*

"Just forget the boxes, Pete, and write down this answer: 234 in base 5 equals 69 in base 10. No, don't worry about it. We'll both get a good night's sleep and tomorrow I'll phone Edward Teller and ask him how I can explain it to you." *(It's immoral, but so is the income-tax code.)*

"What! You've still got more arithmetic!" *(If I hadn't married, on my present income as a bachelor, tonight I could be —.)*

"All right, Peter, so you've got to tell whether these mathematical processes are associative or communicative." *(After you know that, what do you know?)* Now look, Peter, suppose everybody was born with associates instead of parents and commuters instead of ten fingers —." *(Careful! If you cry it may leave him permanently commutatoid — associaphrenic.)*

INTERPRETATION
1. Does the father think the "new math" is illogical? What is his opinion of the "new math"?
2. Is the writer making fun of something? Explain what.
3. Explain what you find amusing about the article.

STYLE AND METHOD
1. Describe the *persona* of the father in this sketch. In what ways is he typical of the twentieth century?
2. What purpose is served by the father's *thoughts,* in contrast to his spoken words? What ironies result from this device?
3. Is this article effective as *exposition?* Explain why or why not.

FOR WRITING
1. Write your own narrative of an experience in which what you said is not what you thought.
2. Write an essay explaining what the father in this article couldn't explain.

IV

Persuasion

◆ Persuasion

Writing or speech that tries to influence the reader or listener to believe or to act differently is called *persuasive*. It usually tries to accomplish its purpose through the use of reason and argument, but sometimes the presentation can be emotional. The campaign speech of a responsible candidate for political office and the harangue of a rabble-rouser both try to persuade the hearer to the speaker's viewpoint, but the rabble-rouser, who relies on loaded words[1] and emotive language to sway his audience, will not persuade the listener who understands the processes of language. He can only be moved by the power of accurate language, clear logic, and honest intention.

That is not to say that emotion should be absent from good persuasion. On the contrary, unless the speaker has deep convictions about his subject, he is not likely to gain anybody's attention. The important point is the writer's sincerity and *his reasons for believing as he does* — and his ability to fuse fact, reason, and emotion into a convincing statement. The James Baldwin letter may seem almost a tear-jerker at first, until we notice how carefully the author has woven history of family and race together and how clear, concrete, and logical his thoughts are. Again, "The Twelve-Foot Ceiling" and "Hooray! Getting Back to Normal" both make use of the author's own felt experience as evidence in the argument — and for this reason they seem more personal — but the emotion is informed emotion based on reason and fact. Still, these selections can be contrasted with an article like Allan Nevins' "From the Ashes, a Solution," in which the facts seem to speak for themselves.

Inevitably, the prose that persuades will start more arguments. If the reader does not *like* what he reads, he may be inclined to discount the validity of the entire argument. But to approach an author with a closed mind, or to refuse to weigh an argument on its merits, is not fair to either the author or yourself. If a writer does not persuade you, take time to ask yourself why.

---

[1] **loaded words:** words that appeal exclusively or primarily to the hearer's emotions of approval or disapproval. See "The Semantic Discipline," page 151.

Harry Emerson Fosdick was a preacher. For many years minister of Riverside Church in New York City, he became famous for his sermons — sermons that always seemed to be filled with common sense about how to live life ethically. Typical of his style is the following sermon which provides some guidelines for deciding whether an act is right or wrong. Like everyone else, you have probably known times when you were perplexed by a situation and were unable to decide whether your action was right or wrong. If so, you may discover here some helpful moral rules of thumb. But read critically; test what Fosdick says against your actual experience. Does he supply any answers to your most urgent problems? How relevant is Fosdick's thought today?

Six Ways to Tell
Right from Wrong

HARRY EMERSON FOSDICK

Our thought starts with the plain fact that it is not always easy to tell the difference between right and wrong. Any pulpit, therefore, which keeps up the traditional exhortation, Do right! Do right! as though, with a consensus of popular opinion as to what right is, all that the world needs is to be urged to do it, is indulging in a futile kind of preaching. Behind a great deal of our modern immoralism is not so much downright badness as sincere confusion as to what is right. In many a dubious situation how we wish that someone would tell us that!

The factors that enter into this condition must be obvious to anybody.

For one thing, change of circumstances. Old customs and old codes of behavior in family life or in the relationships between men and women, let us say, undertake to tell us how to act, but the circumstances in which those codes and customs are supposed here to function are radically different from the circumstances in which they first emerged, so that although their basic principles may be valid their applications are endlessly perplexing. In consequence, old patterns of behavior smash up and old prescriptions for right and wrong do not seem pertinent, and every day human beings, who always like to have their roadways plainly marked, go astray, not because they deliberately want to but because they are honestly confused about which the right road is.

Again, our cosmopolitanism, pouring all the cultures of the earth into one melting pot, has, among other consequences, resulted in ethical confusion. Our Pilgrim forefathers, with a wilderness on one side and a sea on the other, in their comparatively isolated community and with their comparatively homogeneous population, could reach a popular consensus of moral judgment or even a dogmatic certainty as to how men ought to act. But in a city like this most of the ways of behaving known on earth are poured together, so that the issue is not a single clear right against a single clear wrong, but such diverse and competing ideas of right as to befuddle the minds even of the elect.

The upshot of all this is that conscience is not enough. Of course, conscience never has been enough. Many of the most terrific deeds in history, from the crucifixion of our Lord down, were conscientiously done. Listen even to Paul in his first letter to Timothy: "I was before a blasphemer, and a persecutor, and injurious: howbeit I obtained mercy, because I did it ignorantly in unbelief." Paul throughout his life had been conscientious. Toward the end of it he could say to his Jewish brethren, "I have lived before God in all good conscience until this day." That did not mean, however, that as he looked back over his life all the things he had conscientiously done seemed to him to have been right. Upon the contrary, he confessed: a blasphemer, a persecutor, an injurious person, such was I, conscientiously but ignorantly.

Today I propose talking about this matter with homely practicality to my own soul and to yours. We may take it for granted that we would not be here in a Christian church if in general we did not desire to do right. We may even take it for granted that if, as in Shakespeare's *As You Like It*, someone should ask us Touchstone's question, "Hast any philosophy in thee, shepherd?"[1] we would say, Yes indeed, we have; we believe the basic ideas of

[1] Act III, Scene 2.

Christianity about life's meaning — that is our philosophy. But we had better take it for granted also that this general desire to do right and this general acceptance of the Christian philosophy of life do not solve our problem. So as automobilists our problem is not solved when we desire to take the right road or when we hold a true cosmology about the solar relationships of the earth on which the right road runs. Oh, for a homely sign-post now and then, some practical, directive help amid the confusion of competing ways to tell us where to turn! So this morning I invite you to no airplane trip into the lofty blue but to a practical land journey as we set up six homely guide-posts to the good life.

In the first place, if a man is sincerely perplexed about a question of right and wrong, he might well submit it to the test of common sense. Suppose that someone should challenge you to a duel. What would you say? I would advise you to say, Don't be silly! As a matter of historic fact, dueling, which was once a serious point of conscientious honor, was not so much argued out of existence as laughed out. The common sense of mankind rose up against it, saying, Don't be silly! So Cervantes in *Don Quixote* finished off the ridiculous leftovers of the old knighthood, saying, Don't be silly! So Jesus, in his parable of the rich man who accumulated outward things but cared nothing for the inward wealth of the spiritual life, did not say, Sinner! but Fool! — "Thou fool, this night thy soul shall be required of thee: then whose shall those things be, which thou hast provided?"[2]

So, too, more intimately, here is a youth whom you may know, whose behavior burdens with anxiety his family, his teachers, and his friends. They argue with him; they exhort him; they penalize him to no effect. But someday a fine girl for whom he cares says to him, it may be no more than three words, Don't be silly! and lo, something happens in that boy that home and school and church together could not achieve.

What we are saying now is that this is a healthy thing for a man to say to his own soul before somebody else has to say it to him. One wonders how many here would be affected by it. You do not really care anything about drink, and left to yourself you would not drink at all, but it is so commonly offered to one nowadays and is so generally taken as a matter of course, that you are drinking too much. Don't be silly! Or you may have in your hands today a choice between promiscuous sexual liaisons and a real

[2] Luke 12:20.

home where two people love each other so much that they do not care to love anybody else in the same way at all; where romance deepens into friendship and overflows into children; where, as the sun grows westerly, the family life becomes every year more beautiful. And with that choice in your hands you are playing with promiscuity. Don't be silly!

Or it may be that you have a good set of brains and real ability so that if you wanted to you could prepare yourself for some worthwhile work in the world, and just because you are financially able you are trying to be aimlessly happy, not going anywhere, — just meandering, — endeavoring to pick up all the sensations that you can accumulate. I should not think it worthwhile to call you first of all bad, but I am sure it would be true to call you silly.

That is the first test and, alas! twenty years from now somebody here this morning, listening to this and paying no heed to it, will be looking back on life and saying that bitter thing, "God be merciful to me, a fool!"[3]

In the second place, if a man is sincerely perplexed about a question of right and wrong, he may well submit it to the test of sportsmanship. Now, the essence of sportsmanship is that in a game we do not take for ourselves special favors which we deny to other players but, making the rules equal for all, abide by them. In daily life that means that a man should always question concerning his conduct whether, if everybody acted on the same principle, it would be well for all. There is no doubt, then, why it is wrong to crowd in ahead of your turn in a line at a ticket office. Play the game! There is no doubt why it is wrong to cheat the government with petty smuggling or to join whispering campaigns about people when you do not know the facts, or to treat contemptuously a person of another race or color. Play the game! In all such cases we know well that we would not wish to be treated ourselves as we are treating others and that if everybody acted on that principle it would not be well for all. Sometimes one thinks that half the evil in the world is simply cheating. People do not play the game.

Do not, I beg of you, restrict the application of this test within the limits of individual behavior. There are ways of making money in our economic system, not simply illegal but legal, speculative gambling with the securities of the people, using

[3] Edward Rowland Sill: *The Fool's Prayer.*

public utilities as a football to be kicked all over the financial field in hope of making a goal of private profit with it, or betting day after day on stocks that represent genuine values which honest business once created but which now can be used merely for a gambler's chance without creating anything. If everybody acted like that there would be no values even to gamble with and no welfare for anyone. Be sure of this, that this rising tide of public indignation against the economic wrongs has this much justification: we have a right at least to ordinary sportsmanship and in wide areas we have not been getting it. The Golden Rule, my friends, is a grand test. Husband and wife, parents and children, employers and employees, black and white, prosperous and poor, Occident and Orient—what if we did not cheat! what if we did as we would be done by! what if we played the game!

In the third place, if a man is sincerely perplexed about a question of right and wrong, he may well submit it to the test of his best self. Notice, I do not say to his conscience, for the conscience merely urges us to do right without telling us what the right is, but deeper than conscience and more comprehensive is this other matter, a man's best self. For, of course, no one of us is a single self. How much simpler life would be if we only were! There is a passionate self, reaching out hungrily for importunate sensations, good, bad, and indifferent. There is the careless self taking anything that comes along, excellent and vulgar, fine and cheap. There is the greedy self in whose eyes an egoistic want blots out all the wide horizons of humanity beside. But deeper than all these is that inner self where dwells the light that, as the Fourth Gospel says, lighteth every man coming into the world.

Let us illustrate it from biography. You know the story of Pasteur, great scientist, devout Christian, builder of modern medicine. In 1870, when the Germans invaded France, he already had had a paralytic stroke and was a cripple. He could not help repel the invaders. His friends urged him out of Paris that he might not be "a useless mouth" to be fed through the siege. His biographer tells us that sometimes when he was sitting quietly with his wife and daughter, in the little village of Arbois, the crier's trumpet would sound, and forgetting all else, he would go out of doors, mix with the groups standing on the bridge, listen to the latest news of disaster, and creep like a dumb, hurt animal back to his room. What could he do? What ought he to do? "Unhappy France," he wrote to a friend, "dear country, if I could only assist in raising thee from thy disasters!" Then something happened inside Pasteur that has changed the world. He, half paralyzed, a man already warned of his end, determined that he would raise France again to glory by a work of pure beneficence, that he would erect a monument to his country's honor that would make the military monuments of the conquerors seem puerile. In his biography you can read it all, how by years of inspired and sacrificial labor he at last fulfilled his purpose. So Pasteur, wondering what he ought to do, what he could do in a perplexing situation, carried the decision up to that finest self.

Sometimes when I preach here I wonder if there may not be in this congregation a youth who, so choosing his vocation, so testing his ambition, so dedicating his intelligence, will not help to raise America again. She needs it, unhappy country!

Be sure of this, that if, in large ways or small, any one of us does help to ennoble our society and build a better nation for our children and their children to be born into, it will be because we have taken our secret ambitions up to the tribunal of our finest self. There *is* something in us like a musician's taste, which discriminates harmony from discord. There *is* something in us like a bank teller's fingers, which distinguish true money from counterfeit:

> . . . . To thine own self be true,
> And it must follow, as the night the day,
> Thou canst not then be false to any man.[4]

In the fourth place, if a man is sincerely perplexed over a matter of right and wrong he may well submit the question to the test of publicity. What if everybody knew what we are proposing to do? Strip it of secrecy and furtiveness. Carry it out into the open air, this conduct we are unsure about. Suppose our family and friends knew about it. Imagine it publicly talked of whenever our name is mentioned. Picture it written in the story of our life for our children afterwards to read. Submit it to the test of publicity. Anybody who knows human life with its clandestine behavior understands what a searching and healthy test this is.

How often in politics, in church life, in business, in personal character, we see things that remind us of a claque at the theater

[4] *Hamlet:* Act I, Scene 3.

hired to applaud a play! They can get away with it as long as the public does not know it is a claque. It depends on secrecy for its success. What a test publicity is!

Granted that ex-Mayor Walker[5] may not have done anything illegal. Yet all those clandestine funds, those furtive sources of supply, would not stand the test of publicity. Granted that the Insulls[6] may have succeeded in keeping within the margins of the law. Yet all this clandestine juggling with public utilities, this making millions out of the people by speculative greed, which acts as a parasite upon those real values that creative business produces but which produces no value itself, those secret lists of preferred and powerful men who received hundreds of thousands of dollars for reasons not disclosed — all this will not stand the test of publicity.

Do you remember how Phillips Brooks[7] put it?

> To keep clear of concealment, to keep clear of the need of concealment, to do nothing which he might not do out on the middle of Boston Common at noonday, — I cannot say how more and more that seems to me to be the glory of a young man's life. It is an awful hour when the first necessity of hiding anything comes. The whole life is different thenceforth. When there are questions to be feared and eyes to be avoided and subjects which must not be touched, then the bloom of life is gone. Put off that day as long as possible. Put it off forever if you can.

I know one business firm in this city which in a few weeks will crash into a receivership[8] under the tremendous blow of a righteous court decision. Ten years ago that firm did a secret thing which would not stand the test of open knowledge. For ten years those men have lived in deadly fear that it might be known. And now the light has fallen.

Yes, and just the other day in personal conference I talked with an individual on the ragged edge of nervous prostration because in the secret furtiveness of private life something was afoot which it would be disastrous to have known.

[5] **Walker:** James J. Walker, mayor of New York, 1925-32.
[6] **Insulls:** public utilities capitalists, whose collapse was the largest corporate failure in American business history.
[7] **Phillips Brooks:** gifted American preacher who became an Episcopal bishop in 1891.
[8] **receivership:** property, pending court action, taken under the control of a person appointed by the court.

Things that cannot stand sunlight are not healthful. There is a test for a perplexed conscience. How many here do you suppose would be affected by it? Imagine your behavior public.

In the fifth place, if a man is perplexed about a question of right and wrong he may well submit it to the test of his most admired personality. Carry it up into the light of the life which you esteem most and test it there. Why is it that some of us do not like cheap jazz? It is because we have known and loved another kind of music. Why is it that some of us do not think that Coney Island is a beautiful place? It is because on autumn days when the artistry of heaven has been poured out in lavish loveliness upon the trees we have walked in the spacious woods alone with our own souls and God. Why is it that some of us regard with a deep distaste all this promiscuous sexuality? It is because we have lived in homes where love was deep and lasting and dependable.

My friends, it is the beauties and the personalities that we positively have loved that set for us the tests and standards of our lives. Why is it, then, that conduct which seems to some people right seems to some of us cheap and vulgar, selfish and wrong? It is because for years we have known and adored the Christ. There is a test for a perplexed conscience. Carry your behavior up into the presence of the Galilean and judge it there.

If someone protests that he does not propose to subjugate his independence of moral judgment to any authority, not even Christ's, I answer, What do you mean by authority? There are all kinds of authorities — ecclesiastical, creedal, external, artificial — against the imposition of whose control on mind and conscience I would as vigorously fight as you. But there is one kind of authority for which I hunger, the insight of the seers. In science, in philosophy, in literature, in art, in music, not simply in morals and religion, I would, if I might, enrich my soul with the insights of the seers. A modern essayist says of Wordsworth, the poet, that he "saw things that other people do not see, and that he saw with quite unique clearness and frequency things which they see at most rarely and dimly." Aye! More than once some of us have carried our perplexed consciences up into the presence of the Christ and have made a saving use of his eyes.

In the sixth place, if a man is perplexed about a question of right and wrong, he may well submit it to the test of foresight. Where is this course of behavior coming out? All good life, my friends, depends upon the disciplining of clamorous and importunate desires in the light of a long look. We Christians who are trying to be intelligent long since gave up our belief in hell, but one suspects that many of us, throwing over the incredible and picturesque impossibilities of that belief, have dropped also a basic truth which our forefathers carried along in it. Every man who picks up one end of a stick picks up the other. Aye! Every man who chooses one end of a road is choosing the other. Aye! Every course of behavior has not only a place where it begins but a place where it comes out.

Life is like a game of chess. Some youth is here this morning with all his pieces on the board and freedom to commence. They tell me, however, that when a man has once played his opening, he is not so free thereafter. His moves must conform to the plan he has adopted. He has to follow the lead with which he has begun. The consequence of his opening closes in on him until at last, when checkmate is called, See! says the expert, when you chose those first moves you decided the end. Well, with what gambit are we opening our game?

We really do not need to be so perplexed about right and wrong as we sometimes are. To be sure, there is nothing infallible about all this. Goodness is an adventure and "Time makes ancient good uncouth." Nevertheless, the test of common sense, of sportsmanship, of the best self, the test of publicity, of our most admired personality, of foresight,—these are sensible, practical, high-minded ways to tell right from wrong. I call you to witness that in all this I have not been imposing on you a code of conduct; I have been appealing to your own best moral judgment. Alas for a man who neglects that! For though, as in Paul's case, one may come out at last to a good life, it is a bitter thing to have to look back and say, A blasphemer, and a persecutor, and injurious — such was I — ignorantly.

INTERPRETATION

1. What distinction does Fosdick make between an act that might be termed "bad" and one that could be termed "silly"? Discuss his notion of common sense. Does it fit today's world as you know it?
2. Discuss the speaker's concept of the "best self." Can you add any illustrations of your own that would clarify this concept? Do you know any persons who demonstrate this quality? How do they live?

3. Discuss the test of foresight. In what kinds of situations is it most useful? Of all six ways suggested for telling right from wrong, which seems to you most valuable? Explain.

STYLE AND METHOD

1. Review the organization of this sermon. How is it structured? How does Fosdick make the transition from one test to the next one?
2. Can you think of other terms which might have been used to express the six rules in this sermon? Do they mean the same thing? How do you define the terms used in the sermon?
3. Fosdick quotes the Bible and literature generously, alludes to the life of Pasteur and to other public figures and events. For what purpose? How do these allusions affect your view of the speaker? affect the tone* of the sermon? By contrast, which expressions have a popular ring? Explain why these elements, in combination, result in a successful sermon.

FOR WRITING

1. Decide which of the six tests proposed by Fosdick you consider most important. Then write a paper in which you persuade someone that that test is more significant than all others.
2. Select a slogan from popular morality today—example: "Do your own thing." Compare its value as a guideline with one of Fosdick's.

What do you think education is for? Is an educated person necessarily happier than an uneducated one? Must a person be good in order to be happy? And should teachers believe that their students are "wonderful"? You will have to make up your mind about such questions in order to appreciate the original arguments of Mark Van Doren—teacher, critic, and novelist—as he discusses the purpose of education. The title of the essay suggests that education should serve to liberate the mind from something. As you read the author's words, be sure to keep your mind free and open to the challenge of new ideas.

Freedom to Use the Mind

MARK VAN DOREN

This may be a revolutionary viewpoint to express, but I think the purpose of education is to make young men and women happier than they would have been without it. It chills my blood to hear college talked about as if students went there for some other purpose than their own happiness.

Happiness doesn't mean having a good time. Happiness is the most solemn thing, almost, that can happen to anybody. Very few people are happy. The best chance to be happy, I think, is to be educated.

I mean by happiness what the philosophers have meant by it. The Greek philosophers regularly moved from virtue to happiness. Happiness was the highest good, and the good that was nearest to it was virtue, because it produces happiness.

We cannot be happy unless we are good, and I think that education is to make people good and therefore happy. I don't mean good for the world. I mean good in general.

The happiness of a student consists in his achieving to whatever extent is possible the freedom to use his mind. Nothing is more fun than using one's mind. It is my conviction that a student who discovers this is a very lucky person.

"Freedom to Use the Mind," from *NEA Journal*, May, 1960. Reprinted by permission of Mark Van Doren.

A practical result of becoming free to use one's mind is that one tends then to find the world intelligible and interesting in many, if not all, of its parts. The more parts of the world that are interesting to anyone, the more clearly that person is using his mind.

The sign of a good man is that he is interested in many things. There isn't anything, as a matter of fact, that he doesn't seem to be interested in — you can't catch him off base. You can't mention anything that he hasn't thought about at some time or other. Maybe he hasn't thought very much, but he is now delighted to think more with your help.

A good man also has the faith that the world at any point might become intelligible to him if he had a little more time to stare at it, to study it. He isn't in the habit of assuming that most areas of intellectual activity are not for him — that only the experts would know about them.

In college a student learns, I hope, to use his mind. His mind becomes free of the animal in which it is imbedded and now becomes, as it were, a free thing. He can still hold on to it, as a balloon that has a string attached; but still it is a free thing. That is what we mean by not having prejudice.

Changing our mind is the noblest thing that any of us ever does. We learn how to do that by listening to others, and by learning how to listen to others. It is a great art, the art of listening. Reading is a form of listening, too. Without being able to listen or without being able to read, we would never be able to think or change our minds.

Sometimes I get the idea that a student is expected to think about getting educated for the sake of society as if he were not a part of it, as if society were a thing somewhere — in Dayton, Cincinnati, New York, London, or Moscow. But each individual is the most important part of society. I am the most important part of society to me, and you are the most important part to you.

We all have the human mind, and it is the same in all of us. Great people, I think, never have any difficulty in understanding that. Lincoln had no difficulty in understanding that all people had the same mind. Look at the way he wrote for his fellow citizens. He paid them the great compliment of assuming their minds were just like his, and they became so.

A good teacher thinks that all of his students have good minds, at least as good as his, if not better. This is the qualification that the teacher has to have: absolute, childlike faith that his students are wonderful. And they become so.

The doctrine of equality is the greatest of all doctrines. Equality is not easy to understand unless you assume the one thing that makes it intelligible; namely, that we all have something in common with which we communicate, with which we think: We all have the same mind, and each one of us has it in himself. It is what makes a person an individual; that is, one fit to be compared with others who are good and free, and who, to the extent that they are both these things, resemble one another.

Each individual has somehow to discover the mind in him and liberate it. And he has to do this by himself. Nobody can help, except insofar as education can help. And that is what education is for.

The happiness of the individual cannot be separated from the happiness and the good of all. In every good society it is assumed that there is no conflict between the individual good and the general good. It is assumed furthermore that the individual consents to this proposition; he believes that there is no real difference between his good and the good of everybody else.

An old student of mine who now runs a newspaper in Bayonne, New Jersey, prints on its masthead a sentence from Thucydides[1]: "No matter how any man prospers, if the fortunes of his city decline, his fortunes decline." There is no way in which, if the society of which we are a part begins to go to pieces, we can help going to pieces ourselves. We rise and fall with everybody else.

Maybe this is what we mean when we say that there is no conflict between the individual good and the general good. In democratic societies, of course, it is assumed that the most democratic education is simply the best education. It isn't education for democracy; it isn't education for itself, because democracy is for itself.

Democracy has no purpose except to be a good thing. It isn't supposed to accomplish anything, any more than the truth is supposed to accomplish anything. It is its own excuse for being. The strength of democracy is its interest in individuals and in their intellect and freedom and happiness.

A great deal is being said these days about special things that ought to be in the content of education at the moment. We are

---

[1] **Thucydides:** Greek historian c. 471-400 B.C.

often told that education should reshape itself toward a certain end. I believe that it is disastrous to think so. It is the surest way to be beaten by our enemies. Our strength is still in our individual happiness, in the number of us who are happy and free and strong, and very, very intelligent and knowledgeable. That is what we have got to work for.

Much is being said, too, about the importance of science. But there is nothing new about the fact that science is important. Science has always been at least half of our lives, and at least half of all Western thought has been scientific.

The danger in colleges these days is that science will not be enough respected. I don't mean technology, I mean science. Too many interesting, brilliant men and women don't think it is very important, and that had better cease to be true.

It is necessary, too, that scientists and humanists should talk to one another. Despite the idea, which has grown like a cancer among us, that scientists and humanists cannot converse, I believe that if they ever honestly try to talk together, they will have no real difficulty and will discover that they share many problems which can be discussed to their mutual benefit.

The idea has grown, too, that there is too much knowledge for anyone to comprehend. How offensive this is to the human mind, because all knowledge is *in* the human mind; the human mind made it. It is only in our time that we have given up the notion that anyone can know something of everything. I still think this is possible in some practical way.

It would be wonderful if we dropped the notion that the world has become unintelligible to most of us. Let's stop talking about the hopelessness of keeping up with knowledge. If we did this, we might have some great people again. I suspect that the notable absence of great men in our time could be laid to a lack of faith among us that the mind can move in all realms where the mind has been.

The best thing that could happen in the next generation, the thing that would make most people happy, individually and collectively, would be a return to this faith that all men, no matter who they are or how much they know, can tell one another something.

INTERPRETATION

1. According to the first paragraph, what is the purpose of education?

What reasons does Van Doren give for saying: "The best chance to be happy . . . is to be educated."? Do you agree?

2. In the next few paragraphs, Van Doren uses several words and phrases to describe or define education. How are they related? Show how the meaning of *happiness* changes in the discussion.

3. Consider the statement, "The happiness of the individual cannot be separated from the happiness and the good of all." Is it true? What implications can you find in it for your own living? for the life of the nation?

STYLE AND METHOD

1. Van Doren titles the essay "Freedom to Use the Mind," yet throughout the essay he talks about happiness. Why? Discuss the examples and illustrations he uses. How well do they support his generalizations?

2. Discuss the ways in which the word "happiness" is re-defined in the essay. Ultimately, is this essay about happiness, virtue, government, science, freedom, or education? Explain.

3. Look carefully at the manner in which the statements are phrased. Look up the term *epigram*.* Is Van Doren's style epigrammatic? Give some examples.

FOR WRITING

1. Van Doren suggests many meanings for happiness. With these in mind, write your own essay defining "happiness" as it appears to you in the terms of your own experience.

2. Remembering that each of the following statements must be understood in the context of the essay, choose one and write a paper in which you defend or reject it. Be certain to provide examples to support your viewpoint. Examples: "Changing our mind is the noblest thing that any of us ever does"; "Democracy has no purpose except to be a good thing."

What would you think if someone told you that in a democracy
no one should ever feel insignificant? In this essay the columnist
Dorothy Thompson takes issue with this view as expressed by the
famous American architect, Frank Lloyd Wright. Of course,
Wright was talking only about architecture and its effect on
persons, but what if the idea were generalized and applied to all
the arts, as well as to nature? Would this nurture the growth of
the democratic spirit? Not according to Miss Thompson, who
rejects the idea that everything should be adjusted to the level of
the "common man" and his ability to understand or appreciate.

The Twelve-Foot Ceiling

DOROTHY THOMPSON

In a recent publication I read an interview with the famous
architect, Frank Lloyd Wright, occasioned by the unwrapping of
his model for The Modern Gallery of Non-objective Painting. In
the course of the interview he called the big gray Metropolitan
Museum "undemocratic." Public rooms, he explained, should be
only about twelve feet high, so the people will not feel "insignificant."

Mr. Wright is a lover and builder of architecture on broad
horizontal lines, and in his designs has contributed much to the
comfort, beauty and practicality of domestic life. He has also
said many intelligent things about city planning. When Rocke-
feller Center was under discussion, he suggested that it would be
better to tear down what was there and plant the space to grass
and trees. But I wonder whether he wanted only twelve-foot
trees, lest the people, beside a towering elm, should feel "insignificant."

The Metropolitan Museum leaves much to be desired, but not
because its rooms are lofty. The G. I. Joes whom I saw standing
awe-stricken in the great nave of Salisbury Cathedral; or watch-

"The Twelve-Foot Ceiling," by Dorothy Thompson. Reprinted from *The Courage to Be Happy* with
the permission of Morgan Guaranty Trust Company as executor under the will of Dorothy Thompson.

ing the robed procession in Canterbury slowly climb the vast flight of stairs which leads from nave to altar, for the enthrone-ment of the archbishop; or kneeling under the lofty arches of Notre-Dame de Paris; or gazing with saddened, awe-struck eyes into the wreckage of St. Michael's in Munich; or staring upward, in St. Peter's, at Michelangelo's immense dome, were not feeling insignificant. On the contrary, they were realizing that life had a grandeur, beauty and significance above and beyond themselves in which, nevertheless, they could share; the recognition did not demean but expanded them, not in self-satisfaction but in esteem for the possibilities in human achievement.

The terrible heresy of modern democratism is to confound democracy with mediocrity. This is to make the "common man" into the modern tyrant. Everything, it is argued, must be keyed and toned down to his understanding, lest he get an "inferiority complex." Books must be written in the language of the gutter; motion pictures must not appeal "above a mental age of eleven years." The height of inspiration should be put at twelve feet — twice the measure of a tall man; one must not expect him to lift his eyes beyond double his own stature!

This neodemocratism has nothing to do with democracy, nor was it invented by common men, but by panderers who wish to divest the people of their own personalities and make them into masses. You can search America, like Diogenes[1] with his lantern, and you are not likely to find a single American who will describe himself as a member of the masses. The masses exist as the off-spring of modern industrial civilization and commercialism, with their many errors and crimes, but the business of democracy is to turn them into The People again. Every girl or boy, be he a mechanic's child or a hod carrier's, in every moment of intellec-tual, emotional or spiritual awakening, wants to become some-thing other than of the mass; wants to *be,* in full consciousness of personal, individual existence, as something different, apart and therefore precious. He does not want a ceiling put over his life. He says, "The sky's the limit."

Every child wants to adore. His father — what schoolboy fights occur if one boy says to another, "Your dad's no good." What childish woe is more tragic than loss of confidence in father or in mother? The human being responds to what is above, not beneath

---

[1] **Diogenes:** Greek cynic philosopher reputed to have searched with a lantern for an honest man at midday.

him: to the father as the symbol of strength; to the mother, as the symbol of virtue; to the bigger boy; to the girl who is "better than I am." Out of this comes spiritual growth.

The farm lad lies on the hillside and gazes at the fleecy clouds floating in the faraway blueness, or on a starry night identifies red Antares or blue Arcturus from its relationship to the Big Dipper; he loves the broadest, tallest maple tree in the farmyard, and brags that it has stood there for a hundred and fifty years; he loves the ballads of prowess, of which the American folklore is so full — Paul Bunyan, the Gargantuan.[2] He is ever conscious of the danger and grandeur of the elements — of the shattering thunder, and the torrential rain, and the pullets that will drown unless rescued from the range; of the sun calling the earth to fruition or baking the earth on the roots of the crops; of his own inadequacy, often, to do more than endure. He does not learn from Nature that the universe revolves around himself, and at his own rhythm, and to suit his own whims, but that it continually invites him to expand himself into it, mastering, if he can, flood and drought, tempest and storm, and enduring with fortitude what is beyond him to master. That is probably one reason why farm boys grow up to contribute so many names to Who's Who, as inventors, scientists, scholars, educators, artists and managers of great industries.

The measure of a man is never the ceiling of his smug self-satisfaction, but the measure of his humility and reverence, which do not demean but ennoble, and are hallmarks of all noble natures. And the great apostles of American democracy wanted to lift the ceilings, not clamp them down.

Thomas Jefferson, America's first great democrat, lived in what was, in European terms, a wilderness. But he was anti-wilderness and pro-civilization and culture. He did not build himself a log cabin, but Monticello, a large, beautiful mansion; nor did he think the aspirations of the country should be limited to the aspirations of the average. He did not believe in horizontal education; he proposed an educational system whereby all children would be given the education for which their talents fitted them; they would start equal — he never expected they would finish equal, for he was too accurate an observer of nature. He was a slaveholder who hated slavery and believed the slave-

[2] **Gargantuan:** huge, enormous; suggestive of Gargantua, the peace-loving giant prince of Rabelais' satirical romance *Gargantua*.

holders should abolish it, since the slaves obviously could not. He did not go and live in his slaves' cabins, but, recognizing the extraordinary musical talent of the colored people, brought them into his great house, and organized them into an orchestra, and taught them to play Mozart.

Emerson, a philosopher of American democracy, did not advocate a twelve-foot ceiling, but said, "Hitch your wagon to a star." He knew the wagon would never reach the stars. But the height to which a man ascends is commensurate to his ambition; set his ceiling at twelve feet and eventually he will be living underground.

If the limits of art are to be set in advance by the tape measure of mediocre appreciation, by and by we shall have no more art. The essence of art is that it is unique and distinguished—the expression of the most creative moment of a uniquely creative talent and personality. It is begotten of sensitive and humble appreciation of the greatness, not the littleness, of life; of the eternal wonder of birth, death and love; of insight into great laws of rhythm and form, point and counterpoint, in color and sound. It exalts, not men, but Man, not at the average, but at his most creative and Godlike.

All great art—a Beethoven symphony, a Michelangelo or Giotto fresco, a Hamlet or King Lear, the Psalms of David, a Brothers Karamazov of Dostoevski—creates in the beholder not self-satisfaction, but wonder and awe. Its great liberation is to lift us out of ourselves.

In London, when the National Gallery reopened after V-E Day, and only thirty or forty of the very greatest of its pictures were taken from their wartime cellars to hang upon its walls, I watched my husband, himself an artist, before a little picture by Rembrandt that he had long known from reproductions but saw now, for the first time, in the original. Pale with excitement, and unconscious of the surrounding visitors, he stood motionless for half an hour, murmuring, "It's a miracle . . . a miracle."

Why is it a miracle? The subject is a middle-aged woman—a common woman—standing in a pool of water, in a white chemise drawn up to her thighs. It has little color, except browns and golds and the white chemise. But the flesh, one sees immediately, will in a short time have lost its firmness; already it seems to tremble, slightly, away from the bones; the woman will soon be no more woman, but merely old; this common flower will be touched by the inexorable frost; the soft golden light that seems to emanate from her body is a sunset. But how beautiful, tender, loved and lovable — how *miraculous* she is. How compact of sweetness her haunting little smile. Only a painter with a fantastic craft and technique could so have painted flesh. But not alone technique — only technique and vision — could have created the Woman Bathing. It is a profoundly felt and realized experience.

My husband went away from it saddened and elated. Saddened with self-dissatisfaction; elated because what he feels ought to be achieved in painting was achieved. Elated to belong to, and be in the service of, so noble a craft.

All profoundly-realized experience communicates — and to ordinary men. Walt Whitman said all men are poets because all respond to poetry. That is true if the people are not deprived of their natural and naïve relation to art by the abstruse and esoteric patter of professional writers about it, who patronizingly encourage the people to believe that they are incapable of understanding great expressions. When a friend, a great violinist, toured Russia, playing in villages where no artist had ever played before, he found that the people applauded for encores of Bach. No highbrows had ever told them that they could not enjoy what they did not "understand." They merely heard beautiful music. When the Soviet government opened the theaters to the workers, they did not crowd into those designed for the education of the proletariat but into the Grand Opera, the theater of kings, and above all they loved ballet — one of the most refined, and even artificial, sublimations of expression. Homer sang for common men a most uncommon song. Shakespeare wrote for the rabble and the princes. His wit was as broad as a cabby's behind and as fine as King John's delicate hair. But salt is salt on anybody's meat, if it have not lost its savor. The Bible is transcendent language and thus art, but it is still the world's best seller.

And the statesmen whom the people adore are never the ones who talk down to them, putting a twelve-foot ceiling over their words. The Declaration of Independence is not only a great democratic document but a great piece of literature. It will be on the common tongue long after the Potsdam declaration[3] — which, having nothing worthwhile to say, found expression in an execrable style—is forgotten and abandoned. Yet the common people of Jefferson's day did not speak of "self-evident truths" or of a "decent respect to the opinions of mankind." Many of those to whom Jefferson's words were addressed were illiterate frontiersmen. But they understood the meaning and were proud that their hopes and strivings should find elegant and discriminating expression.

The "common man" never invented the patronizing[4] attitude toward himself. Lincoln, the greatest people's President, was also the finest English stylist who ever occupied the White House. The simplicity of his speeches is not the simplicity of a simpleton, but of a man with such exquisite discrimination in words that he could restore the gold tarnished from speech by vulgar use. Churchill mobilized a nation by his speeches; but they were not couched in the language of the streets, but in the highest parliamentary tradition. And Franklin Roosevelt, chosen four times by the people as their President, spoke to them in the tongue of Groton and Harvard; nor did the people hold it against him that their great friend was also a great gentleman.

So let the ceilings of democracy be high; let democratic man be aware of his own insignificance, that he may better measure his great possibilities; let him build more stately mansions for his soul. And let him know, from the examples of his times, that there is no tyranny more dreadful than that of mediocrity over distinction, of mass leaders over and through mass men, which would reduce the people to an ant hill, with a twelve-foot ceiling — and no windows on the "splendid, silent sun," the secret of whose radiation men have mastered, but whose creative beneficence is still beyond them.

INTERPRETATION

1. What is the basic disagreement between Miss Thompson and Mr. Wright? Which one do you agree with? Why?

[3] **Potsdam declaration:** Following Germany's defeat in World War II, Allied leaders met at Potsdam near Berlin to approve earlier agreements on occupation zones and administrations for German territory; the British and Americans drew up an ultimatum to Japan, and Russia repeated its willingness to go to war against Japan.

[4] **patronizing:** condescending.

2. Miss Thompson uses the ceiling image as a symbol.* What does that symbol express in this essay? Do you think the author's development of the idea is well done, or overdone? Explain.
3. Is the author criticizing democracy or attitudes about democracy and the arts?

STYLE AND METHOD
1. By what anecdotes and illustrations does Miss Thompson attempt to convey the emotion experienced by observers of great art? How important is description to her purpose? How successful are her descriptions in this regard?
2. Discuss the illustrations which are provided to show that man needs to have things to admire. Are they all valid? Do they provide a wide or narrow sampling of experience? How is the essay organized?

FOR WRITING
1. If you have ever experienced the feeling of awe and wonder mentioned in the essay, write an account of that experience describing the feeling and what produced it.
2. Write an essay in which you discuss what one of the following symbolizes about democracy: Mt. Rushmore, the tract house, the skyscraper, Disneyland, or the automobile.

Miss America may be a beauty contest to some, but for Shana
Alexander in 1968 it was a degrading spectacle worthy of nothing
but contempt. What has happened to change the complexion of
this annual event that used to be as normal and American as
apple pie? Miss Alexander, a *Life* writer, makes some penetrating
observations on the nature and causes of its decline. But her
style has the indirection of satire*, and you will have to look twice
to catch her meaning when she says, "Hooray! Back to Normal."

Hooray!
Getting Back to Normal

SHANA ALEXANDER

September is everybody's season of shifting down, and after
the rigors of the campaign trail and its final week-long Walpurgisnacht[1] in Chicago, I was more ready than most. Only pastels for
me for a while, gentle sleeps and sips of champagne. Anticipating
a bit of each, I sank down on the sofa, glass in hand, and tuned
the Miss America contest on TV.

Sound came up first — that rich, remembered schmaltz of soggy
strings, brass ooze and Disney choir. Then the Easter-egg colors
brightened into lights, runway, gowns, gloves and girls — those
same dear striding girls in bathing suits and high heels wearing
the same special smiles, each girl so alike with her hard-edge face
of blue eyelids, apricot cheeks and cotton-candy hair you wondered if they all had had the same makeup man or perhaps the
same mother.

Where before (where not?) had one seen that spangled card-
board mountain in center stage, the sequined rainbow bridge, the

---

[1] **Walpurgisnacht:** the night before May 1, associated in German folklore with
a witches' Sabbath.

life-sized gold picture book, slowly opening? Where those judges: Bud Westmore? Donald Voorhees? Now a vintage puff of magic smoke, and bounding out of it a terrifying apparition from the past — ageless Bert Parks in white tie and tails.

One trouble with the ridiculous old Pageant on the Boardwalk is that it takes you a lot farther back to normal than you wish to go. In Atlantic City, nothing has changed. Push the electronic living-color eye of 1968 and you get a perfect glimpse back into 1938.

"A personification of the fine qualities which can be found in a young American girl," lilts a charm-school voice, but where *are* the girls inside these living Barbie dolls with the Styrofoam smiles? Behind every Miss is there really a miss?

And what is behind that smile? Contrary to the propaganda, I suspect that Miss America girls do not have everything. On TV they appear to lack lower teeth, which could account for the dentally arresting composition of gums and uppers known everywhere as the Miss America Smile.

Talent being rarer than beauty in 18-year-old girls, the talent contest places the Smile under a ghastly strain. One girl, a trampolinist, smiled madly upside down. A ballerina smiled her way through "The Dying Swan," somehow suggesting death in a frozen poultry locker. A third girl's talent was to synchronize bubble gum-chewing and the Charleston. At rhythmic intervals her smile was wiped out by a large, wet pink splat.

So many things seem wrong and boring and silly about the Miss America Pageant as it comes across on TV that one struggles to rank the offenses in order of importance. It is dull and pretentious and racist and exploitative and icky and sad. It is fake in everything from wigs to talents to sentiments. It does not worship beauty but beauty products. Though the girls are not fakes, they themselves are treated as products. Beauty contests are not so much antifemale as they are antihuman. The complication of the so-called "talent contest" obliges them to conspire in their own humiliation. And despite all the schmaltz and the sanitizing, there clings to the proceedings a strong taint of the auction block.

Come to think of it, these modern Miss America girls don't seem quite the knockouts they used to seem 20 or even 10 years ago. Is it that the ordinary American girl you see on the street has become so much lovelier? Or that these particular finalists, hampered by the contest's silly, dowdy old Miss America rituals, don't have a proper chance to shine? Maybe the really pretty girls today, or the really smart ones, travel another road.

Perhaps the pageant and the city have been together too long, and like certain souring couples they have begun to resemble each other. Surely Atlantic City would win the title, among all American cities I have visited, of Most Revolting. Miss Most Revolting, in local parlance. But squalid though she is, she still scrabbles for the tawdry tourist's seedy buck, and she gets it. Her huge amphitheater is seldom silent. The miasma of French fries and boiling candy never clears.

Like the city, the beauty contest now is no fun, a joyless pageant both for us and for them. The only recognizably human emotion all night was the anguish on the face of the girl who won, the trampolinist, Miss Illinois. The tears made her nice face ugly, but they made it human, too. For a moment the mask cracked and we saw the girl inside.

For her sake, as well as ours, I wish television could have cut away to some of the interesting things that were going on out on the boardwalk. A few fearless women had set up a Freedom Trash Can and were getting ready to burn their bras, girdles, false eyelashes, curlers and other bits of beauty hard- and software to protest what they called "the degrading, mindless, boob-girlie symbol" inside. And down the boardwalk a ways, another group was electing the first Miss Black America to advertise the fact that in its 47 years the pageant had never included a Negro girl. It's okay to have a Negro Miss Universe, but not a Miss America.

I suppose both the Black Americans and the bra-burners were trying to get things back to normal in their own way. Being by nature opposed to all beauty pageants, amateur nights, diaper derbies, dance contests and other exploitations, my own sympathies were closer to the bra-burners', and I began to wish they'd gone further. Why stop at girdles? Why not get rid of those stockings of knitted string that flay a foot in half a mile? Away with clunky shoes that look as if they'd been cobbled by acid-head elves. Away with wiglets! Away with things that match and junior miss and half-sizes. Away with charm schools and diet pills! Away with all the fake differences between men and women, and hooray for the real ones!

Hooray for normalcy! Why can't things be like they never were?

INTERPRETATION

1. If you have ever watched the Miss America contest, evaluate the author's objections to it in paragraph 8. Why does she compare it to the auction block?
2. What does the writer mean by *normal*? Does she equate *normal* with *natural*? What does her last sentence tell you?
3. In the first paragraph of her article, Miss Alexander describes her own situation a little. Would you say that she herself is more or less "normal" than the Pageant?

STYLE AND METHOD

1. Why does the writer reserve her direct criticisms of the contest until paragraph 8? What purpose is served by paragraphs 2 through 7? Are they effective? Do they support her conclusions? What is the point in describing Atlantic City today?
2. Make a list of the modifiers used to achieve the negative effect, beginning with *schmaltz of soggy strings* (paragraph 2). Would changing the modifiers to "nicer" words change the total effect? Discuss the tone of this editorial as it is affected by the diction. How is the tone reinforced by the title?

FOR WRITING

1. What is your own attitude toward beauty contests? Write an essay evaluating one you have seen.
2. Write an essay defending or criticizing the journalistic style of *Time*, or some other national magazine.

"If the word *integration* means anything, this is what it means:
that we, with love, shall force our brothers to see themselves as
they are, to cease fleeing from reality and begin to change it."
These words, written by James Baldwin to his fourteen-year-old
nephew, sum up the writer's advice to the boy. The letter, both
compassionate and ruthless in its truth, yields a view of a very
difficult world; and although Baldwin never gives a reason for
writing the letter, his intention is clearly to persuade his nephew
to know and to *feel* that his Negro heritage can exalt him both
as an individual and as a member of a race. The advice is
stimulating. It is the kind of advice that any young person might
find invaluable in the search for himself.

My Dungeon Shook

JAMES BALDWIN

Dear James:

I have begun this letter five times and torn it up five times. I keep
seeing your face, which is also the face of your father and my
brother. Like him, you are tough, dark, vulnerable, moody — with
a very definite tendency to sound truculent[1] because you want
no one to think you are soft. You may be like your grandfather in
this, I don't know, but certainly both you and your father resemble him very much physically. Well, he is dead, he never saw
you, and he had a terrible life; he was defeated long before he
died because, at the bottom of his heart, he really believed what
white people said about him. This is one of the reasons that he
became so holy. I am sure that your father has told you something about all that. Neither you nor your father exhibit any
tendency towards holiness: you really *are* of another era, part of
what happened when the Negro left the land and came into what
the late E. Franklin Frazier called "the cities of destruction."

[1] **truculent:** harsh, fierce.

You can only be destroyed by believing that you really are what the white world calls a *nigger*. I tell you this because I love you, and please don't you ever forget it.

I have known both of you all your lives, have carried your Daddy in my arms and on my shoulders, kissed and spanked him and watched him learn to walk. I don't know if you've known anybody from that far back; if you've loved anybody that long, first as an infant, then as a child, then as a man, you gain a strange perspective on time and human pain and effort. Other people cannot see what I see whenever I look into your father's face, for behind your father's face as it is today are all those other faces which were his. Let him laugh and I see a cellar your father does not remember and a house he does not remember and I hear in his present laughter his laughter as a child. Let him curse and I remember him falling down the cellar steps, and howling, and I remember, with pain, his tears, which my hand or your grandmother's so easily wiped away. But no one's hand can wipe away those tears he sheds invisibly today, which one hears in his laughter and in his speech and in his songs. I know what the world has done to my brother and how narrowly he has survived it. And I know, which is much worse, and this is the crime of which I accuse my country and my countrymen, and for which neither I nor time nor history will ever forgive them, that they have destroyed and are destroying hundreds of thousands of lives and do not know it and do not want to know it. One can be, indeed one must strive to become, tough and philosophical concerning destruction and death, for this is what most of mankind has been best at since we have heard of man. (But remember: *most* of mankind is not *all* of mankind.) But it is not permissible that the authors of devastation should also be innocent. It is the innocence which constitutes the crime.

Now, my dear namesake, these innocent and well-meaning people, your countrymen, have caused you to be born under conditions not very far removed from those described for us by Charles Dickens in the London of more than a hundred years ago. (I hear the chorus of the innocents screaming, "No! This is not true! How *bitter* you are!"—but I am writing this letter to *you,* to try to tell you something about how to handle *them,* for most of them do not yet really know that you exist. I *know* the conditions under which you were born, for I was there. Your countrymen were *not* there, and haven't made it yet. Your grandmother was also there, and no one has ever accused her of being bitter. I suggest that the innocents check with her. She isn't hard to find. Your countrymen don't know that *she* exists, either, though she has been working for them all their lives.)

Well, you were born, here you came, something like fourteen years ago; and though your father and mother and grandmother, looking about the streets through which they were carrying you, staring at the walls into which they brought you, had every reason to be heavyhearted, yet they were not. For here you were, Big James, named for me — you were a big baby, I was not — here you were: to be loved. To be loved, baby, hard, at once, and forever, to strengthen you against the loveless world. Remember that: I know how black it looks today, for you. It looked bad that day, too, yes, we were trembling. We have not stopped trembling yet, but if we had not loved each other none of us would have survived. And now you must survive because we love you, and for the sake of your children and your children's children.

This innocent country set you down in a ghetto in which, in fact, it intended that you should perish. Let me spell out precisely what I mean by that, for the heart of the matter is here, and the root of my dispute with my country. You were born where you were born and faced the future that you faced because you were black and *for no other reason*. The limits of your ambition were, thus, expected to be set forever. You were born into a society which spelled out with brutal clarity, and in as many ways as possible, that you were a worthless human being. You were not expected to aspire to excellence: you were expected to make peace with mediocrity. Wherever you have turned, James, in your short time on this earth, you have been told where you could go and what you could do (and *how* you could do it) and where you could live and whom you could marry. I know your countrymen do not agree with me about this, and I hear them saying, "You exaggerate." They do not know Harlem, and I do. So do you. Take no one's word for anything, including mine — but trust your experience. Know whence you came. If you know whence you came, there is really no limit to where you can go. The details and symbols of your life have been deliberately constructed to make you believe what white people say about you. Please try to remember that what they believe, as well as what they do and cause you to endure, does not testify to your inferiority but to their inhumanity and fear. Please try to be clear, dear James, through the storm which rages about your youthful head today, about the reality which lies behind the words *acceptance* and *integration*. There is no reason for you to try to become like white people and there is no basis whatever for their impertinent assumption that *they* must accept *you*. The really terrible thing, old buddy, is that *you* must accept *them*. And I mean that very seriously. You must accept them and accept them with love. For these innocent people have no other hope. They are, in effect, still trapped in a history which they do not understand; and until they understand it, they cannot be released from it. They have had to believe for many years, and for innumerable reasons, that black men are inferior to white men. Many of them, indeed, know better, but, as you will discover, people find it very difficult to act on what they know. To act is to be committed, and to be committed is to be in danger. In this case, the danger, in the minds of most white Americans, is the loss of their identity. Try to imagine how you would feel if you woke up one morning to find the sun shining and all the stars aflame. You would be frightened because it is out of the order of nature. Any upheaval in the universe is terrifying because it so profoundly attacks one's sense of one's own reality. Well, the black man has functioned in the white man's world as a fixed star, as an immovable pillar: and as he moves out of his place, heaven and earth are shaken to their foundations. You, don't be afraid. I said that it was intended that you should perish in the ghetto, perish by never being allowed to go behind the white man's definitions, by never being allowed to spell your proper name. You have, and many of us have, defeated this intention; and, by a terrible law, a terrible paradox, those innocents who believed that your imprisonment made them safe are losing their grasp of reality. But these men are your brothers — your lost, younger brothers. And if the word *integration* means anything, this is what it means: that we, with love, shall force our brothers to see themselves as they are, to cease fleeing from reality and begin to change it. For this is your home, my friend, do not be driven from it; great men have done great things here, and will again, and we can make America what America must become. It will be hard, James, but you come from sturdy, peasant stock, men who picked cotton and dammed rivers and built railroads, and, in the teeth of the most terrifying odds, achieved an unassailable and monumental dignity. You come from a long line of great poets, some of the greatest poets since

Homer. One of them said, *The very time I thought I was lost, My dungeon shook and my chains fell off.*[2]

You know, and I know, that the country is celebrating one hundred years of freedom one hundred years too soon. We cannot be free until they are free. God bless you, James, and Godspeed.

Your uncle,
James

INTERPRETATION

1. What does Baldwin mean by the word "innocence"? (page 211) Whom does he apply it to? He says, "It is the innocence that constitutes the crime." *What* crime?
2. Discuss Baldwin's advice to his nephew concerning the necessity for accepting certain things. Why does he think his nephew is in a better position to understand and act on what he knows than the white people in America? Do you agree?

STYLE AND METHOD

1. How much of the family history Baldwin describes is typical of the experience of the Negro in America? Consider how much of the power of Baldwin's letter derives from this fact—its universal truth.
2. What role is Baldwin playing in the life of his nephew with this letter? Discuss. How does his tone help you determine his role?
3. How does Baldwin modulate his tone in moving from the personal level to a more philosophical level? At what points in the letter do these shifts occur? How are they signalled by shifts in diction (language)?

FOR WRITING

1. You are James Baldwin's nephew. Write a response to this letter. You may agree or disagree, but try to assume the role of the nephew.
2. Write a letter to someone whom you know to be prejudiced. Try to persuade him to change his attitude toward whatever is the object of his prejudice.

---

[2] The source of this line is an old slave song, "You Got a Right" (to the tree of life).

The two following selections—a report and a book review—are placed together here because they represent two different aspects of the same phenomenon. The first is concerned with the social causes that produced the book which is the subject of the second article. Both pieces are persuasive in their claim that the book represents a solution to one of the most acute social problems facing America. Another reason for placing the two side by side is that their different purposes and approaches to the subject help you to sense the urgency and scope of the larger issue. Together they are more than a report and a review; they are a hopeful and revealing comment on life in America.

Dateline Watts: From the Ashes, a Solution

ALLAN NEVINS

As we contemplate the wave of rioting and bloodshed in our cities last summer, we should remember that this is by no means the first time that racial violence has convulsed major parts of the United States. But in the past most of the violence and intimidation has been directed by ethnic majorities against one or another of the subordinate peoples: Negro, Chinese, Mexican, Indian, or Japanese. The violence is not new; its direction is. Today the angry minorities are but faithfully following the example that the majority long ago began teaching them.

This fact and some fundamentals concerning both the outbreaks and the possibility of removing their causes are brought home to us by a striking new compilation of protests from the Watts district in Los Angeles, edited and introduced by Budd Schulberg, under the title *From the Ashes*. These are the voices of the Negroes themselves, raised in grief, expostulation, self-explanation, and occasionally in anger or even in threats. Eighteen Negro writers, who never published anything before, here cry out in deep emotion and fiery sincerity.

When the Watts riots began, Mr. Schulberg had just finished writing a commentary on Nathanael West's novel *The Day of the Locust*. One character in this story was a Hollywood artist and art director whose masterwork was a canvas entitled *The Burning of Los Angeles*. On the hot August night in 1965 when television brought scenes of the Watts rioting into the room where Schulberg was entertaining some Eastern guests, he realized with horror that Los Angeles actually *was* burning. As a social novelist and a supporter of varied reform movements, he felt it his duty, both to the community and to serious literature, to act. He tells us that he realized, from the beginning, that this disturbance was not just a street riot, but a revolt—a revolt against a ghetto, a ghetto of life, full of intolerable wrongs. Schulberg sought a way to help. The means, he found, had a simplicity which recalls the counsel that Lincoln gave to a troubled people at the end of the Civil War, which had ended with guerrilla fighting, violence, and terrorism. A smoldering bed of coals in wide areas of Missouri, Kentucky, Tennessee, and other border states threatened at any moment to break into flame. What Lincoln advised was the use of helpful private action. He suggested that neighbor should call upon neighbor in the disorderly states, that in these calls they should proffer their services and kindly cooperation. Thus a spirit of amity and mutual aid might spread from community to community.

This was precisely the course of action that Schulberg undertook. He secured a building in which he could talk to Negro youths and create a school for ambitious young Negro writers. Many were initially diffident, and some were hostile. But his evident good will won first a few and then more, while his expertise impressed them all. This was neighborliness at its best, with all the constructive values that Lincoln had called for 100 years before.

Schulberg reveals in his eloquent introduction some facts about the Watts ghetto and adjacent parts of Los Angeles that, until the disturbance, were little known. This ghetto was not physically repulsive. It had some wide streets with pleasant stretches of well-kept houses, green lawns, and occasional flower gardens. But, as Schulberg states, the neighborhood did not have a single motion picture house. The people could not see a film without going outside the area. Worse still, the district did not have even one hospital and was devoid of ambulance service. Babies died because they could not be hurried to proper care. Because of inadequate public transportation anyone seeking a job could not reach a possible employer without tremendous cost in money and time. People of Watts did not feel that they were living in a free and hopeful environment. As one of Schulberg's writers says, they felt they were living in a closed and hopeless situation, "entrapped."

Schulberg swung open one door. He helped a growing number of young people to find a mode of self-expression.

Why could this example of constructive neighborliness not be followed by those who possess other types of skill? What Schulberg as a writer did to assist some in writing could be duplicated by different experts: a machinist could conduct classes in various technologies; a scientist could help young people take the primary steps in science; an artist could teach interested Negroes their first lessons in art. This example of neighborliness could spread, as Lincoln said neighborliness would.

Robert J. Donovan, Los Angeles *Times* Washington correspondent, stated on August 3 that an Administration leader had told him the government has not really penetrated the militant Negro youth movement. They do not know its methodology. Schulberg's book suggests a means of learning more about Negro psychology, and a method of raising Negro hopes and aims to a higher level.

From Arson to a Thousand Candles

PIRI THOMAS

"From the ashes, voices of Watts"—what a beautiful realization of the Negro's cry for dignity, a cry not only from the mind but from the soul. This book is to me as close as the aorta through which my heart pumps blood to all parts of my body. It is a freedom cry, expressed in essays, poetry, short stories—the writings of suppressed people who, having no alternative (this I know from my own experience), have been forced, yes, literally forced to react no longer as slaves but as men, with trumpets that blare out loud and clear: "Give us the same liberty that you have claimed for yourselves."

In a brief review it is virtually impossible to salute all those who are heard in this anthology of voices from the ghetto—the Watts Writers' Workshop, writers at Douglass House (named for the great Negro, Frederick Douglass)—voices that white Americans would do well to heed. Since 1965 membership in the Watts workshop has grown to more than thirty, and there have been some thirty-five additional applicants. Think of the contribution already made by this small group and how much greater America could be if their achievement could be multiplied by the thousands.

A short biographical sketch precedes each writer's selection in the anthology, and at times the drama in his history communicates almost as much to the reader as the composition itself. Although many themes recur, the overall screaming message is that poverty and denial of dignity warp, embitter, and destroy millions of lives. By some lovely miracle these "nitty-gritty" writers have been strong enough and articulate enough to write about not only their near defeat in life, but also their faith in ultimate victory.

"From Arson to a Thousand Candles" (review), by Piri Thomas, September 23, 1967 *Saturday Review*. Copyright 1967, Saturday Review, Inc. Reprinted by permission of Saturday Review, Inc. and Piri Thomas.

The individuality of each is particularly evident in the poetry. Guadalupe de Saavedra, the son of Mexican migratory workers, concludes his poem, "The Shoe Shine":

> Someday you'll know
> But you won't like it
> Because things are going to change.
> So let me say it once more.
>
> I shore tanks yo', boss.

Johnie Scott attended Harvard College one year and then returned to Watts to write:

> You become a man when
> you stop all of those faces
> from coming out of your
> mouth and begin shaping your
> lips to sing the recognizable
> features of your own past,
>
> *and what you know is true.*

Jimmie Sherman's poem "Sammy Lee" conveys the same feeling of indignity that I as a dark-skinned Puerto Rican have known. And Blossom Powe's "Black Phoenix" captures the essence of this remarkable book:

> Of this black kind of Phoenix[1]
> With trembling hands —
> Crying! Brooding! Trying somehow
> To create . . . a new mosaic
> From broken bricks and charcoal faces!

The young Negro poet Alvin A. Saxon, Jr., who frequently uses the pen name of "Ojenke," gives honor to the writing profession. "Some men satisfy their longings for a better world by escapism, some by defeatism, and some by coming to grips and defining these terms of existence responsible for man's conditions. The latter is my job as a writer."

The poem that brought tears to my eyes, and I mean real tears, was by Birdell Chew, a woman over fifty years old, born in Texas and one of the earliest members of the Watts Writers' Workshop.

---

[1] **Phoenix:** in Egyptian mythology, a bird said to live 500 to 600 years in the Arabian Desert and then consume itself by fire, only to arise from its ashes young and beautiful to live another cycle.

The poem, "A Black Mother's Plea," closes with these poignant words:

> Please do not give my son a reason to hate, so he will destroy himself while he is still a boy. Allow him a chance to fill his heart with love for all mankind, for he was conceived by woman from man, same as the Whites.

Harry Dolan has already achieved well-earned recognition as a writer and playwright. His short story, "I Remember Papa," echoes what I, growing up in Spanish Harlem, and many ghetto youngsters heard from the lips of their parents:

> "Be careful, boy, there are so many ways to fail, the pitfall sometimes seems to be the easiest way out. Beware of my future, for you must continue, you must live. You must, for in you are all the dreams of my nights, all the ambitions of my days."

At the same time, I really dug the humor blended with the stark reality of the nitty-gritty in Haley Mims's two short stories, "Passing" and "Maggie."

From the Ashes is a monumental work, not of fiction, but in its depiction of the agony and frustration and destruction that have stricken our land. Each of the eighteen writers here represented, along with the others who could not be part of *From the Ashes*, speaks from his or her own heart, yet it is one heart that gives white America another opportunity to listen to the voices of men and women who are determined even unto death that their heritage from America is not to be hunger, pain, sorrow, indignity, and the denial of their full rights as Americans.

A special tribute is due Budd Schulberg for his courage and perseverance in starting the Watts Writers' Workshop and keeping it going. I am sure it will be an inspiration to all such workshops now in existence and yet to be founded all over this country. As Schulberg so eloquently puts it in his introduction:

> His single candle may light a thousand thousand candles. And the light and warmth of these candles may help redeem and re-generate the core of the ghetto, that decomposed inner city, waiting either for a phoenix to rise from the ashes, or for bigger and more terrible fires.

Keep swinging, my brothers and sisters in Watts. Keep wailing! We're gonna reach the mountaintop yet.

INTERPRETATION

1. For what purpose was each of the two preceding selections written? How can Schulberg's project help the country, according to Nevins? How does this project help the Negro, according to Thomas? How does each help America as a nation?

2. What *kind* of information are you given in the Nevins piece? What *kind* of information are you given in the Thomas piece? What kind of conclusions can you draw based on the information from both articles?

STYLE AND METHOD

1. To what does Nevins chiefly appeal, reason or emotion? Give examples of his language and organization to support your answer. To what does Thomas appeal, reason or emotion? Give examples. Which writer is more effective, in your judgment?

2. Compare the organization of the two selections. In each case, what relationship is there between the writer's purpose and his organization?

FOR WRITING

1. Discuss some problem in your school or community for which several possible solutions have been suggested. Choose one solution which you like and write two short papers in which you try to convince your audience that the suggestion is worth trying. Let your argument in one depend on emotion; in the other, on reasoning supported by facts.

2. Write two reviews of the most exciting book you have read or motion picture you have seen. Direct one to the principal of your school and the other to your best friend.

These brief excerpts from Franklin's *Autobiography*, addressed to his son, show how he went about training himself to be a successful user of language. Franklin recognized that the person who understands a few principles of the Socratic method — a method of inquiry into the meaning of terms and ideas — and some of the techniques of word manipulation can usually gain the upper hand in debate with others. As you discover the methods and strategies Franklin employed for improving his writing and conversation, consider whether the approach he recommends may also serve as a formula for success in life. In these few paragraphs you will discover the source of Franklin's reputation both as a candid reporter of truth and as a canny practitioner of whatever would advance his own career.

On Writing and Conversing

BENJAMIN FRANKLIN

A question was once, somehow or other, started between Collins and me on the propriety of educating the female sex in learning and their abilities for study. He was of opinion that it was improper and that they were naturally unequal to it. I took the contrary side, perhaps a little for dispute's sake. He was naturally more eloquent, having a greater plenty of words, and sometimes, as I thought, I was vanquished more by his fluency than by the strength of his reasons. As we parted without settling the point and were not to see one another again for some time, I sat down to put my arguments in writing, which I copied fair and sent to him. He answered and I replied. Three or four letters on a side had passed, when my father happened to find my papers and read them. Without entering into the subject in dispute, he took occasion to talk to me about my manner of writing; observed that though I had the advantage of my antagonist in correct spelling and pointing[1] (which he attributed to the printing-house), I

___
[1] **pointing:** punctuating.

fell far short in elegance of expression, in method, and in perspicuity, of which he convinced me by several instances. I saw the justice of his remarks, and thence grew more attentive to my manner of writing and determined to endeavor to improve my style. At this time I met with an odd volume of the "Spectator."[2] I had never before seen any of them. I bought it, read it over and over, and was much delighted with it. I thought the writing excellent, and wished if possible to imitate it. With that view I took some of the papers, and making short hints of the sentiments in each sentence, laid them by a few days, and then, without looking at the book, tried to complete the papers again, by expressing each hinted sentiment at length, and as fully as it had been expressed before, in any suitable words that should occur to me. Then I compared my "Spectator" with the original, discovered some of my faults, and corrected them. But I found I wanted a stock of words or a readiness in recollecting and using them, which I thought I should have acquired before that time if I had gone on making verses; since the continual search for words of the same import, but of different length to suit the measure or of different sound for the rhyme, would have laid me under a constant necessity of searching for variety, and also have tended to fix that variety in my mind and make me master of it. Therefore I took some of the tales in the "Spectator" and turned them into verse; and after a time, when I had pretty well forgotten the prose, turned them back again.

I also sometimes jumbled my collection of hints into confusion, and after some weeks endeavored to reduce them into the best order before I began to form the full sentences and complete the subject. This was to teach me method in the arrangement of the thoughts. By comparing my work with the original, I discovered many faults and corrected them; but I sometimes had the pleasure to fancy that in certain particulars of small consequence I had been fortunate enough to improve the method or the language, and this encouraged me to think that I might in time come to be a tolerable English writer, of which I was extremely ambitious. The time I allotted for writing exercises and for reading was at night, or before work began in the morning, or on Sundays,

---

[2] **Spectator:** an English periodical published daily from March 1, 1711, to December 6, 1712, and written chiefly by Joseph Addison and Richard Steele. The familiar yet elegant style of the *Spectator* became a model for later journalists and essayists.

when I contrived to be in the printing-house, avoiding as much as I could the constant attendance at public worship which my father used to exact of me when I was under his care, and which I still continued to consider a duty, though I could not afford time to practice it.

While I was intent on improving my language I met with an English grammar (I think it was Greenwood's), having at the end of it two little sketches on the arts of rhetoric and logic, the latter finishing with a dispute in the Socratic method[3]; and soon after I procured Xenophon's "Memorable Things of Socrates," wherein there are many examples of the same method. I was charmed with it, adopted it, dropped my abrupt contradictions and positive argumentation and put on the humble inquirer. And being then, from reading Shaftesbury and Collins, made a doubter, as I already was in many points of our religious doctrines, I found this method the safest for myself and very embarrassing to those against whom I used it; therefore I took delight in it, practiced it continually, and grew very artful and expert in drawing people even of superior knowledge into concessions the consequence of which they did not foresee, entangling them in difficulties out of which they could not extricate themselves, and so obtaining victories that neither myself nor my cause always deserved.

I continued this method some few years, but gradually left it, retaining only the habit of expressing myself in terms of modest diffidence, never using, when I advanced anything that may possibly be disputed, the words *certainly, undoubtedly,* or any others that give the air of positiveness to an opinion; but rather say, I *conceive* or *apprehend* a thing to be so and so; *It appears to me,* or, *I should not think it, so or so, for such and such reasons;* or, *I imagine it to be so;* or, *It is so, if I am not mistaken.* This habit, I believe, has been of great advantage to me when I have had occasion to inculcate my opinions and persuade men into measures that I have been from time to time engaged in promoting. And as the chief ends of conversation are to *inform* or to *be informed,* to *please* or to *persuade,* I wish well-meaning and sensible men would not lessen their power of doing good by a

---

[3] **Socratic method:** method of instruction used by Socrates in his disputations leading by means of questions and answers to a foreseen conclusion or admission damaging to an opponent.

positive assuming manner that seldom fails to disgust, tends to create opposition, and to defeat most of those purposes for which speech was given to us. In fact, if you wish to instruct others, a positive dogmatical manner in advancing your sentiments may occasion opposition and prevent a candid attention. If you desire instruction and improvement from others, you should not at the same time express yourself fixed in your present opinions. Modest and sensible men, who do not love disputation, will leave you undisturbed in the possession of your errors. In adopting such a manner, you can seldom expect to please your hearers or obtain the concurrence you desire.

INTERPRETATION

1. Franklin tells how he learns three lessons. What are they? Paraphrase each paragraph, putting the main idea into one sentence.
2. What was Franklin's attitude toward making mistakes? What did he do about making mistakes? What was his attitude toward using any means available to win his point? Give examples.
3. From your reading of these paragraphs, what kind of person does Franklin seem to have been? Give evidence. Does he give his son good advice? Would you give your son the same advice? Explain.

STYLE AND METHOD

1. Franklin's style, typical of the best English writing of the eighteenth century, is precise and elegant. By comparison with seventeenth-century style, it is also simple, though by today's standards, it sometimes sounds formal—as, for example, when Franklin uses *endeavor* for *try* and *import* for *meaning*. As an experiment, try rephrasing some of Franklin's sentences in the colloquial style of the twentieth century. Is any of Franklin's meaning lost? How is the tone changed?
2. Which of the writing styles you have met so far does Franklin's most resemble? Explain. (To begin, does his writing chiefly express emotion or reasoned judgment?)
3. How important to a convincing argument is a strong and flexible writing style? Give evidence from your reading.

FOR WRITING

1. Have you ever learned to do something by doing it wrong the first time? Explain how you rectified an error of your own as if you are giving advice to someone.
2. Write a character sketch of Franklin from the information in this selection. Let your writing reflect your own estimate of his character.

Mr. Tobin's editorial and his right to express his opinion in this form illustrate one of the cherished freedoms in our national life, freedom of speech. The author uses the editorial to voice his concern for the tendency of some to abuse this "towering privilege," as he calls it. What of the First Amendment? How much freedom does it grant? What does it mean to "abuse" a freedom? Mr. Tobin tries to give his view with a clear explanation of the obligations inherent in the privilege. As editorialist, he is trying to persuade you to his point of view, of course; as reader, your responsibility will be, first, to hear him with an open mind, and second, to judge his argument critically.

"Responsible for the Abuse of That Liberty"

RICHARD L. TOBIN

Along about this time of year in the winter season of 1791-92, the Constitutional Convention brought into force its First Amendment, a proposition that Congress should make no law prohibiting freedom of religion, speech, press, or assembly. This cornerstone of the Bill of Rights from that moment formed the steel girders of the American way and, in consequence, a blueprint for democracies everywhere. If proof were needed, the terror with which authoritarian governments have regarded these freedoms and quickly suppressed them needs no further witness. They are the first rights to be swept away in any dictatorship, Greece being the most recent and surely not the last example.

Justice Hugo L. Black wrote in 1941 that the First Amendment "does not speak equivocally." It simply prohibits any law "abridging freedom of speech or of the press." It must be "taken as a command of the broadest scope that explicit language, read in the context of a liberty-loving society, will allow." Thomas Wolfe, in unpublished papers probably dated 1938, put it this way: "I do not believe in the abolition of free inquiry, or that the ideas represented by 'freedom of thought,' 'freedom of speech,' 'freedom of press,' and 'free assembly' are just rhetorical myths. I believe rather that they are among the most valuable realities that men have gained, and that if they are destroyed men will again fight to have them." And Justice Felix Frankfurter wrote in the Supreme Court in 1946: "Without a free press there can be no free society. That is axiomatic. However, freedom of the press is not an end in itself but a means to an end of a free society. The scope and nature of the Constitutional guarantee of the freedom of the press are to be viewed and applied in that light."

We agree, as we were born and brought up in a newspaper family to agree, with the principles of all three quotations above. To say that censorship of the press is not only dangerous but absurd is ground into the very bones of a newspaperman early in his life. But what is not ground in, and what he usually but not always comes to understand as he matures, is the subtle distinction of Justice Frankfurter's statement: That a free press is there not just for the profession of news and its employees and owners, but as a means to an end for the benefit of the free society it mirrors. We have always liked the wording of Article I, Section V of the Constitution of the State of Connecticut, where we have lived for a quarter of a century. This section, written in 1818, clearly states that every citizen may freely speak, write, and publish his sentiments on all subjects, "being responsible for the abuse of that liberty." In other words, for the privilege of freedom there is a price tag and that price tag is commonsense judgment of what news and information may or may not actually damage or destroy the free society in which one operates. The newsman is, as all but a few of them know full well, as responsible for the abuse of that liberty as for perpetuation of freedom of the press itself.

We never thought it particularly responsible, for example, for a newspaper to publish an eight-column scare headline on a relatively unimportant but highly emotional subject simply for the sake of newsstand sales. Though this is done less nowadays than it used to be done in the worst of the Hearst papers, it is still a sin in the litany of the free press. It is irresponsible, "an abuse of that liberty." Similarly, publication of patently pornographic books and magazines for distribution on newsstands seems to us a clear abuse of the privilege of a free press, and those who profit from these sultry ventures know perfectly well, in spite of self-righteous denials, that this profitable filth will fall under some eyes too young to be exposed to such matters. Our feeling about four-letter words and pornography has always boiled down to a simple equation: We would no more allow this sort of material to fall into the hands of small fry than we would hand them a glass of straight gin. They simply aren't ready for such strong doses of adult stimulant. Yet scarcely a night goes by that network TV does not step over this commonsense line in a medium that goes straight to the heart of every home.

It's an open secret that TV scriptwriters vie with one another to see who can come up with some new cruelty or brutality, usually sex-derived. Sadism and brutalization that would have horrified us all a generation ago now commonly fill prime time, to say nothing of salacious commercials brimming with double entendre[1] and vulgarity. Every conceivable form of torture and hurting and beating and mugging a human being that the mind of man has come upon is available tonight or tomorrow night or the night after that in every home in America. And if the affluent masters of television still claim that this has no relation to the doubling of felonious crime in the past few years, we can only answer that this is the rankest hogwash. TV teaches impressionable minds, adult and young, precisely how these deeds are to be done—and then they are done, in ever increasing number. This is true misapplication of the right of free expression, under Frankfurter's definition.

We are always hearing nowadays about the rights of free speech, the press, and assembly, but the price tag of responsibility doesn't always show. Student rioters who prevent free speech and assembly by others violate the First Amendment themselves, however just their causes. If, as Justice Oliver Wendell Holmes is said to have expressed it, freedom of speech does not include crying "Fire!" in a crowded theater, then it does not include the conscious brutalization of a whole generation who will be worse citizens for it, and it also does not include burning down the community to cook the pig. Freedom of speech, press, or as-

---

[1] **double entendre** (dōō blän tän dr'): word or phrase of double meaning, the less obvious one often of doubtful propriety.

sembly will exist only so long as those lucky few granted this towering privilege exercise it while "being responsible for the abuse of that liberty." It is as simply logical as that.

INTERPRETATION
1. The editorial expresses an opinion about freedom of speech. Try to state that opinion in one sentence. Do you agree with it? Why or why not?
2. What reasons does the writer give for believing as he does? In the light of the seriousness of the issue, are his reasons good ones?
3. What illustrations does the author give of current abuses of the freedom of speech? Do you agree that these are abuses? Explain.

STYLE AND METHOD
1. How much of the editorial is made up of the author's own thoughts and how much of quotations and excerpts from other people? What purpose do the quotations serve? Could the argument be developed without them?
2. Is Tobin's article convincing to you? If it is, what specific ideas in the editorial are most cogent? Explain how the author goes about demonstrating the validity of his ideas.

FOR WRITING
1. List some abuses of freedom that you find in your home life, or in our national life. Write an essay in which you define the limits of freedom that would prevent these abuses.
2. Write a letter to Mr. Tobin in which you express your opinion about any aspect of the editorial with which you either agree or disagree.

What is the difference between science and technology? Do people sometimes condemn the first for the faults of the second? What are the goals of the true scientist? The popular misconceptions surrounding such questions are here attacked by Dr. Lee A. DuBridge, former President of the California Institute of Technology and advisor to several American Presidents. In the course of the discussion, the author makes clear both the limitations and importance of science in today's world, and explains why science can be called "one of man's greatest arts."

Exploring the Unknown

LEE A. DuBRIDGE

After thousands of years of civilized history, it was not until the 17th century that man finally uncovered the fact that nature operated in accordance with laws that could be discovered; laws that were so exact that they could be used to predict with precision the behavior of physical bodies. And at the same time men were uncovering these startling regularities of nature—the grand and beautifully simple laws which nature obeyed—they also discovered the infinite complexity of nature; that there were undreamed-of phenomena awaiting discovery—for those who were willing and able to explore.

And so it was that during the past 300 years scientific knowledge slowly came into being until, at the beginning of the 20th century, the time was ripe for the explosive rise of applied science.

Now this development of applied science has been one of the most spectacular phenomena of our generation. It has revolutionized our way of living—and possibly also our way of dying. It has transformed the lives of millions of people, and has elevated their hopes and ambitions, too. Science has become the new "magic"—it is, some people seem to think, capable of doing anything.

"Exploring the Unknown," by Lee A. DuBridge, from *Frontiers in Science* edited by Edward Hutchings, Jr., © 1958 by Basic Books, Inc., Publishers, New York.

And yet there are disquieting notes mixed in with the growth in public acclaim for applied science. The refrigerators and tooth paste are appreciated and enjoyed. But the scientific knowledge which made all these things possible is forgotten or ignored. The latest gadget for better living is promptly purchased on the installment plan. But when someone mentions weapons for defense, a great cry goes up: "The scientists are trying to destroy us." In fact, in these days it has become feasible in some circles to say we have had "too much science"; that "science is the cause of most of the world's troubles"; that we ought to "return to the liberal arts"; that science ought now to wait a while so that social science can "catch up." The idea is, presumably, that social science or the liberal arts or something will then teach us all how to love one another so that human beings won't end up by atom-bombing themselves off the face of the earth!

To hear some people talk, you would think that science causes nothing but unhappiness, conflict, war; that science denies the finer things of life; is too "technical" to have a place of respect in modern education. You would think that the fate of the world rested on the outcome of some sort of a race between scientists on the one hand and all the historians, philosophers, writers, economists, poets, preachers, and political and social scientists on the other, with the implication that if science wins, the human race will be blasted to oblivion.

Some people talk as though they really believe some or all of these things. In fact, there are some very important people who are making it their business to promote these ideas. I think it is time that we, the scientific community, began to do something about the attacks which have been made on science and on scientists. For they are having profound and even terrifying effects. They have already caused an alarming drop, for example, in the number of high-school students who take mathematics and physics. They have caused many a serious-minded college or university student to avoid all science courses and to look with disdain on those who major in science fields. They have caused well-meaning people to believe that scientists are necessarily so specialized and blind as to be wholly untrustworthy the moment they step out of the laboratory, and to class all scientists and engineers as "narrow-minded technicians."

How then do we go about meeting these charges, these misunderstandings and prejudices?

First, I want to say that I do not think the way to do it is to brag more about the gadgets and devices and weapons which have come about as a result of the systematic attempts to make use of scientific knowledge. I have great admiration for deep freezes and bulldozers and jet airplanes and detergents and penicillin—and even pink and white Cadillacs. But the values of science really do not lie in these things in themselves. Rather, they lie in the way in which pure and applied science contributes to man's physical, intellectual and spiritual well-being. The true values of science lie not in its by-products, but in its goals; not in its dollar value, but in its human value. The value of science will be judged not by how fast it helps us to travel, but where it helps us to go.

In order to get a better look at this problem, I think we should forget about applied science for a moment and think about basic science, the pure search for knowledge.

First let us ask why men are scientists. Why do men spend their lives in pure science? Well, I can assure you it is not because of any desire to destroy the world or even to harm a single human being, or make him less happy. Quite the contrary! Nor is the scientist usually impelled primarily by a desire to make money—though I am sure he looks forward to receiving the monthly paycheck as much as anyone (especially when the fresh Ph.D. today can go out into the first job at $10,000 a year).

On the other hand, I can't claim either that the scientist's objective is wholly or primarily an altruistic[1] one—trying to make the world over into a Utopia,[2] for example. He simply hopes that his work will be some contribution to human welfare.

Primarily, it seems to me, the scientist is impelled by certain basic human urges. One is the urge to explore. The spirit of Christopher Columbus, of Magellan, of Admiral Byrd; the spirit of all those who have first discovered unknown places or climbed unconquered mountains—such a spirit is in each of us to some extent. It is certainly in every scientist, even though few of them have bothered to recognize it.

Another common human urge is the urge to create. Every human being would like to create something new. Just look at the "do-it-yourself" business! Some people create music or poetry; some create beautiful pictures, fine statues, magnificent

[1] **altruistic:** unselfishly devoted to the interests of others.
[2] **Utopia:** a book (1516) by Sir Thomas More, describing an ideal commonwealth; hence, any impossibly perfect society.

buildings, exquisite furniture or jewelry or clothing. So too, a new discovery in science is a creation—and in the eyes of scientists it has a beauty and an elegance all its own. To be able to contribute, even in only a small way, to the building of the magnificent edifice which we call science is a great creative satisfaction.

Add to the urges of exploration and creation the urge of competition—the desire to be the first to find a given piece of knowledge—and one has a good description of a scientist's motivation.

How can it be then that the structure of science, which results from such almost purely aesthetic motivation and which is admired by the scientists as a thing of beauty and a joy forever,[3] can be looked on by the general public as an ugly, mundane, or even dangerous product? It is true, of course, that some works of art are admired only by the artist, and the artist then complains that the public doesn't "understand" his work. So I guess the scientist also sighs that the public does not understand him or what he does. But if science is to have the surging vitality that it should have in modern America, the public should understand science.

Our usual attempts in this direction, however, are often inadequate. We usually try to explain the value of science not by telling why it is beautiful, but only why it is useful. Hence, scientists are mere technicians, specialists, unaware of the finer things of life!

Now, explaining why a thing is beautiful is much harder than explaining why it might be useful. Yet it is worth trying. We can be encouraged, I think, by the great public interest in astronomy. Everyone knows that the Palomar 200-inch telescope has no very "practical" uses. Yet thousands of people journey to Palomar every month to see that magnificent instrument and to hear about the awe-inspiring picture of the universe which it is revealing. Exploring the universe is an adventure which almost anyone envies and admires. And the beauty and grandeur of the universe is at least dimly visible to almost everyone who cares to listen and to look at pictures.

However, I claim there is an equal beauty and grandeur to the picture of an atom of iron or copper or uranium which modern science has revealed. Even more beauty, perhaps, is to be found in the structure of a protein molecule. More still is in the structure

[3] **"a thing of beauty and a joy forever"**: an allusion to the opening line of Keats' poem "Endymion": "A thing of beauty is a joy for ever."

of the gene as it is built up of spirals of nucleic acids all so in-
geniously designed that the gene can make a copy of itself—can
reproduce its kind. With all due respect, I claim there is as much
beauty in such things as can be found in great paintings or fine
literature or music.

In any case, if science were seen and taught in such a light, we
would not see the presidents of great universities (not scientists)
going around the country saying, "There is too much emphasis
on science; let us return to the liberal arts."

Science is one of man's greatest arts and is one which has done
the most to liberate the human spirit. Science, more than any
other subject, has freed men from ignorance and from consequent
fear. Consequently, it has elevated man, intellectually and
spiritually.

How does it happen that many people have just the opposite
conception—that science has been degrading to man; has made
him materialistic, unmoral? Apparently it is because scientists
are wholly misunderstood.

For example, a distinguished religious leader recently said,
"Modern technologists and scientists have come to regard themselves as supreme masters of the universe." Well! That's news
to me. Some scientists might have good ideas about some im-
provements they would make if they were! But the only men in
recent times who have thought themselves masters of the universe (Hitler, Mussolini, Stalin) were certainly not scientists!
Science is a pursuit that makes men humble—because in learning
a few things we come upon so many that we don't know.

But why do these misconceptions of scientists exist?

Personally, I put part of the blame for this on certain mis-
guided philosophers. For example, since the instruments of the
scientists have discovered no non-material or non-physical
aspects of the world, therefore the scientist is accused of saying
that such immaterial things do not exist. Because the anatomist
found no place in the body to house a soul, therefore, says the
philosopher, this proves man has no soul! That's nonsense, of
course. Physical instruments were never intended to measure
non-physical things and, by their nature, they can never do so.
Science thus gives no support to materialism—nor, of course, can
it ever disprove it either. Philosophical theories are just not susceptible to experimental proof or disproof.

Again — philosophers have gone wild speculating about the theory of relativity and its philosophical implications. Now the special theory of relativity is simply a theory in physics which describes how the results of observations made on various phenomena will depend on how the observer is moving relative to what he observes. "Aha!" says the philosopher, "that means everything is relative; nothing is absolute. There are no absolutes physically; therefore there are none intellectually or morally either. It all depends on your point of view."

Nonsense again. Aside from the fact that physical theories have no necessary relevance to moral problems, the philosopher totally misunderstands Einstein's relativity theory. Though the relativity theory did show that many observed quantities were changed when there was relative motion (as had always been known), Einstein found that certain things (the velocity of light, for example) were unchanged. They were "relativistically invariant"; they were "absolutes."

A beautiful physical theory thus has been misunderstood and misused; again science has been misrepresented.

Then, too, there were philosophers who said that the theory of evolution denied the existence of God! No scientific theory can either affirm or deny a spiritual existence, of course.

To me the whole picture of the universe as revealed by science, as well as the picture of the processes that go on within it and of the life that inhabits it, is one of magnificence, vastness, order, splendor, precision, beauty. It is a picture that exalts the Creator of the Universe — and exalts the dignity of the men He created, the men who can discover and comprehend this majesty of creation.

You see, perhaps, why I can claim that science is one of the "liberalizing arts." You see why it deserves a place of respect along with the humanities, the fine arts, and social and behavioral studies as partners and coequals in the intellectual and cultural fields. You see why to dismiss science as too "technical" and too "vocational" is both false and revolting.

However, there are men who say science is still not enough. Of course it isn't. And I do not know any scientist who ever claimed it was. The study of the physical world is one important aspect of man's use of his intelligence and his talents. It is one expression of the urge to know, to create. But the studies of the world of human beings, of the world of beauty and the world of moral values are equally essential activities — all are necessary to the educated and civilized man.

Perhaps, however, the most damaging blows struck by the anti-scientists are those which prey upon the fears and dangers of the modern world which applied science has helped to build. These dangers are indeed real and terrifying. And scientists will do well to continue making factual statements about what these dangers are. Thermonuclear bombs are really horribly devastating weapons — and don't let anyone tell you otherwise.

But the real basis for our fears today is not the human ingenuity that produced terrible weapons, but the human cussedness that threatens to use such weapons against us. The world has never been free from danger. But if we contrast the western world of today with that of 100 years ago, we find much to be proud of. We have eliminated slavery — because our work is now done for us by lumps of coal and pools of oil. We have eliminated much of human suffering caused by ailments and disease — and we will no longer tolerate the existence of suffering caused by human cruelty or neglect.

We have eliminated many evils and many dangers; we face many more of both old and new varieties. But we shall conquer danger not by weeping and wailing, not by stopping or impeding any worthwhile human endeavor, by belittling any noble human aspiration. We shall conquer fear in the end only if we continue to explore the unknown in every field of human endeavor, continue to extend always the frontiers of knowledge, aiming always to elevate the human mind and the human spirit.

INTERPRETATION

1. For what purpose was this essay written? What basic misconceptions about science are mentioned by the author? Do you agree that they are misconceptions?

2. Is there any pattern to the way the author deals with these misconceptions? What are his major arguments in defense of science and scientists? Do his arguments relieve the individual scientist of responsibility for the uses to which his discoveries may be put?

3. What is the purpose of pure science, according to the author? the true value of science? What effect does the pursuit of science have on a man's character or outlook, according to Dr. DuBridge?

STYLE AND METHOD

1. To what audience is this essay directed? Is the author speaking only to the scientific community, or to the general public as well? How do you know?
2. What qualities of style and development help to make the author's argument convincing? Explain.

FOR WRITING

1. Select one of the author's assertions about science or about the people who judge science and explain why you agree or disagree with it.
2. The author stresses the "splendor, precision, and beauty" revealed by the scientist's view of nature. In an essay either (a) describe such a personal experience you have had through science, or (b) contrast the kind of beauty the scientist sees with the kind seen by the painter or poet.

Norman Cousins wrote this editorial in 1959 as a direct result
of a personal experience. Since that time the problem he speaks
about has become more and more a cause for great concern in
many communities. The individual citizen who makes an effort
to help someone in distress is laughed at or thought to be naïve
for "getting involved." The observations the author makes are
just as relevant today — perhaps more so. It is a subject much
written on, but seldom with the clear, restrained — yet urgent —
style of Mr. Cousins. Notice the logical development of his
central idea right up to the last sentence.

The Desensitization of Twentieth-Century Man

NORMAN COUSINS

It happened at the Stamford, Connecticut, railroad station. It
was Sunday evening, at about ten P.M. Some two dozen persons,
among them several young men in uniform, were waiting for the
express to New York.

The door to the waiting room flew open. A woman, shrieking
hysterically, burst into the room. She was pursued by a man just
a few steps behind her. The woman screamed that the man was
trying to kill her and cried out for the people to save her. I was
standing nearest the door. The woman grabbed me, still shrieking. I tried to protect her behind me. The man tried to sweep
me aside to get at her. He rushed at me, caught the woman's
wrist with one hand, tore her loose and pulled her through the
doorway. The woman fell to the ground and was dragged by the
wrist just outside the waiting room. I tried to free her wrist. The
man broke off, grabbed the woman's pocketbook, and fled on foot.

We carried the woman inside the waiting room, sat her down,
then telephoned the police. The woman's eye was badly cut; she

was moaning. I looked around the room. Except for three or four persons who now came up to her, the people in the room seemed unconcerned. The young men in uniform were still standing in the same place, chatting among themselves as before. I am not sure which was greater, the shock of the attack that had just occurred or the shock caused by the apparent detachment and unconcern of the other people, especially the men in uniform.

The next morning, I read in the newspaper of another attack. This one was carried out in broad daylight on a young boy by a gang of teen-agers. Here, too, a number of people stood around and watched.

It would be possible, I suppose, to take the view that these are isolated instances, and that it would be a serious error to read into these cases anything beyond the fact that the bystanders were probably paralyzed by the suddenness of the violence. Yet I am not so sure. I am not sure that these instances may not actually be the product of something far deeper. What is happening, I believe, is that the natural reactions of the individual against violence are being blunted. The individual is being desensitized by living history. He is developing new reflexes and new responses that tend to slow up the moral imagination and relieve him of essential indignation over impersonal hurt. He is becoming casual about brutality. He makes his adjustments to the commonplace, and nothing is more commonplace in our age than the ease with which life can be smashed or shattered. The range of the violence sweeps from the personal to the impersonal, from the amusements of the crowd to the policies of nations. It is in the air, quite literally. It has lost the sting of surprise. We have made our peace with violence.

No idea could be more untrue than that there is no connection between what is happening in the world and the behavior of the individual. Society does not exist apart from the individual. It transfers its apprehensions or its hopes, its fatigue or its vitality, its ennui or its dreams, its sickness or its spirituality to the people who are part of it. Can the individual be expected to retain the purity of his responses, particularly a sensitivity to the fragility of life, when society itself seems to measure its worth in terms of its ability to create and possess instruments of violence that could expunge civilization as easily as ... destroy a village? Does it have no effect on an individual to live in an age that has already known two world wars; that has seen hundreds of cities ripped apart by dynamite tumbling down from the heavens; that has witnessed whole nations stolen or destroyed; that has seen millions of people exterminated in gas chambers or other mass means; that has seen governments compete with one another to make weapons which, even in the testing, have put death into the air?

To repeat, the causative range is all the way from petty amusements to the proclamations of nations. We are horrified that teen-age boys should make or steal lethal weapons and then proceed to use them on living creatures; but where is the sense of horror or outrage at the cheapness of human life that is exploited throughout the day or night on television? It is almost impossible to see television for fifteen minutes without seeing people beaten or shot or punched or kicked or jabbed. It is also almost impossible to pick up a newspaper without finding someone in a position of power, here or elsewhere, threatening to use nuclear explosives unless someone else becomes more sensible.

The young killers don't read the newspapers, true. They don't have to. If they read at all, they read the picture-story pulps that dispense brutality as casually as a vending machine its peanuts. In any case, the heart of the matter is that the young killers do not live in the world of their own. They belong to the larger world. They may magnify and intensify the imperfections of the larger world but they do not invent them.

The desensitization of twentieth-century man is more than a danger to the common safety. It represents the loss or impairment of the noblest faculty of human life — the ability to be aware both of suffering and beauty; the ability to share sorrow and create hope; the ability to think and respond beyond one's wants. There are some things we have no right ever to get used to. One of these most certainly is brutality. The other is the irrational. Both brutality and the irrational have now come together and are moving towards a dominant pattern. If the pattern is to be resisted and changed, a special effort must be made. A very special effort.

INTERPRETATION

1. What is Cousins' main point? Is it about violence or the attitudes of other people toward violence?

2. Which of these three sentences from the article best sums up its ideas? Explain your reasons for your choice. (a) "No idea could be more untrue than that there is no connection between what is happening in the world and the behavior of the individual," (b) "The desensitization of twentieth-century man is more than a danger to the common safety," (c) "We have made our peace with violence."

STYLE AND METHOD
1. Why doesn't Cousins get to his main point at the beginning, and prove it? How does he build his essay? What is the purpose of relating actual incidents at the very beginning?
2. Compare Cousins's diction and tone with that of James Baldwin ("My Dungeon Shook" — page 210) or that of Shana Alexander ("Hooray! Getting Back To Normal" — page 206). Cousins was writing for *Saturday Review;* Miss Alexander for *Life;* Baldwin to his nephew. How would the audience, in each case, affect the author's tone?

FOR WRITING
1. Cousins states that a "special effort" must be made to break the "dominant pattern" of accepting violence and irrationality. Tell what you think that special effort should be.
2. Keep a log for a week of a single source of news information (the same newspaper, television news, etc.). Report on how much of the material is concerned with violence and what general attitude can be found in its treatment.

GLOSSARY OF LITERARY TERMS

allusion: a brief reference to a person, place, or event, real or fictitious, for the purpose of adding color and dimension to the writing.

antithesis: a structure in which the relationship between the two halves of a sentence, or between the clauses or phrases of a sentence, is one of balance or parallelism of grammatical pattern, with a strong contrast implied in the meaning.

argument: (See *persuasion*.)

article: a prose piece on a specific topic, forming an independent part of a book, newspaper, or magazine.

autobiography: a literary work presenting one's own life story.

biography: the history of a person's life, as a work of literature.

character sketch: an essay presenting and illustrating the important character traits of an actual or fictional person.

colloquial: language which is acceptable and correct in ordinary conversation, friendly letters, or informal speeches, but unsuited to formal speech or writing.

connotation: the associated meanings or feelings implied by a word, as contrasted with its denotative (dictionary) meaning. (See *denotation*.)

denotation: that aspect of a word's meaning which names or points to the class of objects (referent) to which it refers. A word's dictionary meaning.

description: the use of sensory details to evoke the scene of the action; depiction of the appearance or character of individuals.

diction: the choice of words used by an author.

document: in writing or speaking, to provide exact references to authoritative information as proof of the statements made. To supply evidence for an assertion.

editorial: a newspaper or magazine essay presenting the opinion of the publisher or editors on a particular event or issue.

epigram: a concise, pithy, cleverly stated thought.

exposition: discourse designed to expound, explain, or appraise analytically. (See page 93.)

figurative: language which makes use of such figures of speech as metaphor, simile, and hyperbole — as opposed to literal language. (See *literal*.)

illustration: example intended to clarify or explain an idea.

irony: a literary device in which the speaker's implied attitudes or values are opposed to those literally expressed — usually with a wry effect.

literal: matter-of-fact language which gives a strict construction and is not exaggerated.

mood: the predominant emotion of a literary work; the atmosphere.

narrative: the recounting of a story as one continuous action or series of actions.

nonfiction: a branch of literature including articles, letters, biography, and the essay; prose works dealing with or offering opinion, conjecture, analysis, or description of actual events, people, or situations.

organization: in literature, the plan or order for the arrangement of ideas, events, or details.

outline: a short summary, often in the form of heads and subheads, which presents the most significant features of a general subject.

paradox: a statement that seems absurd or self-contradictory, but which turns out to have a consistent and logical meaning.

persona: the "voice" adopted by the writer, which reflects his attitude toward his subject and his audience, and is revealed by his tone.

persuasion: a mode of writing intended to influence a person to believe or act differently, through reasoned arguments. (See page 183.)

rhetorical: manner of speech or discourse which emphasizes style, often at the expense of thought.

satire: the literary art of ridiculing foolish or immoral aspects of human behavior for the purpose of holding them up to amusement, contempt, or scorn. The satirist hopes to improve human conduct by showing how it falls short of an ideal.

semantics: a science dealing with the relationships between symbols and their referents, including human behavior in reaction to symbols. Verbal semantics deals with words as symbols.

soliloquy: a discourse made in solitude, to oneself.

structure: (See *organization*.)

style: a distinctive or characteristic manner of writing, often associated with a particular writer.

symbol: something which stands for, or suggests, a larger and more undefinable idea.

theme: the point, conclusion, or implication of a given work; a short essay.

thesis: a position or proposition which must be defended by evidence and argument.

tone: the quality of a writer's words which shows his attitude toward his subject matter or his audience; for example, a writer's tone may be sarcastic, angry, humorous, detached, or awed.

unity: the oneness inherent in the development of a complete idea; unity of form often reinforces unity of thought to make a work a complete whole, closely related in all its parts.

voice: (See *persona*.)